ECONOMIC LIBERALIZATION:
NO PANACEA

WIDER

Studies in Development Economics embody the output of the
research programmes of the World Institute for
Development Economics Research (WIDER), which was
established by the United Nations University as its first
research and training centre in 1984 and started work in
Helsinki in 1985. The principal purpose of the Institute is
to help identify and meet the need for policy-oriented
socio-economic research on pressing global and
development problems, as well as common domestic
problems and their inter-relationships.

Economic Liberalization: No Panacea

The Experiences of Latin America and Asia

Edited by

TARIQ BANURI

CLARENDON PRESS · OXFORD

1991

Oxford University Press, Walton Street, Oxford OX2 6DP

Oxford New York Toronto
Delhi Bombay Calcutta Madras Karachi
Petaling Jaya Singapore Hong Kong Tokyo
Nairobi Dar es Salaam Cape Town
Melbourne Auckland
and associated companies in
Berlin Ibadan

Oxford is a trade mark of Oxford University Press

Published in the United States
by Oxford University Press, New York

British Library Cataloguing in Publication Data
Economic liberalization: no panacea: the
experiences of Latin America and Asia—(WIDER
studies in development economics).
1. Asia. Economic conditions   2. Latin America.
Economic conditions
I. Banuri, Tariq   II. Series
330.951
ISBN 0–19–828678–3

Library of Congress Cataloging in Publication Data
Economic liberalization: no panacea: the experiences
of Latin America and Asia/edited by Tariq Banuri.
p.   cm.—(WIDER studies in development economics)
1. Developing countries—Economic policy.   2. Developing
countries—Economic conditions.   3. Economic stabilization—
Developing countries.   4. Economic development.   5. Latin America—
Economic policy.   6. Asia—Economic policy.   I. Banuri
Tariq. II. Series.
HC59.7.L4185   1990   338.9'009172'4—dc20   89–28344
ISBN 0–19–828678–3

Typeset by Cambrian Typesetters, Frimley, Surrey

Printed and bound in
Great Britain by Bookcraft (Bath) Ltd,
Midsomer Norton, Avon

For Nancy

WIDER Macroeconomics Research Project

EDWARD J. AMADEO, Pontificia Universidade Catolica, Rio de Janeiro.

MASAHIKO AOKI, Stanford University and University of Kyoto.

TARIQ BANURI, WIDER, Helsinki.

AMIT BHADURI, University of Vienna.

SAMUEL BOWLES, University of Massachusetts, Amherst.

ROBERT BOYER, Centre d'Études Prospectives d'Économie Mathématique Appliquées à la Planification (CEPREMAP), Paris.

GERALD EPSTEIN, University of Massachusetts, Amherst.

DUNCAN FOLEY, Barnard College, Columbia University, New York.

ALBERT FISHLOW, University of California, Berkeley.

HERBERT GINTIS, University of Massachusetts, Amherst.

ANDREW GLYN, University of Oxford.

ALAN HUGHES, University of Cambridge.

WILLIAM LAZONICK, Barnard College, Columbia University, New York.

ALAIN LIPIETZ, Centre d'Études Prospectives d'Économie Mathématique Appliquées à la Planification (CEPREMAP), Paris.

STEPHEN A. MARGLIN, Harvard University.

PERRY MEHRLING, Barnard College, Columbia University, New York.

JOSÉ-ANTONIO OCAMPO, FEDESARROLLO, Bogotá.

MIHIR RAKSHIT, Presidency College, Calcutta.

BOB ROWTHORN, University of Cambridge.

JULIET B. SCHOR, Harvard University.

AJIT SINGH, University of Cambridge.

LANCE TAYLOR, Massachusetts Institute of Technology.

PREFACE

THIS volume seeks to understand the obstacles to growth in developing countries. Its basic message has two parts. First, no policy orthodoxy—whether that of openness or dirigism—can provide blanket solutions to the problems of all countries at all times. No orthodoxy, in other words, can substitute for the exercise of pragmatic judgement in particular country situations. The *contextuality of policy* must be the starting point. This contextuality, as the contributions by Tariq Banuri and Edward Amadeo and Albert Fishlow show, is the product of a historical process which policy-makers ignore only at the price of irrelevance, or worse.

Second, it examines in some detail the limitations of the dominant neo-liberal orthodoxy when applied to developing countries. Alan Hughes and Ajit Singh suggest that in the 1970s and 1980s, the most successful countries have strayed far from the path of laissez-faire and openness, at least as these terms are conventionally understood. And, as Lance Taylor argues, development strategy in the next decade is bound to be constrained to an inward-looking path by the lack of access to external sources of capital, at least for heavily indebted countries, and by growing protectionism in the North—unless, of course, an imaginative global strategy, involving debt reconstruction and the recycling of surpluses to debtor countries in support of domestic policy reform, is put in place. This would be necessary to counter the deflationary bias stemming from the correction of the substantial external US deficit under circumstances where the alternative of offsetting expansion in the surplus economies seems unlikely to occur.

If, however, development is constrained by the absence of such a global strategy, several questions arise. In such hostile circumstances, where will countries—especially small, poor countries—obtain the needed stimulus for their development process? How can they reduce their continuing vulnerability to international capital movements? What are the implications for their trading policies and their relationship with the main trading blocks of the North? These are among the key questions posed by the authors of the papers collected in this volume.

Policy-makers in developing countries have been increasingly preoccupied with the difficulties of implementing conventional policy prescriptions. Many well-meaning attempts to apply the prescription have foundered on the rocks of unanticipated political and institutional constraints. One may of course, ignore this experience. This response runs the obvious risk of making policy recommendations increasingly less relevant to the actual political and economic problems faced by the governments of developing countries. The authors of this volume think it more appropriate to change the policy prescription. This requires, as a first step, a much deeper understanding of the specific institutions and history of particular countries.

Thus, much of the research that has gone into this volume has been devoted to displaying the rich variety of the historical and institutional contexts in which policies must operate—and the need to take this into account in framing policy prescriptions. Neglect and misunderstanding of the particular circumstances of particular countries (and thus of what policies are feasible) lie behind the failure of many conventional adjustment programmes emphasizing economic liberalization. On the other hand, ignoring the market altogether has led to the failure of excessively dirigiste and inward-looking strategies, whether in developing countries or the socialist countries. (Another WIDER research project has brought scholars from China, the Soviet Union, and other socialist countries of Europe together to examine the lessons to be learned from the various forms that *perestroika* has taken in the socialist world.) The problem for policy has always been that of finding the proper balance between public intervention and the market and this necessarily varies with particular country situations.

These concerns are illustrated in many ways in the following chapters. I shall single out just three areas: the role of the state, the role of labour unions, and the degree of integration of a country with international financial markets. Albert Fishlow traces several distinct strands in the contemporary analysis of the role of the state (which argues in favour of reduced government intervention) and contrasts these arguments with the plain fact that the state has played a crucial role in virtually all 'late-developing' economies, especially in Latin America. However, given the massive external shocks of the early 1980s, the state faces formidable political and social constraints, and its ability to overcome those constraints has been rather limited. The message of Fishlow's paper is that we must understand the specific environment in which individual states operate in order to understand their potential for encouraging development.

Tariq Banuri and Edward Amadeo point out that the importance of labour markets in developing countries has been neglected by economists, in sharp contrast to the attention given to them in the United States and Europe. Latin American countries have a long history of labour moblization and polarized capital–labour relations, which explains why repeated attempts to destroy labour unions and other popular movements have failed. The true task of governance, they argue, is to reconcile conflicting interests in society—indeed, economic growth itself should be seen as a means to maintain a harmonious society rather than as an end in itself. This has been recognized by the East Asian countries, but not in Latin America.

The issue of international integration is approached from different angles in Lance Taylor's contribution and in the paper written jointly by Alan Hughes and Ajit Singh. The Hughes–Singh paper rejects the view that the problems of Latin American countries can be attributed solely to overvalued exchange rates and unproductive use of foreign borrowing: borrowing itself made the economies of the region more vulnerable. The policy implications are clear: countries are likely to be more concerned with reducing such vulnerability than with the further liberalization of financial markets.

The work embodied in this volume will provide support for policy-makers in developing countries who are committed to domestic economic reforms, but who are at the same time concerned to ensure that the relevant policy packages are viable in their particular institutional and political contexts. Such packages have to be innovative and will require an appropriate degree of flexibility on the part of the international financial institutions with which they have to be negotiated.

Lal Jayawardena
DIRECTOR, WIDER

ACKNOWLEDGEMENTS

The authors of this volume received help from a variety of sources. Financial assistance was provided from WIDER's Macroeconomics Research Project. The members of WIDER's Macroeconomics Research Project, particularly Stephen Marglin, provided invaluable assistance in two ways: by formulating the context of this research, and by offering constructive criticism of drafts of the chapters that follow. The authors would also like to express their collective appreciation of guests at two meetings held in Helsinki in 1985 and 1986. Martina Jägerhorn helped with updating and formatting the text tables for the entire volume. Finally, thanks go to Anne Ruohonen for invaluable assistance in the organization of the project and for keeping everything under control.

In addition to this, Alan Hughes and Ajit Singh would like to thank Michael Ward and Villay Soulatha at the World Bank for providing much of the original data on which the paper is based; and Juan Carlos Moreno for excellent research assistance.

Lance Taylor would like to record his appreciation of Gerry Helleiner's comments on earlier drafts.

Albert Fishlow would like to acknowledge the very helpful research assistance of William Maloney and Menzie Chin.

Tariq Banuri and Edward Amadeo would like to thank Jose Camargo and Charlie Kindleberger for a number of very perceptive comments on preliminary versions of their papers. They would also like to mention the contribution made by Montek Ahluwalia, Jose Camargo, Jose-Antonio Ocampo, Sebastian Saez, and Carlos Winograd in the preparation of the Appendix to Chapter 6. Lastly, the able research assistance of Ricardo Rubinstajn and Martina Jägerhorn is gratefully acknowledged.

CONTENTS

1

Introduction

Tariq Banuri

Politics, as Bismarck once said, is the art of the possible. Development *policy* is a common example of this art in Third World countries and, as one would expect, it has generally been quite sensitive to factors which delimit the range of the 'possible', namely: the nature and history of economic, social, and political institutions in each country, its cultural milieu, and even the nature and history of its ideological controversies. Development *theory*, particularly of the neoclassical variety, has often been disdainful of such imperfections, and since 1970, seems to have become increasingly universal and abstract. At the same time, the self-assurance of the adherents of such views seems to have grown in direct proportion to the distance they have placed between themselves and the 'impurity' of institutional arrangements. This move towards an unquestioning reliance on abstract and universal models and the disregard of institutional specificities is disturbing because it can lead to inferior policy choices and potentially harmful social consequences.

These concerns have assumed exceptional gravity at the present juncture because of the special circumstances created by the global economic crisis of the 1980s. The persistence of this crisis and the seeming inability of many governments, particularly in Latin America and Africa, to manage it is being interpreted by an influential group of development economists as a failure of all alternatives to neoclassical wisdom. Likewise, the ability of East Asian economies to withstand these shocks and to maintain their earlier growth performance has been curiously and erroneously distilled into free trade arguments, providing the basis for pushing Latin American and other unwilling governments into dubious experiments of policy reform, including, under the omnibus title of 'economic liberalization', the virtual elimination of restrictions on international trade, deregulation and internationalization of the financial sector, privatization, de-unionization, and the elimination of all kinds of regulatory arrangements.[1]

Economic liberalization is being offered as a panacea for a country's ills, regardless of its institutional arrangements or historical background, and

---

[1] These arguments have been made in an extensive literature dating from the early 1970s. Prominent names associated with it include Bela Balassa, Jagdish Bhagwati, Anne Krueger, Ronald McKinnon, and more recently, Jeffrey Sachs; specific sources are cited as appropriate below. A succinct statement of this perspective is to be found in Krueger 1986. The IMF has always been a bastion of free-market liberalism; the World Bank, whose attitude had traditionally been somewhat more eclectic, also fell under its hegemony in the 1980s.

regardless even of the costs involved in the cure. Indeed, the broad agenda for policy debate on development is being replaced with the narrow and technical issue of the means and the speed with which liberalization ought to be introduced in the economy. To stretch a metaphor, unlike the economic orthodoxy of Keynes's days, contemporary 'Euclidean geometers in a non-Euclidean world' are bent upon straightening the lines at any cost rather than merely 'rebuking them for not keeping straight'.

Much of this exhortation has been visited upon Latin American governments, partly because the extreme dislocations of their economies following the capital market shocks of the turn of the last decade have rendered them somewhat more suggestible than usual, and partly because their greater dependence upon foreign financial resources has endowed international institutions, such as the IMF and the World Bank, with unprecedented power to force their advice upon reluctant recipients. As Albert Hirschman noted recently,

This is not the first time that the United States, or multinational institutions strongly influenced by the United States, have convinced themselves that they possess the key to progress and development for all those wayward, hence backward, foreign countries . . . But never have Latin Americans been lectured and admonished as insistently as in recent years . . . on the virtues of the free market, of privatization, and of private foreign investment. (Hirschman 1987: 30–31)

The papers in this volume were presented at a conference on global macroeconomics held at WIDER—the World Institute of Development Economics Research—Helsinki, in August 1986. The overall theme of the conference was the causes and consequences of the slowdown and volatility of the world economy since 1970. Another set of papers, focusing more directly on the determinants of the recent slowdown, was edited by Stephen A. Marglin and Juliet B. Schor, and is being published separately under the title, *The Golden Age of Capitalism*. The papers in the present volume are motivated, on the one hand, by the urgent need to address the persistent and deepening crisis in Latin America, and on the other, by grave reservations about the strategy of economic liberalization and openness advocated as a solution by influential theorists.

They examine, through a comparison of the recent experience of Latin American and Asian countries, the differential consequences for the Third World of the recent upheavals in the world economy. Given the prominence of the argument for economic liberalization in discussions of this issue, these papers take as their point of departure the fairly obvious shortcomings of this strategy—its theoretical weakness, the dubious empirical support for its assertions, and the inappropriateness of transferring economic policies from one historical and institutional context to another. While the papers are unified in terms of their underlying concerns as well as in their choice of approach and point of departure, they are far from identical. Indeed, they complement each other—to the extent that the volume has to be read as a whole in order to get the flavour of the argument.

In Chapter 2, Edward Amadeo and I analyse the argument for economic liberalization from the perspective of 'governance'. Using the perspective of the 'state as a mediator of social conflict', we seek to establish a connection between the degree of social tension, the nature of economic institutions, and the feasibility of various economic policies in a country. In particular, we show that given the wide variety of economic and political institutions in the Third World, it is more than likely that policies which prove effective in one context would turn out to be infeasible, ineffective, counter-productive, or even disastrous in other conditions. The paper goes on to argue that since liberalization is an implicit strategy of institutional reform, what is needed is not a set of simplistic cross-sectional comparisons of economic performance; rather, it is the social desirability and political feasibility of the proposed institutional change which needs to be evaluated in the light of the history of each country, particularly that relating to political mobilization and participation.

In Chapter 3, Alan Hughes and Ajit Singh question the validity of many of the empirical assertions which underlie the argument for liberalization. They examine recent macroeconomic developments in nineteen selected countries to demonstrate, first, that the view that Asian countries were hit harder by external shocks is a misinterpretation of the evidence; it ignores the effect of 'positive' shocks to these countries (remittances, Middle East trade), as well as the singularly adverse effect of capital market shocks—interest rate escalation, capital flight, and debt strangulation—on countries with open financial regimes, such as in Latin America. Second, they demonstrate that the supposed relation between exchange rate valuation and export performance is not consistent with empirical evidence; nor is there a close fit between exchange rate policy and capital flight. Lastly, they show that a comparison of large countries—China, India, Brazil, Mexico—reveals the key to superior macroeconomic performance as a cautious attitude towards foreign borrowing and a reduction of exposure to world financial markets.

In Chapter 4, Lance Taylor introduces the important distinction between trade openness and financial openness to evaluate the supposed connection between openness and economic performance. Using a cross-section of fifty developing countries, he shows that while financial openness *is* related to greater vulnerability to external shocks and to the emergence of financial crises and painful adjustment episodes, the relationship is the reverse of what is suggested by proponents of liberalization. Besides this, neither trade openness nor absence of distortions explains superior growth or adjustment performance after controlling for other explanatory factors (e.g. the size of the country). Fast-growing countries are more or less open and have diverse

4 TARIQ BANURI

patterns of specialization, and their success is not obviously led by exports, industrial or otherwise. Taylor goes on to examine critically the various theoretical arguments for increased economic openness, and to show in particular that while the neoclassical argument is far from watertight even on its own terms, the certitude of its conclusions is seriously questioned by structuralist macroeconomic models in which higher trade and financial flows can often lead to slower growth and more costly adjustment.

Albert Fishlow, in Chapter 5, starts with some of the themes touched upon by Hughes and Singh before going on to argue for the reconstruction of 'a Latin American development state that can consistently and effectively implement the right policies, not just register the right prices'. In making this argument, Fishlow questions several assertions underlying the case for economic liberalization, and shows, for example, that the 'dismal' Latin American performance has been exaggerated by the selectivity of the comparison of the whole region against the best Asian performers; that, contrary to the common interpretation, the shocks which struck Latin American countries were more severe than those which affected Asian countries; that faulty exchange rate or trade policies were neither the key to lagging performance nor the central element of Latin American industrial strategies in the 1970s; and that Jeffrey Sachs's conjecture regarding the political weakness of rural interests in Latin America has no basis in the region's history.

In the final Chapter, Edward Amadeo and I follow up on some of the issues raised in our Chapter 2, and in Albert Fishlow's recommendation to reconstruct a developmental state in Latin America, by focusing on the differences in the structure and evolution of labour market institutions in prominent Latin American, South Asian, and East Asian countries. In trying to understand these differences, we steer away from simplistic explanations which rely entirely on differences in government policies and focus instead on differences in historical, social, cultural, and ideological factors, which are often shared by countries within the same region but over which governments have very little control. The analysis indicates the existence of 'hysteresis' in the labour market, whereby the nature of current economic relationships as well as the feasible range of institutional change is limited and constrained by the history of conflict and accommodation. As a result, prescriptions for liberalization, which are increasingly seen as requiring de-unionization as a necessary accompaniment, are not only undesirable in societies with a long history of social and political mobilization but are well-nigh infeasible as well.

The remainder of this chapter sets out the background to the current discussion, namely the mainstream case for economic liberalization and its connection to the recent crisis in Latin America, and the summary features of the critique contained in the chapters that follow.

1.1 THE CASE FOR ECONOMIC LIBERALIZATION

What is the case for economic liberalization? To go over some familiar ground, an early theoretical case was based on the well-known neoclassical result of the Pareto optimality of free trade. In the neoclassical view, government intervention is justified only to correct market failure resulting from externalities, dynamic rigidities, market power, and most importantly, incomplete or missing markets—all of which are present (in spades) in Third World economies—and only if the benefits of the intervention outweigh the costs of interfering with the market. This theoretical argument was bolstered by an empirical heuristic based on the example of Western countries, in which the unfettering of markets and laissez-faire policies of governments had supposedly led to the emergence of capitalism, the consequent rapid economic growth, and generalized social improvement.

In much of the post-war period, however, these arguments were dominated by powerful counter-arguments. In Western countries, the rise of Keynesianism, the increasing legitimacy of social welfare institutions and labour unions, and the acceptance of the need to regulate financial institutions provided justifications for interventionist policies and weakened the ideological support of the Western example for free trade policies in the Third World. The importance of the Western experience was further undermined by the example of socialist countries which appeared to be succeeding in bringing about a dramatic structural transformation of their economies through central planning and pervasive government intervention. Lastly, development economists also provided a justification for government intervention, particularly restrictions on international trade, along the lines of the infant industry argument.[2]

The recent revival of neoclassical wisdom and the growing respectability of economic liberalization among development economists (if not policy-makers) is due largely to the economic crisis of the last two decades, which has undermined confidence in received economic wisdom all over the world. During this period, the example of centrally planned economies lost some of its appeal as they began to run into serious economic and social difficulties of their own. At the same time, Western countries witnessed an erosion of the Keynesian consensus and a growing criticism of stabilization policies, labour unions, social welfare institutions, and regulation of industrial and financial enterprises. (This is somewhat ironic, since the countries which suffered the least disruption in their economies—Austria, Finland, Norway, and Sweden,

---

[2] A more recent argument for protectionism makes the same case by invoking the de-industrializing effects of resource inflows and exchange rate appreciation—the 'Dutch disease' syndrome: see Banuri 1986: ch. 5.

the 'social corporatist' countries—had the strongest and most well developed institutions of the type mentioned here).[3]

More important, the example of the so-called 'Gang of Four' countries in East Asia—Taiwan, Singapore, Hong Kong, but particularly South Korea—was used by neoclassical economists to argue that trade-restricting, import-substituting (IS) policies had failed, and should be replaced with trade-oriented, export-promoting (EP) policies. Later, other forms of liberalization were discovered by these writers as being equally necessary for successful performance.[4] Since the main area of concern here lies primarily in the Third World experience, I shall pursue the last development in more detail.

In much of the post-war period, conventional wisdom in development economics dictated IS as the preferred strategy for autonomous and stable industrialization. Among the central propositions of this strategy were the participation of the state in creating infrastructure, the use of tariffs and quotas to protect selected industries, and, by implication, an overvalued exchange rate and capital controls. During the 1960s, however, as the limits of the domestic markets began to assert themselves, the process of industrialization through IS started showing signs of exhaustion almost everywhere. This forced a choice between three options: lowering the rate of growth, (temporarily) increasing foreign borrowing, or shifting to the new favourite, the EP strategy. Since this happened at a time of increasing international liquidity, many countries, particularly in Latin America, were able to opt for the debt-oriented strategy.[5] This choice requires a few words of clarification.

First, IS meant somewhat different things in Latin America and Asia. In Latin America, the primary motivation behind this strategy was the fear of vulnerability to foreign economic shocks and to foreign political interests. It began as an 'indigenous response' to reductions in import capacities during the two world wars and the Great Depression, and was subsequently provided academic legitimacy by the economists of ECLA (the Economic Commission of Latin America).[6] In Asian countries, on the other hand, the chief motivation behind IS was the desire to expand the domestic industrial

[3] The discussion of analytical and empirical weakness in the neoclassical interpretation of recent history would take us too far afield; Marglin and Schor 1990 provides an alternative interpretation. For a description of the social corporatist experience and a discussion of the relevant issues, see Rowthorn and Glyn 1988.

[4] It is interesting to note that the enthusiasts of across-the-board liberalization of product and factor markets fall over each other in trying to defend the distortions produced by restrictions on free international movement of labor. See e.g. the exchange between Bela Balassa and Jagdish Bhagwati in Bhagwati 1986: 119.

[5] As we discuss later on in this section, Brazil and Colombia did follow the EP strategy during the 1970s, which resulted in their exceptional export performance in the 1980s. See Hirschman 1987.

[6] Coming, as they did, during the populist political phase in Latin America, these policies also proved to be pro-labour, particularly since the insulation of the economy allowed the maintenance of high industrial wages.

sector, and to emulate the production system of Western countries as soon as possible. While it was an 'indigenous response' here as well, the response was to the low industrial base and high import requirements rather than to a fear of dependence or from a generalized hostility to foreign or comprador interests.[7] Thus, while the promise of growth alone was not sufficient to make EP attractive to Latin American economists and policy-makers, in Asia it was; the main question there was not whether it should be adopted, but whether it could be administered effectively and efficiently.

Second, while EP also means different things to different people, and while it seems to have metamorphosed into the broader concept of 'economic liberalization', it has had, from the very outset, a strong association with the experience of the 'Gang of Four' countries, although the link has become increasingly tenuous as the concept has expanded to become almost synonymous with laissez-faire. While the high growth rate, the successful adjustment performance, and the export orientation of the Gang of Four is not a matter of much controversy, there are serious differences among economists over the causes of these phenomena. On the one hand, this experience could be interpreted narrowly as a technical and bureaucratic innovation: an efficient and dirigistic state pushing resources into selected export industries through a combination of government fiat, subsidies, credit controls, and export houses (see e.g. Pack and Westphal 1986). This interpretation would lead, logically, to prescriptions for strengthening state intervention and making it more effective and efficient. On the other hand, it could also be interpreted, as neoclassical economists have consistently tried to do, as a political or ideological innovation in the direction of a free market economy—an interpretation which leads directly to a prescription for wholesale liberalization.[8]

In the neoclassical literature, the title 'export promotion' was affixed retroactively (and very selectively) to the experience of these economies. Initially, when it meant a strategy which promised faster growth than IS, it was used to prescribe import liberalization and devaluation.[9] Later, as economists began to note on the one hand the limited success of import liberalization reforms, and on the other hand the successful adjustment of

[7] In India, the concern was not so much with terms of trade losses as with a bureaucratic desire to move quickly to the production of heavy industrial and capital goods as in the USSR, and to see India as a self-sufficient economic power; in other Asian countries the adoption of this strategy also resulted more from dirigistic concerns than from issues of North–South conflict. See the illuminating discussion in Myrdal 1968: 720–5, 799–806.

[8] A 'political' interpretation of the experience is provided, *post hoc ergo propter hoc*, by Jeffrey Sachs (1985), who argues, in the face of all direct evidence on the ideological position of the South Korean government, that South Korean policies emerged from an alliance of the State and the rural political groups. For a detailed criticism, see Taylor, this volume. See also Pack and Westphal 1986 and Dee 1986.

[9] In terms of concepts popularized by Corden 1971, this required the replacement of 'ordinary' (or tariff) protection with across-the-board incentives to industry generally in the form of 'exchange rate' protection. For an example of these recommendations, see Krueger 1978.

East Asian countries to the recent macroeconomic shocks, a new title, 'outward-oriented policies', was invented to describe and promote policies which promised growth as well as autonomy. These included, in addition to trade liberalization, exchange rate unification, removal of capital controls, and financial liberalization. The last of these recommendations, however, did not have a sound empirical basis, since neither South Korea nor Taiwan had free or open financial markets—unlike most Latin American countries, whose financial institutions had long been open to international capital markets. From 'outward orientation', it was a short step to the most recent transformation, to the notion of 'economic liberalization', which meant virtually a move towards laissez-faire—again, notwithstanding the fact that laissez-faire was hardly an appropriate description of East Asian countries—with the addition of privatization, deregulation, and de-unionization to the list of desirable reforms (see e.g. Krueger 1986).

Today, while the term 'economic liberalization' is used to suggest, ideally, the removal of controls from every market in an economy, the narrow set of markets chosen by most advocates of liberalization includes the markets for foreign exchange (both for current and capital account transactions), the financial market, the labour market, and the market for agricultural commodities (ibid. 16). Some writers, such as Krueger (ibid.) and Balassa (1986a) claim that these changes will facilitate the efficient and effective pursuit of virtually any economic or social goal. Others are less sanguine in this belief, but argue nevertheless that even if government intervention could improve welfare, governments should not be entrusted with such powers (see e.g. Krugman 1987).[10]

All the above writers suggest, explicitly or implicitly, that their arguments are vindicated by the recent successful experience of East Asian economies and the dismal performance of Latin American societies. The broad outlines of the differential performance are not a matter of much controversy; they can be seen from Tables 1.1–1.3, which present figures on the GDP growth rate, the inflation rate, and the debt burden for a select list of countries from three regions of the Third World: East Asia, South Asia, and Latin America. In the latter region, the deterioration in three performance indicators has been quite dramatic: growth has been negative for a number of years, inflation has escalated to historical highs, and foreign debt has assumed alarming proportions. In the other two regions, by contrast, past growth levels have been sustained into the 1980s (and, in South Asia, even exceeded), inflation is moderate, and debt ratios, while high, are still manageable. If the entire difference were due to the illiberal economies of Latin American countries, and the 'open' and 'liberal' policies of Asian governments, it would constitute indeed a formidable case for economic liberalization.

---

[10] These two views are not dissimilar to Franco Modigliani's characterization of the views of extreme monetarists in the US; see Modigliani 1977: 1.

1.2 A CRITIQUE OF ECONOMIC LIBERALIZATION

In the real world, matters are rarely so simple, and indeed there are several problems with this line of reasoning, many of which are brought out in this volume. First, the empirical support for the argument, to put it charitably, is weak and inconclusive. The identification of 'successful' Asia with openness and 'successless' Latin America with illiberalism is little better than a crude caricature. Institutions and arrangements in East Asian countries not only diverge significantly from the neoclassical ideal of laissez-faire, but some of their markets, particularly the market for domestic and international capital flows, have been among the most heavily regulated anywhere—certainly more so than in Latin American countries, which foundered on the rock of capital market shocks precisely because of greater financial openness. Moreover, South Asian countries (and China) succeeded with 'illiberal' economies, while Chile and Argentina languished despite the elixir of liberalization. Indeed, larger samples of countries do not reveal a significant empirical relationship between economic growth and either outward orientation or export-promotion. Second, the supposed relationship between prescribed policies and expected outcomes is not verified by experience. Exchange rate 'rationalization' seems to lead frequently to declines rather than to increases in export shares, and equally frequently to balance of payments crises as to improvements. Policies turn out, often to be ineffective, or, what is worse, counter-effective.

Last, and most importantly, even in the unlikely event that the connection between free markets, government policies, and economic performance in East Asian countries were to prove conclusive, it would still not be clear that the relevant preconditions could be duplicated in other countries, particularly those in Latin America. The neoclassical argument for liberalization rests, ultimately, upon a willingness to believe in the efficacy and optimality of free markets, which provides a way of interpreting recent experience, and, in a circular fashion, using the interpretation to argue for economic liberalization and free markets. Alternative interpretations would have a different view of the efficacy of markets or the role of the government in contemporary societies; the next section brings together in a summarized form the arguments made by the contributors to this volume.

It is fitting to start with a slightly modified version of Lance Taylor's distinction between several related concepts in the literature on openness and liberalization:

1. *Openness* is a description of the economy, indicating its degree of integration with global economic forces. It can be divided into two categories:

    (*a*) *trade openness*, which refers to the exposure of the goods market to the international economy and is measured by the ratio of exports to GDP;

(b) *financial openness*, which indicates the exposure of the domestic financial system to world capital markets and is measured by the volume, nature, and regulation of international capital flows, including such factors as the size of the foreign debt, or the existence of capital controls.

2. *Outward orientation* is a description of government policies—import liberalization, devaluation, changes in bias of trade policy—which supposedly create economic openness.

3. *The 'liberal' economy* is, again, a description of an economy with minimal government restrictions, not only on international trade in goods or assets, but also in domestic financial, commodities, and labour markets.

4. *Economic liberalization* is a strategy of policy reform intended to take the economy from a state of 'illiberalism' to that of 'liberalism', or, in more hackneyed terms, towards laissez-faire.

The case for economic liberalization has rested upon the claim that all of the above contribute to higher growth and reduced dependence of the economy. However, the papers in this volume demonstrate that this claim is not supported by the evidence, and that: (a) neither economic openness nor outward orientation leads to improved economic performance; (b) changes in policy orientation do not lead necessarily to changes in openness; (c) the appropriate degree of openness is different in different societies, and attempts to impose a universal solution by force have been costly as well as ineffective; and that therefore (d) rather than getting hung up on how to liberalize the economy, and at what speed, economists should be looking at the institutional and historical features of different societies in order to understand their functioning, the range of their prospects, and the feasible and desirable directions of policy and institutional changes. The salient features of this critique are summarized below.

1.2.1 Liberalization and economic performance

Lance Taylor looks at the recent experience of fifty Third World countries, to find that neither trade openness nor outward orientation is linked with higher growth or reduced vulnerabilty: 'fast-growing countries are more or less open, have diverse patterns of specialization, and their success is not obviously led by exports, industrial or otherwise'. He also questions the supposed association between economic performance and the World Bank's 'distortion index'.[11] Citing work by Aghazadeh and Evans (1985), Taylor

---

[11] A formal presentation of this index is to be found in Agarwala 1983, and a summary in World Bank 1983. The index was criticized for its selectivity and bias by Aghazadeh and Evans (1985).

argues that not only was the index based on a biased sample of countries, but that only two of the underlying variables—real wage growth and real exchange rate appreciation—were negatively related to output growth. Since these are determined by institutional factors, such as open distributional conflict or the onset of 'Dutch disease', the perceived association represents the impact of historical and institutional factors rather than that of misguided government intervention in the economy.

Hughes and Singh also challenge the mainstream assertion that closed economies are less capable of adjusting smoothly to external shocks. They point out that in looking at the association between openness and vulnerability, one has to distinguish between trade and financial openness. The two are similar in a minor respect: both lead to an increased vulnerability to shocks originating in their respective spheres. However, they are dissimilar in an even more important respect: while trade openness does increase flexibility to cope with financial market shocks, financial openness *reduces* the ability to adjust to any exogenous shocks. The explanation is simple. An external shock creates the equivalent of a transfer problem, which is easier to handle in an open trade regime because of the larger size of the tradable goods sector. On the other hand, financial openness can lead to greater fluctuations in capital flows, and thus to more frequent 'shocks'; more importantly, in the event of a trade shock, financial openness can result in large-scale capital flight, which will exacerbate rather than ease the problem of adjustment.

While most neoclassical economists interpret this as the pathology of the closed economy, the authors here suggest that it derives from the internal inconsistency of an inward-oriented trade structure and an open financial regime. The argument is, that if, for political, structural, or welfare reasons, a country has a relatively closed traded sector, then it should choose a more careful regulation of its international financial transactions as well as a strategy of low foreign debt.

1.2.2 Liberalization and openness

The authors represented in this volume also disagree with the view that the openness of the trade regime is a pure policy variable, arguing that the supposed link between policy orientation and trade regimes is not borne out in practice. Outward-oriented policies do not lead either to trade openness (defined as a high ratio of exports to GDP), or to 'benign' financial openness (absence of capital flight). Furthermore, there are sound theoretical reasons why this should be so.

Edward Amadeo and I introduce the notion of political and social constraints on policy making. The existence of social groups that, to use Joan Robinson's description of the economy, use political action to defend their interests can render some policies ineffective, others infeasible, and yet others undesirable.[12] In particular, as Lance Taylor points out as well, some important economic variables—such as real wages or the real exchange rate—represent underlying social and institutional arrangements, and often cannot be determined by policy alone. As a result, policies which are introduced with the intent of influencing such variables will not produce the same result in all societies.

Hughes and Singh examine the recent experience of a number of countries, from the North as well as the South, to demonstrate that empirical evidence does not support the contention that exchange rate policies influence either export shares or sustained capital movements. These results are consistent with those of the few studies which have examined this link in any detail. Albert Fishlow makes the same argument by looking at other recent experiences. The point is that despite the almost religious belief in this assertion, the bulk of the evidence points in exactly the opposite direction. But then, as Lance Taylor reminds us at the outset of Chapter 4, facts do not win arguments in economics.

1.2.3 The role of the state

The argument over liberalization boils down, eventually, to one over the limits of state activity, and all the papers have something to contribute on the issue. The problem is stated succinctly by Albert Fishlow:

The principal deficiency of the neoclassical approach, however, is its failure to inform about the conditions under which the state can play a positive role. Beyond creating (minimalist) rules to enhance the market, there is no policy advice. Nor, except for resort to authoritarian tutelage, is there guidance about creating and sustaining political support, even for liberalization. There is too much evidence of different types of state action in the course of economic development, successful and unsuccessful, for such a theoretical political economy to suffice. It is a central theme of late-comer development that is not casually dismissed. And, even accepting the conclusion of excess intervention in many countries at the present, there remains the need to establish priorities about what the state should do and not do, and the need to implement them. (Ch. 5, p. 000).

Many writers have pointed to the strong association between economic liberalization and political authoritarianism, partly as a warning but also to

---

[12] E.g. currency devaluation might be unacceptable to a prudent government because its effects are not well understood and often deviate substantially from the predictions of simple models; a shift from indirect to direct taxes may not be possible in the short run (and occasionally, not in the long run either) because of administrative difficulties; and orthodox adjustment programmes might be rejected by democratic governments because of the likelihood of (anticipated or unanticipated) non-economic costs.

suggest the difficulty of implementing these prescriptions in societies with strong democratic aspirations. Rather than withdrawing from the economic sphere, as liberalization enthusiasts hoped, the state in liberalizing societies seems to have begun to invade every sphere of social activity.

In Chapter 2, Edward Amadeo and I address this paradox by arguing that there is a misleading presumption in this literature—that the only choice available to Third World societies is between a 'hard', authoritarian state, which can impose the liberal order without the need for a political consensus, and a 'soft' populist state, which would achieve political solvency through distributional appeasement. Taking the 'Keynesian' perspective of governance, we suggest that it is more appropriate to look at the state as a mediator of social conflict, as an agency which can create the basis for co-operative actions even by groups whose immediate interests are opposed to each other. This perspective helps to distinguish between the (more problematic) situation where the state is characterized by intense differentiation and tension and that where the conflicts are relatively muted. To assume that a simple 'return to the market' will suffice in all possible circumstances is to be wilfully naive and irresponsible. It would require, as indeed it has in Latin American countries, the use of extensive state terror to coerce a highly independent populace into submission; and even then the success of the endeavour is far from assured.

A pertinent illustration of this dilemma comes from the analysis of labour market institutions, taken up by Amadeo and myself in Chapter 6. The argument for liberalization advocates the use of 'tight' (or 'low-wage') labour policies and a move towards the decentralized labour unions existing in East Asian countries. In an attempt to evaluate the consequences of this suggestion, we look at the rich variety of structural and historical features which underlay the evolution of labour market arrangements in various countries. The immense differences in these characteristics indicates quite convincingly that efforts to reproduce one system in another society will end not only in failure, but in disastrous failure. The discussion has special relevance for Latin America, where there have been several attempts in the last two to three decades to roll back the democratic gains made over the last century by the populations in general and working groups in particular.

Now, the kind of institutional change prescribed in many contemporary writings seems singularly inappropriate and undesirable for a region with Latin America's history of conflict, struggle, and reform. Clearly, while institutional reforms may be necessary, even desirable, in these countries, they will have to be something entirely different, something more consistent with this history. Chapter 6 shows that there are other possibilities too, of which the one most consistent with social democracy and popular participation is the Scandinavian model of 'social corporatism', which has been highly successful (in economic terms). The suggestion is intended, however, not to assert the unquestioning superiority of this model over others, but rather to suggest simply that alternatives to the authoritarian solution do exist.

1.3. THE LATIN AMERICAN EXPERIENCE

A major plank in the liberalization thesis has been its claim that the recent downturn of economic activity in Latin America derives from the closed nature of its economies and the unwisdom of the economic policies of its governments. All the authors of this volume find this assertion questionable.

Before we proceed, it may be mentioned that prominent neoclassical writers discussing these issues often divide the countries according to some simple index of policy orientation. However, the problem with this methodology is that the recent economic performance of Latin American countries is fairly uniform, while that of, say, 'outward-oriented countries' is quite variable. Thus, this approach will either not be able to explain the uniformity of regional experience or will obscure it behind a cloud of arbitrary generalizations. The regional uniformity is not at all surprising in view of the fact that countries within a region (but not 'outward-oriented countries') often share similar colonial histories, sustained cultural and social linkages, a lingua franca which facilitates the transmission of ideological controversies, and occasionally even similarities in (physical and human) resource endowments (see e.g. Maddison 1985: 53). Furthermore, it has to be admitted that most analysts writing on these issues focus on the experience of precisely one country, i.e. South Korea.[13] The average performance of any group with South Korea as a member would automatically go up. Recognition of this point would not only make the debate somewhat clearer, but would also help to direct attention towards the hitherto ignored institutional and historical factors which influence policies as well as outcomes.

Returning to liberalization, the neoclassical argument here is that although real incomes of the 'open' East Asian countries were affected more by the trade shocks of the 1970s, they managed to accommodate them without serious impairment of their economies; Latin American economies, on the other hand, despite being better insulated from external shocks by virtue of their low trade shares, were unable to adjust successfully because of the closed and rigid nature of their economies. This assertion is contested here on empirical grounds both by Albert Fishlow and by Alan Hughes and Ajit Singh. They make two points. First, that the 'dismal' economic performance of Latin American countries is somewhat exaggerated; and second, that the direct impact of *all* external shocks was greater, not lesser, on Latin America than elsewhere.

1.3.1 Economic performance

As a guide to economic performance, Tables 1.1–1.3 present figures for the last three decades on the customary indices of performance, growth, inflation and debt accumulation. Table 1.1 shows, first, that while the growth experience of individual countries was quite varied, at the regional level the differences were not very significant until 1980. Between 1960–70 and 1970–80, median regional growth rates changed very little. The dramatic downturn in economic performance came about at the end of the decade: after 1980 Latin American growth fell precipitously, by as much as 4–6 per cent.[14] Subsequent experience has been equally disappointing, Brazil and Chile being the only countries to recover their growth momentum (in 1984 and 1985, respectively). East Asian growth rates also declined but, except for the Philippines, by a modest 2 per cent. In South Asia, the 1980s actually witnessed an increase in growth rates.

Clearly, as far as adjustment to the first trade shock was concerned, the difference between the two regions was not very significant. Yet, looking from the perspective of the 1980s, it cannot be denied that in the long run the Asian growth performance was superior. It must be noted, however, that this perception is relatively recent in origin. Up until 1980, most observers seemed to regard Latin American countries also as examples of successful adaptation to external trade shocks:[15] growth rates were high except in countries plagued by exogenous political disturbances; and while foreign debt was accumulating rapidly, it was being used primarily to finance investment rather than consumption (Sachs 1985). This perception changed dramatically with the onset of the debt crisis in 1982. Not only Mexico, whose default action precipitated the crisis, or even Brazil and Argentina with their large debt burdens, but the entire continent began to be seen as being in a state of crisis.

Coming now to the issue of inflation, it should be stated at the outset that, given the vast differences in political and institutional circumstances of the countries being examined here, it would be simplistic to use it as an indicator of policy adequacy. These differences are reflected in the well-known tendency of Latin American countries towards high inflation, which derives

---

[13] Of the other Gang of Four economies, Hong Kong and Singapore are city-states, and therefore of limited relevance as models for other countries. Taiwan has strong similarities to South Korea but its relevance is complicated by its geopolitical situation, which is even more unique than that of South Korea, and its data are not as readily available as those for other countries.

[14] In at least half of the big Latin American countries, the severe economic decline started in 1982; the exceptions being Argentina (1980), Bolivia (1979), Brazil (1981), Colombia (1981), Uruguay (1981), and Venezuela (1978).

[15] Hirschman (1987) labels the period up to the end of the 1970s as Latin America's *Trente glorieuses*, after the term coined by Jean Fourasti for the French post-war experience. In this regard, see also Ominami 1987.

Table 1.1 Per capita GDP growth rates in Latin America and Asia (% per year)

Country	1960–70	1970–80	1980–7
Latin America			
Major debtors			
Argentina	2.8	0.6	–1.7
Brazil	2.5	6.2	1.1
Chile	2.4	0.7	–0.7
Mexico	3.9	2.1	–1.7
Others			
Venezuela	2.6	1.7	–2.6
Colombia	2.1	3.6	1.0
Ecuador	...	5.8	–1.4
Peru	2.1	0.4	–1.1
Bolivia	2.9	2.3	–4.8
Uruguay	0.1	3.2	–1.8
Paraguay	1.7	5.4	–1.9
Simple average	2.3	2.9	–1.4
Asia			
East Asia			
China	3.3	4.0	9.2
S. Korea	6.1	7.8	7.2
Taiwan	6.6	7.3	4.6*
Philippines	2.1	3.6	–3.0
Malaysia	3.7	5.4	1.8
Thailand	5.4	4.7	3.6
Indonesia	1.9	5.3	1.5
Simple average	4.1	5.4	3.6
South Asia			
Burma	0.4	2.2	2.9
Pakistan	3.9	1.6	3.5
Sri Lanka	2.2	2.5	3.1
Bangladesh	1.3	1.3	1.0
Nepal	0.7	0.0	2.0
India	1.1	1.5	2.5
Simple average	1.6	1.5	2.5

* 1980–5.
Source: World Bank 1982, 1987, 1989.

Table 1.2 Inflation rates in Asia and Latin America (% per year)

Country	1960–70	1970–80	1980–7
Latin America			
Major debtors			
Argentina	21.7	130.8	298.7
Brazil	46.1	36.7	166.3
Chile	33.2	185.6	20.6
Mexico	3.6	19.3	68.9
Others			
Venezuela	1.3	12.1	11.4
Colombia	11.9	22.0	23.7
Ecuador	. . .	14.4	29.5
Peru	10.4	30.7	101.5
Bolivia	3.5	22.3	601.8
Uruguay	51.1	62.3	54.5
Paraguay	3.1	12.4	21.0
Asia			
East Asia			
China	. . .	. . .	4.2
S. Korea	17.4	19.8	5.0
Taiwan	3.5	12.2	3.3*
Philippines	5.8	13.2	16.7
Malaysia	–0.3	7.5	1.1
Thailand	1.8	9.9	2.8
Indonesia	. . .	20.5	8.5
South Asia			
Burma	2.7	11.2	2.1
Pakistan	3.3	13.5	7.3
Sri Lanka	1.8	12.6	11.8
Bangladesh	3.7	16.9	11.1
Nepal	7.7	8.6	8.8
India	7.1	8.5	7.7

* 1980–5.
Source: World Bank 1982, 1987, 1989.

from the more pronounced level of distributional conflict and the existence of inertial propagation mechanisms rather than from failure in adjustment. In any event, the differences in historical experience of various countries are brought out in Table 1.2. Before 1970, only one Asian country, South Korea, experienced double-digit inflation, as against more than half of the larger countries in Latin America. After 1970, while every single country in our sample registered an increase in average rates of inflation, the increase was much more pronounced in Latin America, and became even more so after 1980.

The third index of economic performance is the accumulation of foreign debt. Table 1.3 presents figures on debt–GNP ratios in 1970, 1981, and 1987 for the same sample of countries. While on average the debt ratio in Latin America in 1981 (37.8 per cent) was higher than that in East Asia (12.9 per cent), or South Asia (15.8 per cent), the latter two figures were pulled down by the weight of China and India, which pursued debt-free policies. If these two countries are excluded from the sample, the debt ratios in the three regions seem not significantly different. There are, however, significant differences in debt-servicing requirements, because, first, Latin American countries export a much smaller proportion of their output than do the East Asian economies; and second, a higher percentage of the Asian debt (including that of South Korea) was on fixed interest rates, which provided partial protection against the interest rate escalation of the late 1970s.

This, however, is not the entire story on debt. As it turns out, the rapid accumulation of debt in many Latin American countries is related not to policy or structural factors, but rather to the openness of their capital markets, which allowed large volumes of capital flight—Mexico $26.5 billion (48 per cent of gross capital inflows), Argentina $19 million (65 per cent), Venezuela $22 billion. In Asia, the only country where capital flight is considered significant is the Philippines (World Bank 1985).[16] In contrast, countries with some forms of capital controls (India, South Korea, Brazil, Colombia) suffered far smaller volumes of measured capital flight. In fact, as Sachs (1985) reports in a table reproduced here as Table 1.4, the cumulative current account deficits in Latin American countries were quite comparable to those in Asian countries. Excluding mineral-exporting Indonesia, Malaysia, and Venezuela, Latin American current account deficits are no higher (and, in fact, are somewhat lower) than the East Asian figures, even though their debt ratios in 1981 were somewhat higher.[17] The obvious inference is the existence of capital flight in the former countries.

[16] Notice that illegal capital flight through the black market is more difficult to measure and may be understated, particularly in the case of countries with financial sectors strongly linked to the Western states; see also Sachs 1985.

[17] The debt ratios in Table 1.4 differ from those in Table 1.3 because the latter includes only publicly guaranteed long-term debt. Note here that the Philippines seems once again to be closer to the Latin American norm than the Asian one.

Table 1.3 Debt ratios (total long-term debt/GNP) in Asia and Latin America

Country	1970	1981	1987
Latin America			
Major debtors			
Argentina	23.3	41.8	73.9
Brazil	12.2	24.4	39.4
Chile	32.2	40.6	125.2
Mexico	17.0	23.2	77.5
Others			
Venezuela	8.7	22.7	94.5
Colombia	22.5	16.5	50.2
Ecuador	14.8	42.7	107.4
Peru	38.1	34.5	40.5
Bolivia	47.3	92.0	133.7
Uruguay	12.5	14.9	58.6
Paraguay	19.2*	17.0	54.7
Weighted average, Latin America	18.7	37.8	60.1
Asia			
East Asia			
China	0.7*	0.7*	10.4
S. Korea	23.3	33.0	34.3
Taiwan	. . .	11.3*	7.9*
Philippines	21.1	27.1	86.5
Malaysia	10.9	30.4	74.3
Thailand	11.1	20.6	44.2
Indonesia	30.0	21.7	79.6
Weighted average, East Asia	6.5	12.9	33.8
South Asia			
Burma	5.0	28.5	42.1**
Pakistan	30.8	28.9	47.1
Sri Lanka	16.4*	37.4	72.4
Bangladesh	0.0*	27.5	54.4
Nepal	0.3	10.1	34.2
India	15.4	11.5	18.8
Weighted average, South Asia	15.6	15.8	25.9

* = Public and publicly guaranteed debt only/GNP.   ** = 1985.
Source: World Debt Tables 1988–89.

Table 1.4 External debt indicators: selected countries

	Cumulative current account deficit 1970–80 (% of 1981 GDP)	D/Y 1981	D/X 1981
Argentina	2.3	31.6	334.7
Brazil	22.8	26.1	298.7
Chile	19.8	47.6	290.0
Mexico	13.9	30.9	258.8
Peru	19.3	44.7	223.5
Venezuela	–7.5	42.1	134.0
Weighted average	13.6	31.3	271.5
Colombia	0.4	21.9	182.9
Indonesia	0.6	24.1	87.1
S. Korea	24.6	27.6	76.6
Malaysia	–2.0	27.8	51.8
Thailand	22.4	25.7	103.1
Weighted average	6.4	26.0	77.0
Philippines	18.3	40.6	214.6

Source: Sachs 1985: table 3.

The above data suggest that the decline in Latin American growth performance is quite recent and dates from the complex of real and financial shocks which hit the world economy during 1979–82, not from the terms of trade shocks of the early 1970s. Indeed, both Latin American and Asian countries managed to accommodate to the first oil shock, partly by relying on foreign resource inflows. However, the higher (and increasing) dependence of the former on external financial markets, and the large volume of capital flight from their countries, made further adjustment along similar lines impossible.

1.3.2 Magnitude of external shocks

The second aspect of recent experience which has figured in the advocacy of liberalization policies is the argument that the exogenous shocks which led to the deterioration of economic conditions in Latin American countries were smaller in relative magnitudes than the shocks which hit East Asian countries at the same time. The inference is that the extent of the damage in the former must have been produced by domestic policy factors—in particular, by the closed, and hence rigid, nature of their economies—and not by the shocks themselves. This contention is challenged by Fishlow and by Hughes and Singh, on the grounds, first that the crucial external shock (i.e. debt strangulation) was concentrated entirely in Latin America, and second, that the argument ignores several other shocks, internal as well as external, whose effects were distributed much more favourably for Asian countries.

Conditions in many Third World countries were influenced adversely by a succession of external shocks during the 1970s and the 1980s. These shocks included: (a) the terms of trade effects associated with the increases in price of oil and foodgrains in the period 1972–3; (b) export volume effects of the recession-induced slowdown in world trade persisting, with some interruptions, for almost a decade and a half; (c) the second oil shock in 1979; (d) capital losses and adverse current account effects of the increase in interest rates in world financial markets since 1979; and (e) the financial squeeze due to the drying up of the flow of credit to many third world economies with the onset of the debt crisis in 1982.[18]

The direct effects of the *trade* shocks were generally larger in Asian countries, whose goods markets are more exposed to the world economy;[19] those of the *interest-rate* shock were more equally distributed between the continents, while the effects of *debt strangulation* have been felt primarily in Latin America. This result has been established in many recent studies including Balassa (1986b),[20] Balassa and McCarthy (1984), Helleiner (1986), and Sachs (1985), as well as by Lance Taylor in this volume. Thus, while external shocks in general could not have caused the crisis in Latin America, debt strangulation might have had a role to play.

The second point is that the external shocks mentioned above were not the only exogenous source of disturbance for Third World economies in the last two decades. First, with the exception of Pakistan and Bangladesh (which were recovering from a traumatic civil war and the partition of the country in 1971), and later the Philippines, the period from 1973 to 1985 was one of remarkable political stability in Asian countries, while Latin America

---

[18] Most analyses have, however, focused attention on the first four shocks and ignored the debt shock, presumably because they saw it as the consequence of policy and adjustment behaviour of the affected countries rather than of purely external circumstances.

[19] See Sachs 1985: 5–7, esp. Table 2; also Taylor, this volume, esp. Tables 4.4 and 4.5. While both sets of data are in broad agreement on the 1979 shocks, Taylor also quotes figures on the 1973 shock which differ from those for the 1979 shock only in that disruption in Chile is greater than in most Asian countries.

[20] For instance, Balassa 1986b showed that the average adverse impact of the two external shocks (excluding the debt strangulation) on 'outward-oriented countries' (OOCs, which included only Chile and Uruguay from Latin America), as a percentage of GNP, was between two to three times that on 'inward-oriented countries' (IOCs, which included Argentina, Brazil, Mexico, Peru, and eleven others).

witnessed an exacerbation of political tension almost everywhere: Argentina, Brazil, Chile, Ecuador, Peru, and Bolivia, not to mention the expanding conflict in Central America. As Fishlow suggests, these political conflicts could not but affect economic performances.

Second, as Hughes and Singh show, several Asian countries received 'positive' economic shocks during this period. Pakistan, Sri Lanka, India, Bangladesh, and to a lesser extent South Korea and the Philippines registered substantial increases in the receipt of worker remittances from their nationals working overseas and benefited from the expanded market for agricultural and other imports in the oil-exporting countries of the Middle East. Furthermore, many Asian countries (Pakistan, Bangladesh, Malaysia, Thailand) registered strong agricultural growth during this period for reasons unconnected to the external environment, and the resulting increase in exportable surpluses helped moderate the effects of the terms of trade shocks on payments balances.

Third, as Hughes and Singh also point out, Latin American countries received other adverse shocks during this period in addition to political disturbances. These included the 'contagion effect'—the Mexican default leading to a cut-off of loans even to those Latin American countries which had not defaulted; 'Dutch disease'—the relatively greater incidence in Latin America of the adverse effects of foreign exchange bonanzas; the equally higher incidence of capital flight, which has already been mentioned; and the initiation in the Southern Cone countries of Latin America—Argentina, Chile, and Uruguay—under the urging of neoclassical economists, of a programme of liberalization, which may have had even more of an impact on their domestic situation than the external shocks.[21]

1.3.3 Policy errors

Lastly, there is the view that the debt crisis emerged in Latin America because of the inappropriate commercial policies pursued by governments during the adjustment process. The adjustment policies used by various countries in recent years have been characterized in terms of demand contraction, expenditure switching, and debt accumulation by many writers including Balassa (1986b), Helleiner (1986), and Taylor (Ch. 4 this volume). Demand contraction was not used significantly during the first shock period by countries in either region but had become important everywhere by the time of the second shock.[22] With respect to the choice between the other two

[21] The story of these experiments has been related in several recent papers. For an excellent structuralist analysis, see Foxley 1983. For a sophisticated neoclassical defence of the experiments, see Khan and Zahler 1985.

[22] Within the rubric of aggregate demand management, however, there are some interesting patterns: Several countries in Asia (S. Korea, Thailand, the Philippines) as well as in Latin America

options—expenditure switching and debt accumulation—there are significant differences between Latin American and Asian countries. Balassa (1986b) reports that 'Outward Oriented Countries' (OOCs, a term that includes most East Asian economies) relied primarily on expenditure-switching policies, while Latin American countries used foreign borrowing to offset the adverse consequences of the shocks. Balassa, however, looks at the behaviour of the affected variables (output, trade, debt, etc.), rather than at the policy variables (exchange rates, budgetary variables, etc.), where the differences are not as significant.

In principle, it is possible for the same observed level of accommodation to be introduced immediately (in one or two years), gradually (spread out over a longer period), or belatedly (at the end of a period of worsening conditions). Naturally, looking at discrete data separated by a few years would tend to obscure this pattern.

The pattern in expenditure-switching policies becomes clear from Table 5, which presents data on the movement of the real exchange rate[23] in selected countries between 1978 and 1983. Most countries registered a real devaluation of 20–50 per cent over this period, the exceptions being resource-rich Venezuela and Thailand, war-torn Argentina, and the somewhat anomalous Colombia.

The interesting picture, however, is the dynamic one of a slow appreciation of Latin American currencies (except the Brazilian cruzeiro) following the 1979 shocks, and a massive real depreciation with the start of the debt crisis in 1982. In Asian countries, on the other hand, the oil shock was followed by an immediate, though smaller, real depreciation, in most cases maintained throughout the period.[24] The only exceptions to this regional pattern were the Philippines, which was close to, but less extreme than, the Latin American experience; Brazil, which had a massive devaluation immediately after the second shock and maintained it thereafter; and the OPEC countries

(Chile, Uruguay, Argentina) reduced consumption but raised investment, in many cases by an even larger amount, in response to the first shock, and did the reverse of this action in response to the second one.

[23] It should be noted that much of the perversity of the Latin American response to the onset of the crisis in the late 1970s can be explained by experiment of global monetarism in the Southern Cone countries of Latin America, which had been started at the behest of the very economists who were later to deplore the dismal performance of their client countries. This project led these countries to experiment with fixed exchange rates in order to influence price expectations and therefore the rate of inflation by refusing to validate the latter. For a review of these experiments, see Diaz-Alejandro 1981, or Hirschmann 1987. For the Chilean experiment, see Foxley 1983.

[24] Sachs 1985 suggests that one reason for this difference is the fact that Latin American economies continued to maintain their parity with the US dollar during the period when it was appreciating with respect to other hard currencies, while Asian economies were quick to shift to a basket of currencies and managed to hedge themselves against this appreciation.

Table 1.5 Real exchange rate movement (end of year)

	1978	1979	1980	1981	1982	1983	1984	1985	1986
Latin America									
Argentina	100.0	68.3	47.7	90.5	231.5	254.3	227.9	264.9	239.3
Brazil	100.0	181.3	269.9	270.6	287.7	465.4	505.2	529.2	490.8
Chile	100.0	85.4	72.1	70.4	124.6	121.9	162.3	181.0	173.4
Colombia	100.0	94.1	93.1	96.9	106.7	116.4	147.6	153.7	166.8
Mexico	100.0	90.7	78.4	76.1	185.1	149.3	128.2	165.6	232.8
Uruguay	100.0	75.1	64.1	62.5	166.7	145.0	160.1	157.7	137.1
Venezuela	100.0	89.8	78.4	76.4	80.1	78.9	117.6	114.1	126.9
South Asia									
Bangladesh	100.0	100.9	101.1	122.6	140.5	144.3	133.9	143.6	138.6
India	100.0	90.9	89.3	102.7	107.3	111.4	129.0	121.9	120.9
Pakistan	100.0	103.1	101.8	100.7	127.5	131.7	142.0	144.2	152.1
Sri Lanka	100.0	93.9	99.4	103.0	102.4	106.9	96.0	104.7	104.7
East Asia									
Indonesia	100.0	82.3	69.5	66.0	71.9	94.4	95.0	95.5	116.4
S. Korea	100.0	91.1	108.4	109.6	116.7	123.7	128.6	138.3	133.9
Malaysia	100.0	96.3	99.8	109.1	117.4	117.4	119.2	125.1	150.3
Philippines	100.0	94.9	91.8	97.8	107.5	152.6	149.3	126.2	137.2
Thailand	100.0	97.7	92.4	104.5	107.7	108.5	131.2	130.4	128.7

Source: IMF 1987.
Note: The real exchange rate index is calculated by deflating the dollar exchange rate with the ratio of the domestic to the US GDP deflator index. An increase in the index means a real devaluation.

in the sample (Venezuela and Indonesia), which maintained the values of their currencies more or less to the end.[25]

These data might suggest that expenditure-switching policies in Asian countries were timely, while those in Latin American economies were delayed by reliance on debt finance until the increasing difficulties due to the debt crisis and loss of credit-worthiness made further postponement impossible;[26] alternatively, they could indicate that, given the domestic rate of inflation, particularly of wages, and the nature of social conflict, it was impossible for Latin American countries to enforce a real devaluation without running the risk of the exacerbation of tensions and the incurrence of

[25] A similar result is reported by Khan (1986), who estimated real effective (against a trade-weighted basket of currencies) exchange rates for two groups of countries, that of industrial exporters (East Asian), and those from the Western hemisphere.
[26] See for instance, Balassa 1985, 1986*b*; Sachs 1985; Khan 1986; and Bianchi, Devlin, and Ramos 1987.

excessive social costs. However, the general recognition of the economic crisis enabled the emergence of a consensus in which massive depreciation could, and indeed did, take place. In any event, it is not clear whether this path would have turned out to have been so fraught with adversity in the absence of capital flight.

The picture which emerges from the above discussion is the following. While it is generally believed that Asian economies were hit harder by the recent external shocks (due to their greater exposure to the international economy), there are good reasons to doubt this assertion. When domestic political events and other exogenous factors are taken into account, it would seem that Latin American countries found themselves facing a particularly unfortunate conjunction of events in the 1970s. The situation of Asian economies, while similar with respect to the international terms of trade shocks, was otherwise more comfortable than that of their Latin American counterparts. As such, while there are significant differences in growth performance between the two regions, it is not entirely clear that these differences can be attributed solely, or even primarily, to differences in policy choices or to the relative degree of openness of the different economies.

1.4 CONCLUSIONS: POSSIBILITIES FOR THE FUTURE

Abraham Maslow once said that if the only tool you have is a hammer, everything begins to look like a nail. The prescription of liberalizing all conceivable markets in countries in every conceivable political circumstance is beginning to look increasingly like the application of Maslow's hammer. The argument of the papers presented in this volume is that these prescriptions are neither feasible nor desirable, and are likely to cause greater damage than the malady itself. Having said that, however, it must be stressed that the need for urgency in the search for a solution to the stalemate in Latin America is readily apparent. The attempt here to point out the limitations of economic liberalization is intended not as a counsel of despair, but rather as a step in the discovery of more fruitful ways of handling the situation.

The proposals which emerge from this volume focus on three aspects of the situation: (a) short-run solutions to the immediate crisis; (b) long-run (structural) solutions pertaining to the links with the international economy; and (c) long-run solutions of an internal character. On the short-run issue, Lance Taylor speaks for all the authors when he stresses the urgency of instituting some form of debt relief so that the flow of resources from the North to the South can recommence (or, at least that reverse flows can be arrested). Unless concerted international effort is undertaken to initiate some form of recycling (Okita, Jayawardena, and Sengupta 1986), or debt write-off or write-down, the only alternatives may be overt or veiled repudiation. The

point is that without some concerted international effort in this direction,
most Third World countries will be starved for investment resources and will
suffer slow growth for the foreseeable future.

On the international aspects of the long-run solution, Taylor as well as
Hughes and Singh are explicit in their recommendations for the 'selective
delinking' of the economy. This is not because selective policies are
unproblematic, but rather because they are less risky in current circumstances.
The idea is that each country should be able to choose an optimal degree of
openness to the international economy, one which would allow the utilization
of benefits from trade without exposing the economy to excessive dependence
upon external events beyond its control. One area of clear agreement is the
desirability of some form of insulation from fluctuations in the international
capital markets. For larger countries, the optimal strategy may include, in
addition, an 'inward-oriented' trade strategy as well, but this will not be
feasible for smaller countries (defined by Taylor as having a population of less
than 20 million). This indicates that the current dim prospects for world
trade pose the greatest threat to the smaller countries, and some means will
have to be sought to offset their disadvantage. South–South trade may be one
solution, but it is not likely to be a major factor in the immediate future.

On the structural solutions of an internal character, the proposals revolve
around Albert Fishlow's notion of reconstructing a developmental state.
Such a state would seek to manage rather than to suppress or ignore social
conflict, and would encourage the construction of institutions which facilitate
this task. The urgency of institutional development would depend, of course,
on the nature of social conflict in each country, but two generalizations can be
advanced. First, in labour markets, given that the object of social institutions is
to enable labour and capital to reach stable and credible compromises; in this
model, the effort should be to strengthen rather than to weaken the labour
movement and to incorporate it into national economic decision-making so
that a larger number of social decisions can be reached in a co-operative rather
than a conflictual manner. In addition, the idea is for labour unions to shoulder
the burden of social responsibility to complement their often unacknowledged
but real influence over social and political life in the country.

Similarly, when it comes to assets markets, greater liberalization means
the unfettering of the financial sector from the imperatives of industrial
development, whether state-led or not. An alternative solution is a co-
ordinating role for the state, by maintaining some form of regulation over the
financial sector (including such elements as nationalization of banks and
other financial institutions), some form of control or restrictions over
international capital movements and maintaining a policy regime which can
keep up with the development of informal financial institutions. The parallels
and analogy between the two sets of propositions may be evident.

To summarize, the authors of this volume believe that current attempts to seek a universal approach to the problems of Third World economies based on neoclassical prescriptions of liberalization and openness are seriously misguided in that they ignore the important role of institutions and history—as opportunities as well as constraints. Recognition of these factors would lead us to examine more closely the special circumstances of each country or region in order to discover its particular strengths and weaknesses, and to chart out a desirable direction for social change. This is not a new message, by any means, but it bears repetition precisely because it is all too readily forgotten. G. W. F. Hegel warned us a long time ago that 'the only thing we learn from history, is that we learn nothing from history'. This collection of papers is, among other things, an effort to avoid the consequences implicit in this warning.

2

Policy, Governance, and the Management of Conflict

Edward J. Amadeo and Tariq Banuri

2.1 INTRODUCTION

This paper is concerned with a simple puzzle. Why have Latin American economies proven so remarkably fragile in the face of the macroeconomic shocks of the 1970s and 1980s? Even a decade ago, there was great optimism in the region. Growth was high, per capita incomes compared favourably with the rest of the Third World, industrialization and urbanization were proceeding apace; even though there were problems, they did not appear insurmountable. Today, that optimism has disappeared. In many countries growth has been negative for a succession of years, inflation has skyrocketed, and foreign debt has reached alarming proportions. No one today places much faith in the ability of the governments or economists in Latin America to find a way out of this deepening quagmire.[1] In contrast, Asian countries have been able to maintain respectable rates of growth despite the recent crisis, and in some cases even to exceed their earlier performance.

The contrast between the crisis in Latin America and the relatively 'successful' outcomes in Asia has been explained by a group of neoclassical economists as the result of massive government interventions and erroneous and misguided policies by governments of the former group of countries. Part of the motivation for writing this paper is our profound disagreement with this line of reasoning. Our argument is that the crisis emerged not from the use of 'wrong' policies, but because the nature of political constraints on policy-making in Latin America had rendered most conventional policies ineffective, infeasible, or undesirable. Thus, in a sense, policy-makers were right in refusing to adopt the policies recommended by neoclassical advisers and bureaucrats, since their results would not have been very wholesome. On the other hand, Latin American governments were not entirely blameless, since they had failed to create arrangements which would allow effective policy intervention when it was needed. In other words, we see the failure of Latin American policy-makers not in short run, contemporary terms, but in

[1] Of course, Latin American countries are not the only ones in trouble. Africa is in a similar crisis, and even most of the industrialized countries have not recovered from the recent recession; Africa's fragile ecology, persistent droughts, and civil wars are reasons enough. In the industrialized countries, too, growth has been variable, not consistently negative. Clearly, Latin America is a case apart.

historical terms—in not creating institutional and political bases for effective action when the opportunities still existed. In this perspective, economic liberalization and openness can be interpreted as one among many different ways of re-recreating policy effectiveness, but one which is neither very desirable, nor even feasible, in the circumstances prevailing in Latin America today.

To make this argument, we shall use the concept of 'governance', namely of a perspective which sees the goal of state action in a contemporary society to be the maintenance of economic and political stability, the management (not elimination) of social conflict, and the creation of institutions and arrangements in which various social groups can co-operate with each other in the economic life of the country. This is by no means a radical perspective. The problem of governance was central to much of Keynes's writings, and distinguishes the Keynesian perspective on economics from its competitors.

The organization of this chapter is as follows. Section 2.2 presents a political model of economics, which is then applied, in Section 2.3, to the analysis of political constraints on policy-making. Section 2.4 applies the lesson to the crisis of policy-making in Latin America, and Section 2.5 summarizes the argument and provides some concluding observations.

2.2 A POLITICAL MODEL OF ECONOMICS

There is a curious inconsistency in the neoclassical attitude towards government policy. On the one hand, the government is seen as being completely omnipotent and unique in its ability to *choose* policies and to pursue macroeconomic objectives; on the other hand, it is seen as being almost completely impotent and incapable of actually *improving* anything (except when they chose policies to ensure the freedom of markets). The extreme political *naïveté* of this view, which underlies much of the theorizing in favour of economic liberalization, has been noted by many influential writers, including economists as well as political scientists.[2]

We believe that in most areas of social activity, contrary to what is suggested by economists' monistic vision of politics, governments are neither all-powerful nor completely powerless. On the one hand, polities as well as governments are characterized by differentiation and tension, rather than by monolithicity of structure and function. In order to understand the functioning and consequences of social decision-making, it is important to

---

[2] A symmetrical criticism can be made of those non-neoclassical economists, who believe in the omnipotence of government policy, and its impotence in maintaining 'truly' free and competitive markets. Indeed, Albert Hirschman (1987) places the blame for the economic disasters in Latin American countries not on the use of policies considered by economic theorists to be wrong, but rather for following too religiously policies considered by theorists to be right— of the structuralist variety in the 1960s, and the neoclassical one in the 1970s and 1980s.

replace monistic perspectives with more plurastic views; to make greater use of analytical tools, particularly those of political scientists, which are designed to analyse conflict; and to see policy-making as the constrained decisions of one among many actors operating in a situation of conflict and tension, rather than autonomous actions of an independent and omnipotent actor.

On the other hand, the government plays an important and unique role in maintaining social peace, managing social conflict, and facilitating social co-operation. The ineluctability of this role invalidates the perception of the powerlessness of governments to achieve any social ends whatsoever: even if one believes the neoclassical assertion that governments cannot optimize social welfare, it is still possible to argue that governments can be more, or less, successful in managing conflict and pursuing the goal of social peace— and not only by freeing markets.

The view that the nature and intensity of social divisiveness and polarity can constrain the autonomy of governments to use certain policies or to pursue certain objectives has been expressed by many influential social theorists. Vito Tanzi for example, has argued that policy prescriptions for developing countries differ inherently from those for industrial countries because, *inter alia*, changes in policy instruments are often neutralized by the reaction of forces outside the control of the government, and that authorities often find unacceptable the policies which are seen as desirable by economists (see Tanzi 1986). Margaret Weir and Theda Skocpol (1985) similarly suggest that the structural features of the state affect the ability of the government to innovate, institutionalize, and implement different types of economic strategies.

On the other hand, the pragmatic role of governments in facilitating social co-operation has also been emphasized by many writers, most notably by Albert Hirschman, who has repeatedly questioned the theoretical certitudes of economists and social theorists and has shown that governments have erred most often when they gave up a pragmatic attitude in favour of blind obedience of theorists' prescriptions (see Hirschman 1987). Tony Killick draws upon a vast literature in political science and sociology to argue that

decision making in the face of major divisions becomes a balancing act rather than the search for optima; a process of conflict-resolution in which social tranquility and the maintenance of power is a basic concern rather than the maximization of the rate of growth or some such . . . The maintenance of government authority and social peace will tend to be dominant themes, with adoption of a development objective conditional on the extent to which it furthers these higher-priority, 'non-economic' concerns. (Killick 1983: 360)

A conceptual framework for the above line of reasoning has recently been provided by Jukka Pekkarinen (1988), who draws upon the work of Weir and Skocpol to suggest an illuminating distinction between the 'theory model' and the 'policy model' of economics in Scandinavian countries (which can just as easily be applied to Third World countries). While the term, 'theory model' refers to a conventional, axiomatic theoretical system (neoclassical, neo-Keynesian, or neo-Marxian), a 'policy-model' is defined as a nationally specific and coherent framework of ideas, which comprises structural, ideological, cultural, and institutional factors, and

is *not* the kind of closely-specified conceptual framework that is characteristically developed by economists. Rather, it consists in a more diffuse set of cultural biases that delimit the agenda of economic policy-making. Professional economists who rely on international economic theories, can meet serious problems of communication with these diffuse, yet powerful, policy models. If hostile to the policy views implied by an economic theory, the policy model usually does not generate an analytic argument but rather a broad consensus that the economic theory is 'unrealistic' or 'irrelevant'. (Pekkarinen 1988: 3)[3]

Given this perspective, one can understand why the adoption of liberalization packages, for example, has taken place in but a handful of countries (and that too under considerable duress),[4] in spite of the immense intellectual and financial pressures on Third World governments from major international institutions. As we argue in Chapter 6, Latin American countries, with their high levels of political tension and their long history of political mobilization and organization along functional lines, are faced with a problem quite different from that confronted by East Asian countries, where these developments are extremely recent, or by South Asian countries, whose long history of political mobilization is not characterized by a similar evolution of functional organization and polarization. The reluctance to accept liberalization has derived, arguably, not from some deep-seated pathology in these countries, but rather from the greater sensitivity of policy-makers to the specific institutional arrangements prevailing in their countries, or from the 'policy models' of their economies, which seem to differ considerably from the 'theory model' of neoclassical advisers. We now turn to a discussion of the underlying determinants of this 'policy model'.

2.2.1 A taxonomy of policies and states

In analysing the connection between politics and economies, use has often been made of Gunnar Myrdal's illuminating distinction between 'hard' and

---

[3] This distinction as well as its problematic implications are not unique to macroeconomic policy. Stephen Marglin 1988 has drawn a very important distinction between two forms of knowledge, which he calls 'episteme' and 'techne'. The former, like Pekkarinen's 'theory view', is impersonal, axiomatic, analytic, articulated, cerebral, non-contextual, and with a strong claim to universality. The latter, like the 'policy view', is personal, intuitive, implicit and indecompasable, practical, and contextual. Marglin shows that there is ubiquitous belief in the Western world that 'epistemic' knowledge is superior to 'techne', indeed that it is the only form of knowledge. He goes on to argue that many contemporary social problems can be traced back to this belief.   [4] For a complaint of this nature, see Krueger 1986.

'soft' states. While we are critical of the simplistic manner in which this distinction has often been used, it would not be out of place to describe its evolution in the literature. Myrdal argued that the latter term described most South Asian governments—Burma, India, Indonesia, Pakistan, Sri Lanka (then Ceylon)—which were reluctant to impose social discipline in their societies, the implication being that these governments dealt with social conflict by seeking to postpone rather than to manage or control it.[5] He contrasted these countries unfavourably in this respect with Japan and China—supposedly hard states, willing and able to impose social discipline (i.e. to suppress social conflict)—and suggested that softness was an aspect of underdevelopment which these societies would have to overcome to modernize themselves. (South Korea had not yet caught the eye of economists, but presumably Myrdal would have approved.)[6] He was careful, however, to explain that the nature of the state depended upon cultural and structural features of the larger societies (in addition to, say, the regime's willingness to use force), and that these underlying features are not transformed completely into their opposites overnight. Nevertheless, given the tenor of the times, particularly the unequivocal priority of growth and modernization in national agendas, such views could not help but give strong ideological support to emerging authoritarian regimes in various parts of the Third World.

In recent years, the optimistic view of hard states has been questioned, partly because of their association with social repression but more importantly because attempts to construct hard states in countries with a high degree of political mobilization seems to have resulted in endemic political instability.[7] In an influential monograph published in 1976, aptly entitled *No Easy Choice*, the eminent political development theorists Samuel Huntington and Joan Nelson argued that neither of these two choices was internally stable. Populist (soft) regimes brought about improvements in economic and political equality at the cost of rising aspirations and declining incomes, while bureaucratic-authoritarian (hard) regimes improved economic growth at the cost of political repression and worsening inequalities.[8] Both led to increasing political instability and a swing towards the other extreme.

[5] See Myrdal 1968, esp. ch. 18, sects. 13–14; ch. 19, sects. 3–4; app. 2, sect. 20.

[6] The model of hard states spans the (Western) political spectrum from right-wing authoritarian regimes (e.g. South Korea, Taiwan, Singapore, Chile 1973–88, Argentina 1976–83, Brazil, 1964–78), which denigrate, if not ignore entirely, the role of social conflict or human rights of their citizens; to left-wing regimes (e.g. China, North Korea, Burma, Vietnam), which rely on central planning by an efficient state to introduce desirable forms of social change in the country.

[7] As has recently been discovered by numerous authoritarian leaders, including the Shah of Iran, Ferdinand Marcos of the Philippines, U Ne Win of Burma, Jean-Claude Duvalier of Haiti, Leopoldo Galtieri of Argentina, and perhaps even Chun Doo-Hwan of South Korea.

[8] The concept of bureaucratic-authoritarianism was introduced by Guillermo O'Donnell (1973), to describe the spate of military regimes which came into power in Latin American countries in the 1960s and early 1970s.

In economic terms, hard states would be expected to take the 'economically correct' policy decisions, with little regard for their political consequences. For example, if it is believed that adjustment to external shocks requires a change in the distribution of income through changes in real wages or the real exchange rate, or reductions of subsidies or transfers, the government will try to bulldoze the decision through over the heads of representative groups.[9] In the presence of organized political forces, repeated instances of this nature can lead to growing unrest even culminating in the overthrow of the regime by populist groups.[10] Soft regimes, on the other hand, would resort to any number of *ad hoc* regulatory actions to protect incomes and to avoid having to face conflict. But this has problems as well. Although there will be instances when the conflict simply disappears with time, the more common situation will be that postponed conflicts will accumulate and eat into the political and fiscal resources of the state until they cannot be postponed any longer. This would create an opening for groups which favour hard regimes to come into power.

There are exceptions, however. On one hand, three of the four successful East Asian countries (Singapore, South Korea, Taiwan) are said to have stable authoritarian regimes, going back almost three decades or more; Burma, China, Indonesia, and Thailand provide other examples. On the other hand, India and Mexico have had stable and soft states for an even longer period.[11] The presence of such exceptions has created the hope that they could be replicated in other, hitherto less stable, polities; and also that the adverse features of either type of state would turn out to be transitory and disappear over time—hard states would become more democratic, and soft states more efficient in economic terms. These hopes have been surprisingly persistent, despite repeated refutation by experience.

The advocacy of economic liberalization, like the promises of political development experts of the 1960s, stems precisely from the hope that stable as well as hard regimes (such as South Korea) can be created everywhere and will generally benefit society. The strong association of liberalization experiments with political authoritarianism, particularly in Latin America, has been noted by many writers (see e.g. Sheahan 1980; Hirschman 1981). This is not surprising, since the hard state is the one most compatible with economists' monistic view of politics; since there is only one 'right' theory, there is no scope for conflict on what is desirable for society.

It seems to us, however, that the contrast between hard and soft states is a false dichotomy, and that most regimes fall into a third category, which can

[9] While this is not intended as a normative exercise, concern must be expressed about the denial of democratic and participatory rights entailed in this vision of the state, bordering, in extreme cases, on torture, terrorization, and brutal repression.

[10] Recent examples include the Bhutto regime in Pakistan, the Aquino regime in the Philippines, or the Garcia regime in Peru.

[11] On the political economy of India, see Bardhan 1984.

be entitled a 'pragmatic' state, and which may occasionally include nominally hard or soft states.[12] The unstable exceptions to this generalization are provided by governments which blindly obey the advice given by social scientists on the basis of their theoretical priors; or, to use Pekkarinen's categories, governments which will accept the replacement of their 'policy model' by the 'theory model' of theoretical economists. Albert Hirschman has brilliantly analysed the growing crisis in Latin American countries as the result of precisely such a blind adherence to theoretical dogmas.[13] The same analysis could easily be applied to similar cases in other regions—Pakistan during the 1960s, the Philippines during the martial law period (1972–85), India during Indira Gandhi's emergency rule (1974–7), and several countries pursuing the liberalization dogma in recent years.

The notion of a 'pragmatic' state is derived from the perspective of 'governance', which was central to Keynes's writings on political economy. In contrast to hard and soft states, which seek, respectively, to repress or postpone social conflict, pragmatic states seek to manage conflict, not to eliminate it. In purely economic terms, the idea can be expressed in the form of a support for government intervention to guarantee economic stability. This perspective has always distinguished Keynesian economists from their neoclassical counterparts. For example, a leading Keynesian economist, the Nobel laureate Franco Modigliani, used the following words to describe the difference between Keynesians and monetarists (in the United States):

[Keynesians] accept what I regard to be the fundamental practical message of *The General Theory*: that a private enterprise economy using an intangible money *needs* to be stabilized, *can* be stabilized, and therefore *should* be stabilized by appropriate monetary and fiscal policies. Monetarists by contrast take the view that there is no serious need to stabilize the economy; that even if there were a need, it could not be done, for stabilization policies would be more likely to increase than to decrease instability; and, at least some monetarists would, I believe, go so far as to hold that, even in the unlikely event that stabilization could on balance prove beneficial, the government should not be trusted with the necessary power.[14]

In broader, socio-political terms, it means that in order to live together people have to co-operate with each other, conflicting interests notwithstanding; that this can be accomplished only through institutions which can

---

[12] This is not meant as a moral approval of these regimes. What is possible, given the political, moral, and ideological circumstances of a particular country, need not lie within the bounds of the morally desirable.

[13] See Hirschman 1987, which argues that the rigid reliance on structuralist/Keynesian theories was just as harmful to Mexico as the adherence to monetarism was to Chile and Argentina in the 1970s. Hirschman finds the recent turn to pragmatism in Latin America a reason to be optimistic about the future.

[14] The excerpt is from Modigliani's presidential address to the American Economics Association, 17 Sept. 1976. See Modigliani 1977: 1 (emphases in original).

channel incipient conflict into manageable directions; and that the state is the paramount social agency which can contribute to such institutionalization.[15]

Most regimes try to manage social conflicts with available political, economic, bureaucratic, and ideological resources. Given that the nature of conflicts, as well as the nature and magnitude of available resources, differs from country to country and from time period to time period, the requirements of governance will be different as well. The failure of a state does not derive from its refusal to adhere to a theoretical dogma. On the contrary; it derives, in the short run, from its abandonment of the goal of governance in favour of theoretical certitudes; and in the long run, from its inability or unwillingness to create or modify institutions to facilitate the management of conflicts which are forever changing in form and intensity.

This can be stated differently. The existence of political pressure groups makes the task of governance that much harder by creating countervailing forces which can nullify the effect of given government policies. A pragmatic state will try to shift to alternative policies; but if the (unsuccessful) short-run solution becomes permanent, allowing the underlying imbalance to persist and to grow increasingly unmanageable, a problem emerges. The next section tries to illustrate this argument with an example.

2.3 THE POLITICAL ECONOMY OF CONSTRAINTS

To discuss the issue of 'governance', and in particular, the failure of Latin American governments in this respect, we shall begin by looking at the conditions which determine the effectiveness of government policies. Whether a policy can be implemented at all, whether if implemented it will have the desired effect, and whether or not it will be associated with undesirable side effects, is determined by the nature of economic institutions and the balance of political forces in a particular country.

For this purpose, it is convenient to think of an economy not as a collection of markets, but rather, as Joan Robinson once described it, as a collection of groups that use political action to safeguard (or increase) their legal rights to a share of the total output,[16] by *direct* action (e.g. industrialists raising output prices), or *indirectly*, by imposing costs on other groups or on society at large. The ability of a particular group to protect its share within a given amount of time will depend on the specific institutional arrangements and the nature of political organization, and will generally differ from country to country and

[15] Many of these ideas are expressed in the recent literature on social corporatism. See e.g. Przeworksi 1987.

[16] We restrict the discussion to conflicts over income distribution only for purposes of simplicity. In many countries, other forms of conflict—e.g. minority groups' fears about cultural domination by the majority—may be more significant.

from situation to situation. Two conflicts which are prominent in economic analyses are those between labour and capital (the Marxian conflict) and between finance and industry (the Keynesian conflict). Recognition of these conflicts implies that government policies which affect the distribution of income between these groups could have unanticipated consequences. In particular, policies which seek to alter key relative prices—the real wage rate, the real exchange, and the real interest rate—which in turn affect the income shares of labour, capital, and finance will be less effective, and often counter-productive, in more conflict-ridden societies.[17]

These two conflicts are relevant to the discussion of policy effectiveness, particularly in the context of economic liberalization, because they have a bearing on the choice between market-oriented and regulatory policies. It is well known in the political economy literature that labour will often oppose government policies based entirely on market considerations, while financial institutions are generally perceived as being the bastion of laissez-faire ideas and staunch opponents of interventionist or regulatory policies. Industrial capital falls somewhere in the middle of the spectrum. While an extensive discussion of the reasons for this preference would take us too far afield, the simple explanation is that the income of the financial sector, as well as its ability to influence national economic and political choices, derives precisely from its anarchic nature, from its quickness and flexibility, its ability to take advantage of transient profit opportunities without being bogged down by longer-run considerations and obligations. On the other hand, while industrial capital requires a stable environment in order to be able to translate potential profit opportunities into realized profits, it does need room for manœuvre to be able to take advantage of these opportunities. Lastly, labour's earnings depend upon a stable and growing economy; its ability to affect economic outcomes derives from the need for co-operation in production activity, while its influence on national choices emerges mainly from its organizational capacity. In general, therefore, labour will support regulations which try to create stability and to encourage growth; industry will support stability-seeking policy interventions and restriction of competition, but will oppose the extension of similar privileges to others—workers, foreigners, and so forth; while finance will tend to favour laissez-faire and the existence of maximum possible opportunities.

Parenthetically, a curious asymmetry may be pointed out here. Economic liberalization proposals typically recommend the liberalization of capital as well as labour markets. However, while the liberalization of labour markets is

---

[17] Much of economic policy is concerned with the proper exercise of the government's control over the nominal value of these prices. We argue that the link between nominal and real prices is determined by underlying political processes and institutional arrangements in addition to market forces. Other relative prices which hide underlying conflict include the terms of trade between agriculture and industry and those between traded and non-traded goods.

intended to weaken the influence of the workers *vis-à-vis* the state, financial liberalization has the opposite effect of *increasing* the influence of the financier class in economic and social decision-making. Thus, the liberalization proposal, far from being politically neutral, is strongly biased in favour of groups whose commitment to the local economy is the least secure.

Be that as it may, the question for the state is, first, how to minimize the adverse consequences of these conflicts without stifling either the willingness of various groups to co-operate with each other or the incentive for them to contribute to national economic and social progress. A second question is how to ensure that the need for policy intervention is minimized and the effectiveness of such intervention enhanced. Both these tasks require management of the conflicts which exist in society. Conflicts between labour and capital were handled typically by (*a*) encouraging organization, nego-tiation, and bargaining; (*b*) legal guarantees of income stability; and (*c*) macroeconomic policies designed to reduce economic instability. Conflicts between finance and industry were addressed through the institution of central banks, which restrained destabilizing speculation, guaranteed liquidity, helped insure deposits, and regulated and supervised financial institutions. However, as the nature of conflict changes, the demands of governance also change. The differences between Latin American and Asian countries reflect precisely the different circumstances surrounding these two conflicts, and therefore differences in the demands which governance places upon the governments in the two regions. We shall examine each of the two types of conflict below.

2.3.1 Wage resistance

The effectiveness of government policies will be affected by the nature and intensity of the conflict between capital and labour, which, while conditioned by the existence of labour organizations and labour legislation, does not emerge only because of these institutions. Since production requires co-operation between a large number of people, a conflict over wages can affect labour productivity and profits, even in the absence of labour organizations, through a widespread reluctance to co-operate voluntarily.[18] The economic consequence of this type of conflict is *wage resistance*.[19] A clarification is necessary before proceeding further. Wage resistance is not the same as wage rigidity, which is defined as the empirical observation that

[18] In his discussion of wage rigidity, Keynes emphasized that this did not depend upon the existence or strength of formal trade unions. Non-union resistance can effect labour productivity, and hence profits, presumably through the absence of motivation, deliberate slowdown of work, or even sabotage. Some of these ideas have recently been taken up in the efficiency wage literature. See e.g. Akerlof and Yellen 1986.

[19] To simplify the discussion, we focus only on the effect of the capital–labour conflict on wages, ignoring e.g. conflicts over the pace and intensity of work, or control of the labour process.

(real or nominal) wages do not change. Rather, it means that *smooth and sustained changes in wages are resisted by political factors and can be overcome only by political means*, such as consensual agreement, political concessions by workers in an emergency or crisis, or even direct repression.[20] In what follows, we develop a simple model which illustrates the impact of wage resistance on the effectiveness of protectionist and adjustment policies.

Consider an economy with three sectors, a non-traded sector (services), an exportable goods sector (agriculture?), and an importable goods sector (manufacturing?), with output prices, p_n, p_x, p_m respectively (all variables are in rates of change).

$$p_x = e + p_x^\star = q_x + w \qquad (2.1)$$

$$p_m = e + t + p^\star = q_m + w \qquad (2.2)$$

$$p_n = w \qquad (2.3)$$

$$p_x^\star = p_m^\star = 0 \qquad (2.4)$$

The starred variables are the (rates of change of) world prices of the two traded goods (assumed constant), e is (rate of depreciation of) the exchange rate, t is the (proportional increase in) the tariff rate, w the (growth rate of) money wages (assumed to be the sole determinant of the changes in the non-traded goods price) and q_x and q_m are the prices of export and import goods normalized in terms of the wage rate. If labour is the only input in production, the normalized prices will also index the rate of increase of the profit share, and thus of the level of protection for each industry.

Now, consider the situation where the government wishes to shift the terms of trade in favour of tradable goods, i.e. to increase q_m, or q_x, or both. There can be three different reasons for seeking this outcome. One would be the desire to stimulate the import-substituting or the export industry in the pursuit of economic growth. A second reason may be the desire to correct persistent balance of payments deficits, which necessitates the contraction of demand for and the expansion of supply of the traded goods sector, both of which, in the conventional approach, are approached through changes in relative prices: a real devaluation of the exchange rate, which influences the economy largely through a reduction of real wages.[21] Third, the need to adjust to an external terms of trade shock may also necessitate a depreciation

---

[20] Latin American countries, for example, have been characterized by wage resistance but not by wage rigidity in recent years: despite the existence of a strong labour movement and other impediments to unilateral reductions of labour's share of income, real wages have declined by as much as 50 per cent in some episodes of the recent adjustment crisis. Indeed, it could be argued that in polarized or conflictual situations, one of the consequences of wage resistance must be the absence of wage rigidity, or at least the presence of a high variance in the observed real wage. If non-political means are not sufficient to bring about a decline in wages, the government might be inclined to overcompensate whenever it has the opportunity to bring about such a reduction.

[21] This will accomplish both ends—a fall in consumption, and a rise in the profit share—and hence, it is to be hoped, will increase investment and output in the traded goods sectors.

of the real exchange rate (i.e. an increase in the relative prices of the two traded goods), in order to stimulate the traded goods sector.

In a static economy, either of these will require a transfer to the traded goods sector from some other sector. In general, the transfer is expected to come out of a decline in the wage share,[22] and the success of the policy is expected to depend on the behaviour of wages. Given that foreign prices are stable, if nominal wages are constant as well ($w = 0$), a devaluation (i.e. an increase in e) will raise both q_x and q_m, while an increase in the tariff rate, t, will raise q_m alone.[23] These will fulfill the objectives of the policy, but only by retarding the share of wages in income. This means, first, that the success of the policy will depend upon the willingness of workers to accept a decline in their incomes (which will differ from place to place); and second, there may be no such thing as 'appropriate' or 'equilibrium' real wages, since it is not necessary that a certain level of wages produce both internal balance (full employment) and external balance (payments balance), in addition to being acceptable to workers. The discussion will focus on the implications of the last point.

To discuss real-wage resistance, assume that wages adjust with a lag to increases in the domestic price level (a weighted average of the prices of the three goods).[24] This could be represented by the following formula.

$$w_{+1} = a_x p_x + a_m p_m + a_n p_n; \qquad a_x + a_m + a_n = 1. \qquad (2.5)$$

After some manipulations, this will yield a dynamic equation describing the path of normalized trade goods prices, $q_x = a_n (q_x)_{-1}$. In other words, the positive impact effect of the devaluation on relative prices will erode over time, at a speed determined by the share of the non-trade goods prices (or the pure wage sector) in the economy. This means that the maintenance of a desired level of the terms of trade between traded and non-traded goods will require repeated devaluations, and consequently a constant rate of inflation. However, if this leads to a progressive shortening of the lag between the devaluation and the wage adjustment, then an ever increasing level of inflation will be needed to produce the same effect.[25]

---

[22] In a dynamic analysis, an increase in wages could also provide a stimulus through aggregate demand effects. See Marglin and Bhaduri 1990. We are abstracting from these issues here because in Third World countries, the aggregate demand stimulus applies mainly to the non-traded goods sector, while the contractionary effect of higher wages applies primarily to the preferred traded goods sector.

[23] These two policies are the simplified versions of the textbook recommendations on export promotion and import substitution policies, respectively.

[24] The three weights (a_x, a_m, a_n), which add up to unity, can be thought of as shares of the three goods in the consumption basket.

[25] For example, in indexed countries such as Brazil and Argentina, conflicts developed over the speed of indexing since the greater the retardation in relative prices, the more slowly nominal prices adjust to the price level.

If wages adjust instantaneously, some other sector in the economy will have to bear the resource burden of the protection. Assume that real wages are constant, i.e.

$$w = a_x\, p_x + a_m\, p_m + a_n\, p_n; \qquad a_x + a_m + a_n = 1. \qquad (2.5a)$$

In addition, at least one price in the economy, say p_n, adjusts with a lag. Or,

$$p_n = w_{-1}. \qquad (2.3a)$$

In this case, since the lagging sector will bear the distributional burden of the protection, its size will determine the short-run effectiveness of policies.[26] The remaining results are similar to the previous case.

Lastly, devaluation will be completely ineffective in two cases. First, if wages as well as relative prices adjust instantaneously, devaluation cannot produce any change in relative prices. Second, if the traded sector is effectively isolated and wages are tied to the exchange rate, i.e. $w = e$ (although in this case, tariffs could help protect the import sector). The last assumption is not intended as a curiosum, however. In many Third World countries the exchange rate is a 'sensitive' price, changes in which will often trigger immediate adjustment of a wide range of domestic prices (see Katseli 1986). In fact, the shift towards somewhat flexible exchange rates in these countries may have the hidden advantage that it has helped 'desensitize' this price, and therefore made it possible for small changes in it to have real effects.

To go from prices to output, protection will stimulate industry only if output adjusts more rapidly than relative prices. If the expansion of output depends on the installation of new capacity, the long-run effect will depend crucially on expectations of future profitability, which, in turn, will be based on expectations of future protectionist policy and changes in speed of adjustment in lagging prices. If the policy is successful in offsetting any increases in domestic factor costs and is credible, output will expand in the long run. In the short run, however, the expansionary effect will be negligible, and will generally be swamped by the contractionary effect of macroeconomic policies which accompany devaluations.[27] Be that as it may, the extent to which factor costs can be restrained by government policy will

[26] This can be demonstrated readily. Substituting from (2.1), (2.2), and (2.3a) into (2.5a), and setting t, $p_x{}^*$, and $p_m{}^*$ at zero, we get: $q_m = q_x = a_n(e-w_{-1})$. The larger is a_n, the larger is the protective effect on the traded goods industries.

[27] This pattern in the impact of devaluation on output is well recognized in the literature as the J-curve effect: output first declines (due to contractionary macropolicies which normally accompany devaluations during adjustment phrases), and then rises as the response to stimulative effects filters through. The effect was first demonstrated by Cooper (1971) in a classic article. Recent theoretical explanations from somewhat different perspectives are to be found in Krugman and Taylor 1978, and van Wijnbergen 1986. The importance of restraining wages in a successful devaluation has been emphasized by Khan and Lizondo 1987, Blejer 1979, Connolly and Taylor 1976, and Rodriguez 1978.

depend on the nature of labour market and other institutions, and therefore will differ from country to country.[28]

Furthermore, even if the policy is successful in restraining wages, it could be counter-productive in the face of worker resistance. It could actually lead to *lower* profits, because of strikes, work stoppages, and a general decline in productivity. It would thus fail to stimulate investmentor output; indeed, the decline in wages could restrain aggregate demand, and thus lead to lower output and employment (see Bowles and Boyer 1990; Marglin and Bhaduri 1990).

This approach can be extended to analyse anti-inflationary objectives. As has been argued in well-known structuralist macroeconomic models, lowering the rate of inflation requires the retardation of one of the relevant nominal prices, which can be accomplished only if relative prices are flexible and, in particular, if workers are willing to accept a decline in their purchasing power (see e.g. Ros 1987). If workers resist the decline and demand higher money wages, inflation will tend to increase and the real devaluation will be short-lived.

Where do the above considerations lead us in terms of the choice between various policy options? First of all, recognition of institutional and political sources of wage-resistance would lead to the exercise of a certain amount of caution in the use of policies which rely on the retardation of the wage rate in order to be effective. Whenever wages are not determined solely by market forces or solely by government fiat, however significant the two might be, such policies will be relatively ineffective, and policy-makers will tend to resist using them no matter how ardently they are espoused by the orthodoxy of the times.[29] Secondly, as already mentioned, the emergence of real wage resistance means that changes in the general price level will no longer have the effect of redistributing income and expenditure, nor of moderating the conflict over the distribution of income between wages and profits. If the adjustment mechanisms adjust money wages with a lag, then only an increase in the rate of *inflation* will have a redistributionary effect; but this effect will also erode over time, as the increase in inflation generates pressures to shorten the period between successive wage adjustments.

There are two interrelated solutions to the dilemma. First, the problems related to growth strategy could be avoided by resorting to ordinary or tariff protection. Since this seeks to protect only a subset of the traded goods

[28] Comparison of two different experiences, then, would generally be irrelevant unless one is willing either (*a*) to argue that the two sets of supporting institutions are broadly similar, or (*b*) to prescribe that the 'successful' country's institutions be reproduced in the other country. Most mainstream analysts assume both (*a*) and (*b*).

[29] For example, Krueger 1986 identifies the 'liberalization' of labour markets as an essential component of the desired policy reform. Fields 1984 showed that export promotion policies were successful only in countries which had low-wage (or 'tight' labour) policies, and not in countries which had high-wage (or 'loose' labour) policies.

sector, it requires lower resource transfer. A simple version is to examine the effect of a neutral tariff, which discriminates only between exports and imports but not among different imports. The impact effect of such a tariff on the imported goods price is $p_m = a_n (t-w_{-1}) + a_x t$; recall that an equivalent devaluation will produce $p_m = a_n (e-w_{-1})$, which is smaller. However, the effect will not be that much different if the export sector is too small to provide an adequate surplus, or if it is sufficiently organized to resist the extraction of this surplus.[30] Moreover, since part of the burden is taken up by the export sector, even though the protection erodes over time it never goes to zero. The protection will be even higher, and the resistance less, in the more realistic case of selective tariffs; however, these will create incentives for rent-seeking as well as other efficiency costs.

Second, it might be possible to maintain growth rates, or to avoid adjustment dilemmas, by resorting to foreign borrowing. This will keep wages high by allowing the maintenance of an overvalued exchange rate, and will keep profits (and hopefully investment) high by protecting import-substituting industry with tariff and other barriers. In general, this will require some selective forms of protection to single out industries where investment is highly elastic to profit rates, and where it might be socially most desirable. Foreign borrowing can be increased indefinitely as long as the real interest rate is less than the growth rate of the economy,[31] and as long as the financial markets consider the country to be a good credit risk. If borrowers cannot respond quickly to short-term fluctuations in perception of credit risk, or to overvaluation of the currency or other policy measures, the economy will be reasonably insulated despite the debt exposure.

However, with the emergence of financial openness, this channel can become weaker. Financial openness can lead to destabilizing speculative runs on the currency, i.e. to destabilizing capital outflows. Such capital flight can be caused by the overvaluation of the currency, expectations of a devaluation, the use of low interest-rate policies at home, or political disturbances which influence expectations of future variables. Under fixed exchange rates, capital flight will of course lead to rapid increases in foreign debt and may help impair the creditworthiness of a country. Under flexible exchange rates, we get back to the earlier problem of wage resistance. If exchange rates are flexible, capital flight will induce depreciation and initiate a wage–price inflationary spiral. More important, if there is real wage resistance it may not be possible to protect the industrial sector by government policy.

---

[30] Such resistance can be political (lobbying, political unrest, conflict between states and the federation, etc.), or economic (decline in output or shift towards smuggling and capital flight through currency black markets, thus creating balance of payments difficulties).

[31] This condition simply means that the debt/GNP ratio can be stabilized at any level if further borrowing becomes unnecessary. If the interest rate is higher than the growth rate, then the debt/GNP ratio will explode even without fresh net inflows.

2.3.2 Financial openness

Unlike the capital–labour conflict, which revolves around the maintenance of a given distribution of income of the two groups, the finance–industry conflict revolves around the maintenance of *conditions* under which each of the two groups is best placed to maximize its profit opportunities. Thus, the political and economic influence of financial groups will be aimed not at the effectiveness of government policies which seek to reduce a particular level of income, but at those which affect the rules of the game and inhibit the unencumbered pursuit of profit. Whether or not such political influence will exist, or will be called into play, will depend on the nature of the financial system in a particular country.

Consider the relationship between finance and industry, taking 'industry' to mean the productive sector of the economy, comprising manufacturing, construction, and non-financial services, especially merchandise trade; while 'finance' refers to the financial intermediation sector, covering banks, insurance companies, investment banks, and commodities, stock, and bond markets. The traditional view of the relationship of these two sectors is that of 'finance as a handmaiden to industry and trade'; in other words, of finance as a passive activity which accommodates itself to the imperatives of the active sectors. In this perspective, the task of finance is to transfer resources from surplus economic units to deficit ones, and to ensure the optimal distribution of risk across the economy. The return to finance is then equivalent to the social value of channelling resources and assuming the risk of the transfer from one level to another.

This, however, is a non-institutional view of finance, which ignores the effect of specific features of financial intermediation arrangements upon rates of return as well as on the quality of the service and the nature of the outcomes. To look at these effects, one can start with a distinction between 'dependent' and 'autonomous' financial institutions, where the degree of dependence or autonomy derives from the degree of control of the state or of industrial capital upon decision-making in financial institutions.

'Dependent' financial institutions can be further divided into 'bureaucratic' or 'industry-dominated' systems. The former refers to a financial system comprised mainly of government bureaucrats, and which therefore tends to represent and implement the economic and other objectives of the government. The efficiency and quality of the service will depend upon the degree of efficiency in the public sector in general. South Korea and Taiwan are illustrations of an efficient bureaucratic financial system, while Bangladesh, India, and Pakistan have competent but inadventurous institutions.

'Industry-dominated' institutions correspond to the case where financial institutions have strong symbiotic ties with industrial houses, particularly when they are the subsidiaries of these industrial houses. The Philippines is the best example of this pattern, although many countries went through this stage in the early period of financial development—e.g. the United Kingdom in the eighteenth and nineteenth centuries, the United States in the nineteenth and early twentieth centuries, Pakistan in the 1950s and 1960s.

'Autonomous' finance can also be subdivided into 'conservative' (or 'bank-dominated'), and 'anarchic' (or 'market-dominated') systems.[32] The former represent domination by conservative, quasi-bureaucratic personnel of commercial banks, who take a long-run view of the economy and resist actions, no matter how profitable, which would overextend the system or overexpose their financial portfolios. Japanese and continental European financial systems, particularly until the 1970s, could be placed in this category. 'Anarchic' financial systems are dominated by internal groups, who perceive their role, in classic Smithian fashion, as one of profit maximization as an end in itself, and one which is independent of any connection to industry, the state, or to industrial labour. The United States in the 1970s and 1980s has begun to resemble this pattern, as have many Latin American countries.

In other words, while there is often a symbiotic relation between industry and finance, on occasion this relation can break down. In such a case, finance can become a source of macroeconomic instability; and the desire to avoid instability will result in an excessive solicitude for the concerns of financial groups. This has become increasingly the case since the breakdown of the Bretton Woods system. As many observers have noted, we increasingly seem to be living in a world in which capital flows have a dominating influence on the conditions under which production and trade takes place. The reasons are not hard to discover. The Bretton Woods system was built upon extensive domestic arrangements for regulating and supervising the financial sector, and ensuring its domestic orientation; the breakdown of this system was at the same time a cause and an effect of the increasing autonomy of the financial systems of key member countries.

The ability of finance to influence the economy stems from two sources: the stock market, which is very sensitive to investor psychology (but which is relatively unimportant in the Third World); and international capital flows, which figure very prominently in policy discussions and economic analyses of Third World countries. This influence is higher in countries whose financial systems are relatively more autonomous and those where there is greater financial openness, i.e. where there are strong connections between domestic and international financial markets and where there are limited or ineffective capital controls.

The view of the role of the financial sector is in direct contrast to the neoclassical position, such as that presented by Ronald McKinnon (1973),

---

[32] In terms of behaviour, these categories correspond, roughly, to Frankel and Froot's (1986) distinction between 'fundamentalists' and 'chartists' in the currency market.

who sees financial activity as necessary not only for the mobilization and efficient allocation of resources but also as a stabilizing force in the economy. The neo-classical perspective leads unequivocally to a prescription for deregulating and privatizing the financial sector, while the Keynesian perspective leads in some instances towards regulation and in others towards deregulation. At issue in the former view is the removal of distortionary controls, while the latter view is concerned not with controls but with governance, the requirements for which could vary in different circumstances.

Thus, autonomous finance, particularly when it acquires an 'anarchic' orientation, can create problems for economic policy and performance. Speculation will tend to become destabilizing in nature, and economic instability will increase as even small and transient changes in economic performance, future expectations, or investor psychology will lead to large swings in economic activity.[33] More importantly, it will influence economic and political decision-making at the national level. An increase in interest rates (and the return to finance) is likely to result,[34] as is the inability of governments to pursue protectionist policy (see e.g. OECD 1982: 58–61). In fact, it is well known that the election of pro-labour governments in Western countries affects the economy adversely through the reaction of the stock markets.

Given this situation, consider a government which seeks to stimulate economic growth or to facilitate macroeconomic adjustment by one of the following actions: (a) low interest rates combined with preferential access of industrial investors to institutional credit; (b) currency devaluation; or, (c) an overvalued currency combined with tariff barriers and preferential access of industrial investors to foreign exchange. In the presence of financial openness, none of these policies will be effective. High capital mobility will permit capital flight if the domestic interest rate is lower than the world interest rates. Because of the possibility of large international capital flows, exchange rate policy will become purely reactive rather than active, in order to avoid speculative pressures and balance of payments problems (high debt, reserve losses). Furthermore, even trade restrictions will be difficult to sustain without capital controls, since easy availability of foreign exchange can facilitate low-cost smuggling operations (Banuri 1988). In this case, therefore, governments will be unable and unwilling to pursue such social objectives as income distribution or economic stability whose urgency and need is not perceived as such by financial groups.

---

[33] This view has come to be associated with Keynes (even though it pre-dates Keynes) and with prominent Keynesian economists, most prominently, Hyman Minsky. See Minsky 1975.

[34] The interlocking nature of financial institutions means that there will be considerable variation in the distribution of benefits as well as in institutional support for higher interest rates. For example, during the 1970s in the US, the savings and loans associations were badly hit by the rise of interest rates, because of the nature of their portfolios, which had short-term liabilities and long-term assets.

To summarize, we have made two points. First, the existence of well-organized labour groups will, by creating wage-resistance in the economy, erode the effectiveness of 'market-type' economic policies; most advocates of economic liberalization have implicitly recognized that in order for their prescriptions to be effective and successful, the political influence of organized labour will have to be considerably diminished. Second, the existence of financial openness will reduce the effectiveness and increase the costs of interventionist and regulatory policies. This, too, is well known from another context, namely the opposition of financial groups to interventionist policies. In the next section, we shall apply these results to an analysis of the Latin American situation.

2.4 THE LATIN AMERICAN CRISIS

The relevance of the above analysis to the current crisis derives from the differences between Latin American and Asian countries in terms of wage resistance and financial openness. In Chapter 6 we examine the nature of labour-market institutions in Latin American and Asian countries, to discover that the former are characterized by a long history of worker mobilization and extensive legislation guaranteeing rights and benefits to workers; while in South Asian countries, although such legislation has existed for a significant number of years, the labour movement is fragmented vertically as well as horizontally; and, in East Asia (except the Philippines), labour mobilization has a relatively shorter history, and labour laws are weak and often loosely enforced. It can be ventured, then, that there would be a strong element of real wage resistance in Latin America and relatively little in East Asia; in South Asia, since the labour movement has been unable to organize itself at the national level or to acquire a national identity, the main form of wage resistance is at the enterprise level, and pertains to nominal rather than real wages.

2.4.1 Financial openness

Contrary to the impression obtained by looking at trade shares, it turns out that the financial sectors of countries in East Asia are relatively more 'closed' than those in Latin American countries. While the nature of financial institutions has been changing very rapidly in Latin America,[35] at the time of the recent crisis period (1979–82) most Latin American economies had open

[35] For instance, Chile, Argentina, and Uruguay initiated a process of financial liberalization in the early 1970s, but some controls were reintroduced in the 1980s with the worsening of the economic picture. On the other hand, Mexico which had always had an open capital account and a privately owned banking sector, nationalized its banks, ended the convertibility of dollar accounts, and introduced capital controls in 1982.

capital markets. The two exceptions, Brazil and Colombia, are often singled out for strong economic performance and low incidence of capital flight. The presence of foreign-owned banks,[36] currency black markets, and multinational corporations[37] has also been much more extensive in Latin America.

In Brazil, although the process of the internationalization of the financial system was far more timid than, say, in Chile or Argentina, it has come a long way since 1964 when the new military regime, despite its nationalistic rhetoric, opened the Brazilian economy to foreign capital. While there are stringent capital controls (which are being opposed by the financial institutions), there are other links to the international financial system. Despite the legal restrictions on foreign banks, their participation in the economy increased dramatically during the last two decades. In 1970, 11.6 per cent of the deposits, and 13.3 per cent of the lending, were made by purely foreign-owned banks; by 1980, these numbers had increased to 15.2 per cent and 28.9 per cent respectively. The number of banks with foreign *participation* increased from 11 in 1970 to 22 (out of 40) in 1980; and their share of the total credit went up from 44 to 67 per cent in the same period. The number of foreign banks with representative offices in Brazil increased from 67 in 1969 to 408 in 1981. The exposure of the Brazilian economy to international capital has also been influenced by the influx of transnational corporations (which financed a significant part of their investment with foreign capital) and by the rolling over of the foreign debt after 1977.

In Asia, only Indonesia and Malaysia have no restrictions on capital outflows. India, Pakistan, Bangladesh, and South Korea have always had strong capital controls. All four countries have had a nationalized banking structure since before the first oil shock, and have had low participation of foreign banks in the domestic financial sector. In all four cases, however, there has been a gradual move towards liberalization, beginning in the early 1980s. Capital restricitions have been eased, as have been the restrictions on foreign banks, and dollar accounts have been allowed in limited cases.

Take the case of Korea. As Cole and Park (1984) have so painstakingly documented in their study of financial development of Korea, until recently all major financial decisions were controlled by the government or the central bank. 'The government allocates anywhere from 50 to 70 percent of domestic credit, depending on the classification of "directed" or "policy" loans, to predesignated sectors, industries, and uses. The remainder is then, in theory, allocated at the discretion of the D[eposit] M[oney] B[ank]s, but, in reality,

---

[36] Except for Brazil, no Latin American country placed strong restrictions on the ability of these banks to do domestic business.

[37] In their influential reference volume, *International Finance Handbook*, George and Giddy remark that these enterprises can and do transfer funds in and out of a country with much greater facility because they can enter into reciprocal contracts with similar institutions abroad that need to transfer money into the country.

these banks exercise little control over even the residual banking funds' (Cole and Park 1984: 173).[38]

The Taiwanese financial institutions are remarkably similar to those of South Korea. As Cheng notes, 'whereas other Pacific Basin nations have liberalised their financial regulations since 1980 in the face of domestic and international market forces, Taiwan, China stands nearly alone in the region in retaining a system dominated by bureaucratic government banks, continuing to ration credit at below market-clearing interest rates under behind-the-scenes direction of the central bank' (Cheng 1986: 143).

In other words, the Latin American financial system would be characterized as 'autonomous', while the financial systems in East and South Asia are generally of the 'bureaucratic-dependent' type. The autonomy of the former derives in large part from the links between domestic and international financial markets.

2.4.2 Policy ineffectiveness

The upshot is that Latin American countries are generally characterized by wage resistance as well as financial openness; South Asian countries by wage resistance but not financial openness; and East Asian countries by neither. Policy effectiveness will therefore be highest in East Asia and lowest in Latin America, and any objectives of economic policy (say, adjustment), will be more difficult to pursue in the latter region.[39]

This is where the choice between hard and soft options becomes relevant. A hard option, as in the neoclassical prescription of liberalization, is to eradicate wage resistance and to re-establish market forces in labour–capital relations. In this scenario, the government would, for example, cease the automatic wage increases of indexation mechanisms, leaving the decision entirely to employers. Alternatively, it might freeze wages, while allowing prices to increase or even devalue the currency. This could require using police or military force to deal with labour unrest, strikes, lockouts, productivity declines, and riots. This strategy was employed in Chile and Argentina during their liberalization episodes, with disastrous consequences: decline in output, increase in unemployment, capital outflows, capital flight, payments crises, exchange rate depreciation, and inflation. However, the adoption of this strategy is often based on a willingness to accept short-run

[38] However, the situation is changing as South Korea proceeds towards its stated policy objective of complete financial liberalization and openness. Already banks have been given almost complete autonomy in loan sanctioning, and are allowed to engage in foreign exchange transactions. The stock market and other domestic markets for financial assets are also to be opened up to international investment and competition.

[39] It should perhaps be clarified that this does not mean that governments in Latin America do not do anything. When either the disturbances or the impact of policies are small, they will generally be effective. It is only when a major reordering is called for that policy effectiveness becomes an issue.

economic as well as political costs, under the assumption that in the long run the new rules of the game will be accepted by all parties, and that such conflicts will not recur in the future. The experience of the Southern Cone countries does not bear out even this limited degree of optimism.

An alternative policy is the soft option of postponing the conflict by relying on *ad hoc* measures such as increasing foreign borrowing, selective protection for industries in crisis, social welfare spending, consumer subsidies, or selective credit controls. It must be stated that this option is not without its strengths. First, in the case of temporary shocks it may be wiser to incur a balance of payments deficits rather than to seek to modify the economic structure.[40] Second, political resistance notwithstanding, selective policies will work without significant social or political costs. Third, the dynamic efficiency of expanding output could offset static inefficiencies of selective policies.[41] Lastly, if it is conceded that in a situation of polarization and confrontation, the acceptance of controversial policies by social groups is facilitated by the shared perception of a crisis, then the postponement of conflict could be the pragmatic choice: if the shock turns out to be temporary or if production responds to growth incentives, there will be no problem; if the shock is permanent and the long-run stimulative policies do not work, the resulting crisis will mobilize public opinion behind the need for corrective measures.

The problem is, however, that rarely is postponement of conflict a long-run option. Perhaps this is best explained by an example—the relatively greater propensity of Latin American countries to use inflation and foreign debt for resource mobilization. In a situation of differentiation and tension, inflation and debt can play an important role in maintaining social harmony and postponing social conflict. Inflation enables the postponement of conflict primarily through its ambiguity: it can help retard real wages and redistribute income from workers to capitalists and from the private to the public sector, but not through an explicit mechanism which is likely to be resisted by the affected groups. Similarly, foreign debt accumulation can postpone conflict because those who will pay for it in the future are not mobilized at the time the debt is contracted and are not likely to resist the initial action. As a result, these two processes are of great potential use to a government faced

[40] This may constitute something of a problem since it is difficult to know *ex ante* which shocks will be temporary and which permanent. The two oil shocks are an illustration that general perceptions may be more often wrong than right: many economists expected the 1973 oil price increase to be temporary, and the 1979 increase permanent, but the first turned out to have permanent consequences, while the second soon reversed itself. For a discussion of these perceptions, see Bianchi, Devlin, and Ramos 1987.

[41] For example, in the 1970s Brazil and Colombia adopted a strategy to maintain a high and stable aggregate demand and used selective policies to shift incentives towards investment in the traded goods sector. As Hirschman (1987) and Bianchi, Devlin, and Ramos (1987) have shown, it led to their relative success in expanding exports in the 1980s.

with escalating tensions without adequate institutional means of managing them.

The level of inflation in Latin American countries was significantly higher than in the rest of the world, even in the 1950s and 1960s, and can be argued to have resulted from the need to transfer resources to the industrial sector without excessive social cost in terms of heightened conflict. Beginning in the mid-1970s, however, inflation appeared to have lost its efficacy in Latin America as a tool for mediating social conflict. The inflation rates escalated from one-digit to two-digit to three-digit and even to four-digit levels in some countries. A major reason for this was the ubiquity of indexing arrangements, which considerably weakened the distributional effect of inflation and hence its effectiveness for resource mobilization. As a result, serious efforts began to be made to bring down the level of inflation, often at high cost.

Similarly, most Third World countries with access to the expanding international credit market in the 1970s borrowed extensively to finance investment while maintaining (or even expanding) consumption, thus effectively postponing the distributional conflict which would have been precipitated by the high investment programme. However, from the late 1970s onwards, the changes in world interest rates, the perception of increased risk in Latin American borrowing, private capital outflows, and finally the debt crisis ensured that debt had also outlived its utility as a tool for maintaining social harmony. Analogously to the earlier situation, efforts began to be made, perhaps under duress, to bring down the level of the debt—often, indeed always, at a high cost.[42] In other words, while inflation and foreign debt accumulation were not irrational choices, given their importance for maintaining social peace in several countries, what the emerging crisis has revealed is that such solutions cannot work forever.

Thus, we are back at the earlier dilemma. The hard option is costly in the short run and ineffective in the long run. The soft option is less costly in the short run, but equally costly, and perhaps more costly, in the long run. To see our way out of this dilemma, we shall have to go back to the notion of governance with which we started this chapter.

2.5 CONCLUSIONS: THE CASE FOR PRAGMATISM

In order to discuss the notion of the pragmatic state, a few points have to be noted. First, the analysis is relevant mainly for major conflicts which impact upon the nature of the society as a whole: the conflicts between labour and

---

[42] At the risk of gross oversimplification, it could be argued that just when inflation ceased to be effective as a social lubricant, foreign debt came along, but when debt ran out of steam a few years later, no other instrument emerged to take its place. Hence the crisis.

capital, between finance and industry, or even between various ethnic groups in culturally heterogenous societies. Unlike smaller or local conflicts, which can be handled by all but the most inept of governments, these conflicts cannot be suppressed without adequate firepower (and the willingness to use it) relative to the organizational and other resources of countervailing social groups. Nor can they be managed unless institutional arrangements exist to facilitate management. Finally, even postponement requires the expenditure of fiscal or communicative resources of the state, which may not always be available in adequate magnitude (especially when the conflict has been postponed too many times and for too long). Where a conflict of major proportions can be neither suppressed nor postponed nor managed, the result is a breakdown of the civil order, such as in Lebanon or in some African states.

This brings us to the crux of the issue. Faced with an unmanageable conflict, a pragmatic state may, in the interest of social peace, choose either appeasement and postponement or neglect and civil war, or even confrontation and suppression; but it will make the choice not as a permanent solution to the crisis but rather as a tactic to buy time in which to construct appropriate institutions for managing similar conflicts in the future. Latin American and South Asian governments were right in refusing to pursue policies which would not have worked in their institutional and political circumstances; but they erred in not trying to create institutions which would have facilitated social co-operation and restored policy effectiveness. In talking about the economic instability which can be produced by the instability of wages, Keynes once said that it was fortunate that workers, though unconsciously, were instinctively more reasonable economists than the classical school. In an analogous manner, it could be said that it is fortunate that (some) policy-makers, though unconsciously, are instinctively more reasonable economists than the neoclassical school.

The mainstream analyses of the Latin American dilemma are not ignorant of this dilemma, even though they do not talk about it overtly. The suggestions of Balassa, Krueger, or Bhagwati can be understood as attempts to achieve wage flexibility by weakening trade unions and rolling back the so-called impediments to the smooth functioning of labour markets. Likewise, in Jeffrey Sachs's venture into political economy, the alliance of the state with rural groups is identified as the key to effective policy-making in East Asia, and by implication as the appropriate direction of political reform in Latin America. Our suggestions differ from those of such authors mainly on account of our different reading of the region's history. Both the mainstream proposals require a concerted effort aimed at weakening the political and economic influence of industrial labour. Implicitly or explicitly, the first group allocates this task to the power of the state, which is expected to railroad over any opposition. Sachs is more ambivalent in his prescriptions, but the obvious implication is that the alliance with rural groups will provide a counterforce to the political influence of urban groups.

What is missed in these analyses is the fact that urban labour *is* politically influential in Latin America, partly because of its organizational strength, and partly because of a shared consciousness emerging from a long history of conflict and struggle. The task of destroying this political influence is not comparable to policy-making in the *absence* of such influence in South Korea or in the rest of East Asia. First, while the actions of the latter governments can be considered 'pragmatic' in nature, Latin American governments would have to be 'hard' (and, therefore, unstable) states in order to be able to accomplish the tasks set for them by neoclassical theorists. Furthermore, just as policies are often constrained by institutional factors, the feasible range of institutional reform is also conditioned by the history of political conflict and reform. As is revealed by the example of liberalization experiments in the Southern Cone, attempts to destroy union organization and influence were, in the final analysis, unsuccessful in addition to being undesirable and costly. They did not succeed in changing the perceptions of industrial workers of their rights and responsibilities in a democratic society. The problem with history is that it is often resilient to the frequent attempts by interested groups to rewrite it.

The strengthening of the financial sector also appears in a new light from this perspective. By making government policy reactive rather than active, it has the effect of inhibiting legislation protecting the rights of industrial workers, and thus of reducing their influence. However, given the nature of the social consensus, the result has only been a stalemate.

To discuss alternative paths of institutional development, the state will have to acknowledge the high level of mobilization and political influence of organized labour as well as the ability of finance to resist policies which appear to be against its interests. The question for a pragmatic government is how to channel these sources of influences into economically fruitful directions—in other words, how to create conditions in which these powerful groups will be willing to co-operate with each other and with other groups in society. Noting that both the economic stalemate and the ineffectiveness of economic policies derive from the emergence of wage resistance and financial openness, policy reform will seek to minimize the effect of these two factors in a manner which is politically feasible.

First, the restoration of wage flexibility does not require the destruction of labour unions. It does, however, require that the flexibility be based on a credible and stable compromise between labour and capital. For this purpose, it will be important to institutionalize the political influence of workers into more manageable channels. Thus, instead of seeking to destroy labour unions and to push wage-bargaining down to the plant level in an attempt to divide and weaken the workers, the government would encourage participation in national level negotiations to agree on real wages, employment, investment, and growth. This is an analogue of the rise of labour unions within each plant. Instead of destroying the unions and bringing down the wage negotiations to the level of each worker, the strengthening of the unions allowed the money wage bargain to be made at the centralized level of the plant at discrete intervals, thereby ensuring long periods of peace as well as improvements in productivity because of an increase in worker loyalty. This did not mean that the conflict between labour and capital disappeared—indeed, the current crisis is in part a result of the success of the earlier compact—nor that the conficts between workers were also taken care of. It simply meant that the most potent form of conflict was neutralized for the time being.

Latin American governments in the 1930s and 1940s were successful in constructing precisely such institutional arrangements, but they were overtaken by an ideological shift in favour of hardness and repeated (though ineffective) attempts to destroy these institutions. The optimistic aspect of the current crisis is that the mood of polarization and confrontation has given way to a new period of search for social peace through participation, democracy, negotiation, compromise, and consensus. The greatest danger posed by liberalization attempts is their potential for derailing these new initiatives.

Second, most countries would be well advised to maintain some form of barriers against international financial flows, and some central control or influence over the domestic financial sector. This would require regulation or mediation by the central bank, which should not only supervise the activities of financial institutions but should also act as their representative in national decision-making. The idea behind this reform is also to compensate the actual level of influence of a social group with an equal amount of social responsibility.

It should be noted here, however, that the changes in the international financial arrangements, as well as the increasing sophistication of internal financial markets (both official and unofficial) in Third World countries, are such that it may have become impossible for any government to maintain overvalued exchange rates or to protect itself against sustained pressures on its currency. This means that our proposals for maintaining restrictions on capital flows is intended not as a long-term policy instrument, but rather as a means of insulating the economy from the short-run instability which these flows can generate. As the OECD 1982 report on capital controls points out, capital controls can perform useful functions even in this limited role. First, in normal times, they may help to influence capital flows sufficiently to ensure that minor disturbances causing pressure on exchange rates or domestic capital markets are minimized. Second, in the event of a major disturbance, they might help to gain time while more fundamental policy adjustments are being made. Third, they can help the government politically by demonstrating that action is being taken to stem the more obvious channels of capital outflows and to prevent windfall gains to speculators.

Similarly, regulation of financial institutions is proposed not to enable the government to pursue arbitrary policies, but to give it leverage in meeting unanticipated crises. Likewise, the managerial approach to labour organization will lose its effectiveness if it is used consistently in the interest of political expediency.

The generality of these suggestions is meant to underscore the fact that detailed solutions will have to be found for each country in the context of its own political and institutional development. For too long, the Third World in general, and Latin America in particular, has served as a testing place of universal social theories which deny the uniqueness of every experience. It is time that the Third World began to write its own history.

3

The World Economic Slowdown and the Asian and Latin American Economies: A Comparative Analysis of Economic Structure, Policy, and Performance

Alan Hughes and Ajit Singh

3.1 INTRODUCTION

Since the slowdown of world economic growth, beginning in 1973, two outstanding features of the economic experience of developing countries have attracted the attention of economists. First, the developing countries were able to withstand the first oil shock and the consequent upheavals in the world economy reasonably well, but were affected much more adversely by the trade and financial shocks, which hit the world economy during the period 1979–82, and the associated economic slowdown in industrialized countries. After the first shock, whereas the trend growth rate of industrialized economies nearly halved—from an annual average rate of 4.9 per cent in 1960–73 to 2.8 per cent in 1973–9—the developing countries suffered only a relatively small decline in their pace of economic expansion: from 6.3 per cent during 1960–73, to 5.2 per cent in the later period, between the two oil shocks.[1] However, the impact upon the Third World of the changes in the world economy during 1979–82 have been devastating. At the bottom of the recession, in 1982 and 1983, the aggregate GDP of developing countries grew at an annual rate of only 2 per cent, below the rate of population growth.[2] Although growth did resume in 1984, because of the recovery in the US economy and the pick-up in OECD economic growth, it lost momentum again in 1985 and 1986 (World Bank 1986).

The second important aspect of the Third World's economic experience is the differential performances of the different parts of the Third World, particularly since 1979. As Table 3.1 indicates, economic growth did not slow down in the 1980s in all parts of the South. Indeed, China, India, and other low income Asian countries managed, on average, almost to double their pace

---

[1] World Bank 1984. There is no suggestion here that the oil shocks were the 'cause' of the deceleration in world economic growth in the 1970s and 1980s. For full analysis of the reasons for the world economic slowdown, see Glyn *et al.* 1990.

[2] In fact, 1982 was the first year since the Second World War when per capita GDP in the developing countries actually fell.

of economic expansion—from 4.0 per cent during 1965–80, to 7.8 per cent during 1980–6; in middle-income East Asian countries as well, although there was a decline in the trend of economic growth in the 1980s compared with the 1960s and 1970s, the growth record is still respectable. It is the economies of Latin American and Sub-Saharan countries which have performed particularly poorly in the 1980s. In the Latin American and Caribbean countries, GDP per capita fell at a rate of more than 4 per cent per annum for three consecutive years—1981, 1982, and 1983. For the region as a whole, per capita GDP levels in 1983 were lower than in 1977, and in some countries as low as in the 1960s. Similarly in the sub-Saharan African countries per capita GDP has contracted at a rate of almost 5 per cent per annum in each of the years 1982, 1983, and 1984. Reduced economic growth has, not surprisingly, been accompanied by large falls in levels of consumption and employment, and in a number of African and Latin American countries by enormous under-utilization of industrial capacity and massive de-industrialization.

The reasons why the Third World countries as a whole were able to withstand the first oil shock and the associated turbulence in the world economy relatively well are not far to seek. Firstly, they were able to borrow on the private capital market at an unprecedented scale, and at extremely low real interest rates. Secondly, the recession in the industrialized countries which followed the 1973 oil price rise was sharp but of short duration, compared to the shallower but more prolonged recession following the oil price rise of 1979 and the associated mix of contractionary economic policies.[3] Lastly, the availability of private foreign capital which had permitted many Third World countries to maintain economic growth between 1973 and 1979 declined sharply after 1981.

This chapter is concerned with the second aspect of the South's economic experience outlined above, i.e. the question of differential economic performance. In particular, the question asked is why the Asian economies apparently coped with the world economic crisis in the 1980s so much better than the Latin American countries?[4] Is it mere coincidence—a matter of good luck—or are there more systematic forces at work, deriving from economic structure, initial conditions, or economic policy, which can help explain the differences in economic performance in the countries in the two continents?

---

[3] After the first oil shock, the recession in industrialized countries lasted for two years, 1974 and 1975, when GDP growth fell (from the 1973 level of 6.1%) to 0.8% and −0.4% respectively; in 1976, it was 4.7 per cent, almost back to its trend level. In comparison, after the second oil shock, the growth rate went from 3.3% in 1979, to 1.3% in 1980 and 1981, −0.5% in 1982 and only 2.3% in 1983.

[4] The differential economic performance of the sub-Saharan African countries is not considered in this essay because the initial level of economic development and the structural characteristics of these economies are rather different from those of Latin American countries. For a study of the sub-Saharan African countries, see Singh 1987.

Table 3.1 Population, GDP, and GDP per capita, GDP growth rates, various country grouping

	GDP	Population	GDP/cap.	GDP growth rates (average annual % changes)						
	1985	1985	1985	1965–80	1980–5	1980	1981	1982	1983	1984*
Developing countries	2,027.0	3,681.5	550.6	6.1	3.3	2.5	2.4	1.9	2.0	5.4
Low Income Asia	500.7	2,026.0	247.1	4.0	5.5	6.3	5.2	5.6	8.6	10.2
China	265.5	1,040.3	255.2	6.4	9.8	6.1	4.8	7.3	9.6	14.0
India	175.7	765.1	229.6	3.7	5.2	6.9	5.7	2.9	7.7	4.5
Low Income Africa	84.4	312.0	270.5	2.9	0.7	1.3	1.2	0.5	0.3	0.7
Middle-income oil importers	906.9	718.8	1,261.7	5.2	1.7	4.3	0.9	0.7	0.8	4.1
East Asia and Pacific	239.1	192.4	1,242.6	7.5	4.5	3.6	6.7	4.2	6.4	6.4
Middle East and N. Africa	27.1	46.8	579.9	3.7	3.5	4.2	-2.4	5.5	2.9	4.1
Sub-Saharan Africa	23.4	34.8	673.3	5.6	2.9	5.5	3.9	1.1	-1.4	-1.1
Southern Europe	163.0	97.2	1,677.4	5.9	1.8	1.5	2.3	0.7	0.9	2.7
Latin America and Caribbean	370.8	316.1	1,173.1	4.7	-0.3	5.8	-2.3	-0.4	1.7	3.7
Middle-income oil exporters	533.1	523.3	1,018.7	7.1	1.0	-2.4	2.4	0.9	3.1	2.5
High-income oil exporters	170.3	18.4	9,255.4	7.8	-2.2	7.4	0.0	xxx	-7.1	1.3
Industrial market economies	8,568.9	737.3	11,622.0	3.6	2.3	1.3	1.3	-0.5	2.3	4.6

Source: World Bank 1987; IMF 1987.
* = Estimated

In view of the obvious analytical and policy significance of these issues, they have recently been investigated by a number of scholars (e.g. Balassa 1984; Maddison 1985; Sachs 1985; Singh 1985b). Section 3.2 briefly revies this literature and outlines the competing hypotheses. Section 3.3 examines comparative economic performance for a more comprehensive group of Asian and Latin American economies than has been attempted in earlier studies. Differences in economic structure, initial conditions, and the nature of the economic shocks suffered by the two groups of countries are considered in Sections 3.4 and 3.5. Section 3.6 offers some comments on economic policy differences between the countries. Section 3.7 briefly analyses the individual economic experience of the large semi-industrial countries in the two continents—China and India in Asia, Brazil and Mexico in Latin America. The main conclusions are summarized in Section 3.8.

3.2 THE REASONS FOR SUPERIOR ASIAN PERFORMANCE: ALTERNATIVE HYPOTHESES

In the analysis of East Asian success and Latin American failure to cope with the recent economic shocks, most economists have come to focus on a single issue—the degree of openness of the economy. Neoclassical economists have maintained, first, that the main reason for the difference in economic performance was the openness of East Asian economies to international trade and financial flows, and the relatively closed nature of Latin American economies; and second, that this openness was determined solely by the nature of economic policies in the two regions, and particularly by exchange rate policies which have a significant effect on the competitiveness of the tradable goods sectors. Other writers have argued that the issue is much more complex, and that the relationship between economic openness and vulnerability to external shocks depends upon the nature of the openness, the nature of the shocks, and the state of the international economy.

The mainstream views on this issue are best contained in the works of Bela Balassa, Anne Krueger, and Jeffrey Sachs. While the first two writers criticize interventionist governments for creating inefficient, 'inward-oriented' or 'illiberal' economies, Sachs places the blame squarely upon commercial policies, namely, overvalued exchange rates in Latin American countries which not only reduced competitiveness but also encouraged capital flight.[5] For example, Sachs (1985) writes:

The most important differences seem to centre on exchange rate management and on the trading regimes. Latin American and Asian countries have differed not only in the amounts borrowed, but also the uses to which the loans were applied. Simply put the

---

[5] Indeed, he goes even further, to suggest, on the basis of rather weak evidence, that the superiority of the policy regimes in Asian countries stems from the supposedly greater dominance of rural interests in these policies. For a criticism of this argument, see Taylor, ch. 4 this volume.

Latin American countries did not use the foreign borrowing to develop a resource base in tradable goods, especially export industries, adequate for future debt servicing.

These writers also argue that openness to world trade may reduce rather than increase the vulnerability of the economy to external shocks. Balassa, for example, writes:

At any rate, one should not exaggerate the vulnerabilty of an economy with a high export share. Thus, during the 1974–75 world recession, export-oriented developing countries in general, and South Korea in particular, fared relatively well, since they had more of a margin to spare as far as imports are concerned. By contrast, countries which went the farthest in import substitution, and limited imports to what appeared to be absolutely necessary inputs, suffered serious production setbacks because of their inability to procure these inputs as their balance-of-payments situation deteriorated.

Finally, as the author has elsewhere noted, the degree of instability of the world economic system should not be overstated. 'This is because the confluence of the circumstances existing in 1974—the quadrupling of oil prices and the doubling of grain prices, together with a deep world recession, partly caused by reactions to the sudden oil price increase and partly the consequence of the super boom of the years 1972–73—cannot be expected to recur.' (Balassa 1981: 355–6)

Balassa's second point above need not detain us: the post-1979 experience of the world economy has shown him to be conclusively wrong on this issue. However, on the first point, leaving aside for the moment his empirical assertion, he has a more reasonable a priori case. The theoretical argument is very well put by John Williamson, as follows:

A country with a very small trade sector generally has a limited range of exports based on resource-intensive products that are exploiting some local comparative advantage bestowed by geology or climate. These products tend to exhibit both inelastic supply and inelastic demand, so there is a very little possibility of export expansion at the margin. Import capacity tends to be entirely preempted in importing intermediate goods, including oil, that are necessary to keep industry going for the domestic market. Hence, there is minimal elasticity in the trade structure to permit adjustment to trade shocks. This is the basic, though not the only, reason why the size of the trade sector is significant in enabling countries to overcome external shocks. (Williamson 1985: 569–70)

An alternative analysis of differential performance of Latin American and Asian economies, which also stresses the role of openness as well as that of economic policy, is provided in Angus Maddison's (1985) fascinating historical comparison of the effects of the recent decade of slow growth in the world economy (1979–83), with an earlier downturn in 1929–39. Maddison finds that the effect of economic openness and orthodox policies was essentially reversed in the two crises. During the Great Depression of the 1930s, Latin American countries achieved a much higher rate of economic growth than Asian countries, despite being subjected to relatively larger exogenous shocks. According to Maddison, this was partly because of the greater protection provided to the domestic economy by Latin American policies, and partly because of the orthodox contractionary economic and financial policies of the colonial governments in Asia. In Latin America, 'the sharp experience of recession in the independent countries of Latin America induced a change in attitudes towards the liberal international economic order, and [fostered] an inward-looking developmentalism . . .' He goes on to argue that 'in the conditions of the 1930's, the verdict must be in favour of the import-substitution policies, for openness to the world economy of the type Cuba was compelled to follow meant large scale unemployment of productive resources' (Maddison 1985: 23).

However, the position is reversed in 1973–83. Maddison believes that the less favourable record of the Latin American countries during this decade is essentially due to the poor quality of their domestic policies. He writes:

In Latin America, most governments still rely on inflation as a way of raising revenue . . . In Asian countries [fiscal], monetary and exchange rate policies were more cautious, trade deficits and foreign borrowings were much more modest . . . Because of better domestic policy, these countries have not been plagued by massive capital flight by their own nationals, as Latin America has been. (Maddison 1985: 46)

Maddison's analysis helps to bring out the contextual nature of the argument for openness and its relationship to economic vulnerability. These issues were also emphasized in an earlier study by one of the co-authors of this Chapter (Singh 1985b). This study examined the recent experience of five large, semi-industrial economies—Brazil and Mexico in Latin America, and India, China and South Korea in Asia—to argue that India and China performed better than Brazil and Mexico precisely because they were less closely integrated with the world economy. These two countries had long followed the path of 'self-reliance' and import-substitution industrialization; they also depended relatively little on foreign debt. In contrast, the two large Latin American countries chose to follow outward-looking industrial strategies based on multinational investment and foreign debt. The result was that

when the world economy was growing rapidly, these countries benefitted from their greater integration with it in much the way orthodox economics extols the virtues of increased trade and specialization. However, their industrial structures which were suitable for an expanding world economy and world trade also left them vulnerable to prolonged economic disruption when the international economy ceased to grow. (Singh 1985b: 3)

It is true that among the countries which opted for an outward-oriented strategy, South Korea was far more successful than the others, but its success was due less to the exchange rate policies than to the direct state promotion of exports. The present study builds on the earlier work by using a larger sample of countries and by focusing more directly on the issues thrown up by the above disagreements.

To review the foregoing discussion: the differences between the various perspectives can be traced back to two underlying issues. First, how is 'openness' or 'the degree of integration with the world economy' to be defined? Does the concept simply refer to foreign trade as a proportion of GDP, or does it also encompass foreign investment and foreign debt? It seems to us that if the second definition is used, the supposed empirical relationship between openness and economic performance breaks down.

Related to the first question, and perhaps of greater importance, is the question of the relationship between economic vulnerability and the degree of integration with the world economy. Neoclassical logic, positing that the greater the openness, the lesser the vulnerability to international economic fluctuations, seeks reassurance in South Korea's recent experience. On the other hand, the experience of the large countries, as well as the regional pattern during the Great Depression, suggests the opposite.[6] Moreover, as the following analysis will show, the relationship also depends critically upon the precise nature of the external shock: most countries adjusted to the trade shocks without much difficulty, but were severely impaired by the shocks originating in the financial markets.

3.3 THE COMPARATIVE ECONOMIC PERFORMANCE OF ASIAN AND LATIN AMERICAN ECONOMIES

In this section, we shall review briefly the background to the subject of discussion, namely, the differences in economic performance in Latin American and Asian countries. We shall focus most of our attention on nineteen of the larger countries in the two continents. The information is assembled in Tables 3.2–3.5 and suggests that the major differences in economic performance emerge after 1980, when Latin American growth dropped precipitately, while Asian countries maintained or even improved upon their earlier growth performance. The differences in underlying behavioural variables do not become significant until the 1980s, and this too largely because of the sudden increase in the debt repayment burden.

Table 3.2, which compares the long-term rate of growth of GDP of the selected countries, for three periods (1960–70, 1970–80, and 1980–7), reveals not only the superior performance of Asian countries in the current decade, but also the remarkable uniformity of economic experience within each

---

[6] However, as noted specifically in Singh 1985*b*, a country's vulnerability is not just a function of the size of its trading sector but depends on the nature of its exports and imports as well as a host of other factors.

Table 3.2 GDP Growth rate in Asian and Latin American countries (% per year)

	1960–70	1970–80	1980–7
Asia			
China	5.2	5.8	10.4
India	3.4	3.6	4.6
Indonesia	3.9	7.6	3.6
Korea	8.6	9.5	8.6
Malaysia	6.5	7.8	4.5
Pakistan	6.7	4.7	6.7
Philippines	5.1	6.3	–0.5
Sri Lanka	4.6	4.1	4.6
Taiwan	. . .	. . .	. . .
Thailand	8.4	7.2	5.6
Median	5.2	6.3	4.6
Latin America			
Argentina	4.2	2.2	–0.3
Bolivia	5.2	4.8	–2.1
Brazil	5.4	8.4	3.3
Chile	4.5	2.8	1.0
Colombia	5.1	5.9	2.9
Ecuador	. . .	8.8	1.5
Mexico	7.2	5.2	0.5·
Peru	4.9	3.0	1.2
Venezuela	6.0	5.0	0.2
Median	5.1	5.0	1.0

Source: World Bank 1982, 1989.

continent. For neither group were the 1960s significantly different from the 1970s (which included the period between the two oil shocks—the so-called inter-shock period, 1973–9). After 1980, however while the median[7] annual rate of economic growth plummeted in Latin America, from 5 per cent to one per cent during 1980–7, in Asia it fell only slightly from 6.3 to 4.6 per cent). Indeed, four Asian countries—China, India, Pakistan, and Sri Lanka—managed actually to increase their rate of economic expansion during the last decade of turbulence in the world economy.[8]

[7] Since economic policy is carried out at the individual country rather than the continental level, and the focus of the study is inter-country comparisons, the median is a better summary measure of central tendency than the weighted average (weighted by GDP) used in Sachs 1985. The latter measure will simply reflect much more the experience of the larger economies.

[8] The improvement over historical trends was much more significant for China and India, whose economies were the least integrated into the world markets. It is arguable that these two countries have been even more successful than South Korea in coping with international economic fluctuations.

Table 3.3 Rates of inflation in Asia and Latin America, 1960–1987 (average annual % growth of consumer price index)

	1960–70	1970–80	1980–7
Asia			
China	. . .	. . .	4.2
India	7.1	8.5	7.7
Indonesia	. . .	20.5	8.5
Korea	17.4	19.8	5.0
Malaysia	–0.3	7.5	1.1
Pakistan	3.3	13.5	7.3
Philippines	5.8	13.2	16.7
Sri Lanka	1.8	12.6	11.8
Taiwan	3.5	12.2	3.3
Thailand	1.8	9.9	2.8
Median	3.4	12.6	7.3
Latin America			
Argentina	21.7	130.8	298.7
Bolivia	3.5	22.3	601.8
Brazil	46.1	36.7	166.3
Chile	33.2	185.6	20.6
Colombia	11.9	22.0	23.7
Ecuador	. . .	14.4	29.5
Mexico	3.6	19.3	68.9
Peru	10.4	30.7	101.5
Venezuela	1.3	12.1	11.4
Median	11.1	22.3	68.9

Source: World Bank 1982, 1989.

Besides the Philippines—the only Asian country to suffer a sharp decline in its growth rate—and Indonesia, a member of OPEC, all the Asian countries managed to register an annual growth rate of close to or over 5 per cent during 1980–6. On the other hand, only one of the nine Latin American countries achieved a growth rate of more than 3 per cent in the same period (and only Brazil and Colombia were above 2 per cent). This continental uniformity in economic performance is all the more significant in view of the wide inter-country differences in economic structure, economic policy, and even in the basic economic system.[9]

Table 3.3 records the well-known inflationary experience of Latin American countries, where the median annual inflation rate doubled from

[9] This is particularly true in Asia, where countries like China, India, and South Korea not only have different economic systems, but the two market economy countries (India and South Korea) have traditionally followed very different economic strategies.

11 per cent in the 1960s to 22 per cent in the 1970s, and tripled again to 69 per cent in the 1980s. In Asian countries, while the 1970s witnessed a quadrupling of the median inflation rate, this increased it only from 3.4 to 12.6 per year; from which level the rate fell in the 1980s, to 7.3 per cent. During 1980–7, only one Latin American country, Venezuela, managed to achieve a lower inflation rate than the Asian country with the highest inflation rate, the Philippines.

Tables 3.4 and 3.5 report on two indicators of debt burden for the two groups of countries—the debt/GDP ratio and the debt service/export ratio (DSR). The debt figures for each country refer to the gross external liabilities and include both short- and long-term debt. In the inter-shock period (1973–9), while the average debt/GDP ratio in Asian countries was greater than that in Latin American economies—South Korea, Indonesia, Pakistan, Sri Lanka, and Philippines had higher ratios than Mexico and Brazil—the formers' average DSR was only about half that of the latters'. This is explained,

Table 3.4 Total External debt/GDP ratios in Asia and Latin America (%)

	1973–9	1980–3
Asia		
China	. . .	. . .
India	14.2	13.5
Indonesia	35.5	30.8
Korea	31.9	50.6
Malaysia	. . .	. . .
Pakistan	52.5	38.7
Philippines	31.1	58.2
Sri Lanka	46.7	55.3
Taiwan	. . .	. . .
Thailand	15.2	30.6
Median	31.9	38.7
Latin America		
Argentina	17.8	46.2
Bolivia	. . .	. . .
Brazil	21.3	33.8
Chile	43.1	64.6
Colombia	21.6	25.2
Ecuador	. . .	. . .
Mexico	26.7	45.1
Peru	53.1	55.8
Venezuela	24.9	46.2
Median	24.9	46.2

Source: World Bank Data Bank.

Table 3.5 Public foreign debt service/export ratios in Asia and Latin America (%)

	1973–9	1980–5
Asia		
China	. . .	1.0*
India	13.7	9.8
Indonesia	10.0	12.4
Korea	11.5	13.7
Malaysia	5.0	7.9
Pakistan	19.3	22.6
Philippines	9.4	12.8
Sri Lanka	13.9	10.1
Taiwan	. . .	. . .
Thailand	3.1	9.5
Median	10.7	10.1
Latin America		
Argentina	19.5	25.4
Bolivia	. . .	30.8
Brazil	22.9	31.9
Chile	26.3	23.7
Colombia	12.0	18.7
Ecuador	. . .	28.6
Mexico	38.8	34.4
Peru	27.1	25.7
Venezuela	6.6	13.6
Median	22.9	25.7

Source: World Debt Tables 1986–7.
* = 1980–4.

partly, by the softer loan conditions (the greater role of official development assistance) for Asian countries, but more significantly by the higher degree of trade openness (i.e. larger exports/GDP ratios) in Asian countries.

In the 1980s, while the DSR did not change by much, the debt/GDP ratio increased appreciably in both continents, much more so in Latin America than in Asia. In the Latin American case, this increase reflects three factors: the effect of higher real interest rates (a larger fraction of the Latin American debt was on variable interest rates), a large volume of capital flight, and a decline in the rate of growth of GDP after 1980 (Table 3.2). The increase in the Asian debt ratios is explained more simply as the result of higher current account deficits in the 1980s as we shall see below (Table 3.7). This increase was not uniform across the continent, however, as India (and China[10])

[10] The comparable figures for China's debt are not available in the World Bank data bank. However, see Section 3.7 below.

continued to have relatively very small debt burdens throughout the 1970s and 1980s. This was not fortuitous but the result of a deliberate act of economic policy, as will be discussed in Section 3.7.

3.4 EXPLANATIONS OF DIFFERENTIAL ECONOMIC PERFORMANCE

Tables 3.6 and 3.7, which present investment and savings rates, respectively, in the countries of the two continents, indicate three things: first, the similarity of investment rates across the two continents during the 1970s; second, the recent decline in Latin America, significant (from 25 per cent of GDP during 1973–80 to only 20 per cent during 1980–5), but less pronounced than the fall in growth rates (in fact, four countries registered modest increases in investment ratios in this period); and third, a more

Table 3.6 Investment performance of Asian and Latin American economies (Gross domestic investment/GDP, %)

	1965–73	1973–80	1980–5
Asia			
China	. . .	. . .	. . .
India	18.4	22.6	24.4
Indonesia	15.8	24.5	29.4
Korea	25.1	31.8	30.7
Malaysia	22.3	28.7	36.1
Pakistan	16.0	16.5	16.2
Philippines	20.6	29.1	25.8
Sri Lanka	15.8	20.6	28.9
Thailand	23.8	26.6	24.4
Median	19.5	25.5	27.3
Latin America			
Argentina	19.8	21.8	16.3
Bolivia	25.4	24.9	16.0
Brazil	26.1	26.2	20.4
Chile	14.4	17.4	17.5
Colombia	18.9	18.8	20.0
Ecuador	19.0	26.7	23.2
Mexico	21.4	25.2	25.4
Peru	27.7	28.9	28.0
Venezuela	29.3	32.6	19.9
Median	21.4	25.2	20.0

Source: World Bank 1987.

Table 3.7 Domestic savings in Asian and Latin American countries (gross national savings/GNP %)

	1965–73	1973–80	1980–5
Asia			
China	. . .	. . .	. . .
India	17.9	22.3	22.6
Indonesia	13.7	24.6	26.6
Korea	21.5	26.4	26.9
Malaysia	21.6	29.3	27.3
Pakistan	. . .	10.9	12.5
Philippines	20.6	24.3	20.0
Sri Lanka	14.6	13.5	17.1
Thailand	22.6	21.5	18.5
Median	20.6	23.3	21.3
Latin America			
Argentina	19.7	21.2	11.3
Bolivia	29.2	18.2	6.9
Brazil	24.3	21.7	16.9
Chile	12.9	12.2	6.9
Colombia	17.2	19.2	15.0
Ecuador	16.3	21.2	18.3
Mexico	19.9	21.3	23.5
Peru	27.2	24.9	23.7
Venezuela	30.0	34.5	24.9
Median	19.9	21.3	16.9

Source: World Bank 1987.

uniform decline in national savings rates. Part of the decline in Latin American investment and savings rates is explained by the increase in interest payments on foreign debt from fairly low levels in the 1970s to as much as 3–4 per cent of GNP in the 1980s (and, in some cases, even to 7 per cent). In Asian countries, despite the world economic slow-down, the trend of increasing investment ratios has been maintained in the 1980s, rising from less than 20 per cent of GDP in 1965–73 to 25 per cent during 1973–80 and over 27 per cent in 1980–5. Table 3.7 shows, however, that although Asian countries performed better than Latin American countries, savings mobilization did not match the improvement in investment demand.

Taken together, the investment and growth records suggest an increase in the average incremental capital/output ratio (ICOR) in both continents. Table 3.8 indicates that there was in fact a rise in ICORs during the 1970s for almost every group of countries in the world economy, the largest increase

Table 3.8 Incremental capital–output ratios in world market economies at 1975 prices

	1960–5	1965–70	1970–5	1975–80	1960–70	1970–80
World market economies	4.1	4.7	7.1	6.4	4.4	6.7
Developed economies	4.3	5.1	8.3	6.7	4.7	7.4
Developing countries	3.2	2.9	3.8	5.4	3.0	4.6
Developed economies						
North America	4.1	6.9	7.9	5.7	5.4	6.6
Africa, Asia, and Oceania	3.3	3.1	8.1	7.0	3.2	7.5
Europe	4.8	5.2	8.8	7.6	5.0	8.1
Major industrial economies	4.2	5.2	8.4	6.4	4.7	7.2
Other developed economies	4.4	5.0	7.8	8.8	4.8	8.2
European Economic Community	4.9	5.2	9.2	7.3	5.0	8.1
Developing countries						
Latin America and the Caribbean	3.5	3.4	4.1	5.5	3.5	4.9
Africa	2.7	2.5	6.2	4.8	2.6	5.2
West Asia	1.6	1.7	2.0	10.7	1.6	4.5
Asia and the Pacific	4.5	3.3	4.1	4.1	3.7	4.1
High-income	2.8	2.6	3.6	6.1	2.7	4.8
Medium-income	2.8	3.3	3.8	4.4	3.1	4.2
Low-income	6.1	3.5	4.9	4.6	4.3	4.7
Least developed	4.1	6.1	5.2	4.0	5.1	4.4
Capital-surplus energy exporting	0.9	1.0	1.9	13.3	1.0	5.2
Other net energy exporting	2.8	3.0	4.1	4.5	2.9	4.4
Net energy importing	4.2	3.5	4.2	5.1	3.8	4.7
Petroleum-exporting	1.9	2.0	3.2	6.0	2.0	4.7
Newly industrialized	3.7	2.7	2.9	4.4	3.1	3.7
Agricultural product exporters	4.8	3.8	5.2	5.7	4.2	5.5
Mineral product exporters	2.8	3.7	7.1	6.3	3.3	6.6

Source: UN, reproduced from Raj 1984.

being for the developed market economies. Given the low capacity utilization in Latin American countries in the 1980s due to the severity of the balance of payment constraint, the average ICOR is bound to have risen above the levels reported in this table.

Table 3.9 provides data on the current account balances of the countries in the two continents. In 1973–80, they were broadly similar, but after 1980 the deficits increased somewhat faster in Asia than in Latin America.[11] This does not reflect superior international performance on the part of the Latin countries, simply that the debt crisis obliged many of them to sharply and often precipitately reduce their deficits. However, the similarity of current

Table 3.9 Current account balance in Asian and Latin American countries, 1965–1985 (current account balance/GNP %)

	1965–73	1973–80	1980–5
Asia			
China	. . .	. . .	. . .
India	–0.5	–0.3	–1.8
Indonesia	–2.2	0.1	–2.8
Korea	–3.6	–5.3	–3.8
Malaysia	–0.7	0.6	–7.6
Pakistan	. . .	–5.6	–3.7
Philippines	0.0	–4.8	–5.9
Sri Lanka	–1.2	–7.2	–11.8
Thailand	–1.1	–5.1	–5.9
Median	–1.1	–5.1	–5.9
Latin America			
Argentina	0.0	–0.6	–5.0
Bolivia	–0.2	–6.7	–9.1
Brazil	–1.7	–4.5	–3.5
Chile	–1.4	–5.2	–10.6
Colombia	–1.8	0.4	–5.0
Ecuador	–2.7	–5.5	–4.9
Mexico	–1.5	–3.9	–1.9
Peru	–0.5	–4.1	–4.3
Venezuela	0.7	1.9	5.0
Median	–1.5	–4.1	–4.9

Source: World Bank 1987.

[11] The comparable Chinese figures are not available in Table 3.9, but as will be reported in Section 3.7, the Chinese ran a current account surplus for much of the period and had accumulated enormous reserves by the early 1980s.

account balances in the two regions obscures the more severe balance of payments problems of Latin American countries because of capital flight. For example, Venezuela, which registered on average a current account surplus in all the three periods, ended up contracting enormous debts because of capital flight. The question of capital flight will be considered in Section 3.6.

Tables 3.10 and 3.11 summarize the main characteristics of the economic and industrial structure of Asian and Latin American countries in 1985. The exceptional features of the South Korean economy are evident, not only from the high exports to GDP ratio but more importantly from the uniquely low share of primary goods in its merchandise exports. Even ignoring the oil-exporting countries in the sample (Indonesia, Ecuador, Mexico, and Venezuela), South Korea's 10 per cent share of primary goods exports is far below those of Latin American economies, which range from a low of 59 per cent for Brazil to over 90 per cent for Bolivia and Chile; or even the slightly lower Asian figures, which vary from 37 per cent (Pakistan) to 73 per cent (Sri Lanka).

As for the importance of the trade sector in general, the medium-sized Asian countries, including South Korea, have higher exports/GDP ratios than comparable Latin American economies. However, the larger countries in both continents have, as one would expect, relatively smaller trade ratios. For example, the Indian ratio of 6–7 per cent in the 1980s is less than half of the most closed Latin American economies; and even China and Pakistan, with 11 per cent were well below Brazil (14 per cent) or Mexico (15 per cent). In fact, these two figures can be combined to yield a significant source of difference between most Latin American and Asian countries, the share of *non-primary* exports in GDP. In the Latin American sample, this share is below 3 per cent for all countries except Brazil (5.7 per cent) and Mexico (4.3 per cent), while in Asia only India (3.0 per cent), Indonesia (2.5 per cent), and Pakistan (4.7 per cent) lie below 5 per cent; the South Korean figure is an extraordinary 33 per cent.

To sum up, the last two sections have shown that while there was a significant worsening of economic conditions in Latin America after 1980— as measured by standard indicators, growth, inflation, foreign debt—the differences from the more 'successful' Asian countries in terms of savings and accumulation rates and current account behaviour were much less pronounced. In the mainstream literature, it is suggested that although the relatively closed nature of Latin American economies reduced the direct impact of the external trade shocks, it made adjustment even to these smaller shocks more problematic. We found, however, that while regional differences in export performance were quite significant, the relative success of closed economies like China, India, Indonesia, or Pakistan cast doubt on this explanation. With this background, we can turn to an examination of the two analytical

Table 3.10 Indicators of economic and industrial structure in Asia, 1985

	China	India	Indonesia	S. Korea	Malaysia	Pakistan	Philippines	Sri Lanka	Taiwan	Thailand
GNP per capita, $	310	270	530	2,150	2,000	380	580	380	...	800
Distribution of GDP, %										
Agriculture	...	31	24	14	...	25	27	27	...	17
Industry	...	27	36	41	...	28	32	26	...	30
Manufacturing	...	17	14	28	...	20	25	15	...	20
Services	...	41	41	45	...	47	41	46	...	53
Value added in manufacturing										
Food and agriculture	...	12	20	9	18	...	28	44	...	23
Textiles and clothing	...	26	7	17	6	...	23	15	...	...
Machinery and transport equipment	...	19	7	29	28	...	10	4	...	12
Chemicals	...	11	6	11	4	...	21	7	...	8
Others	...	32	60	35	42	...	18	31	...	56
Share of export of goods and non-factor services in GNP	11	6	23	36	55	11	22	26	...	27
Share of primary commodities in merchandise exports	46	51	89	9	73	37	49	73	...	65

Source: World Bank 1987

Table 3.11 Indicators of economic and industrial structure in Latin America, 1985

	Argentina	Bolivia	Brazil	Chile	Colombia	Ecuador	Mexico	Peru	Venezuela
GNP per capita, $	2,130	470	1,640	1,430	1,320	1,160	2,080	1,010	3,080
Distribution of GDP (percent)									
Agriculture	...	27	13	...	20	14	11	11	8
Industry	...	30	33	...	30	42	35	38	42
Manufacturing	...	19	...	...	18	19	54	20	21
Services	...	42	54	...	50	45		51	50
Distribution of value added in manufacturing									
Food and agriculture	24	36	19	27	45	39	28	26	28
Textiles and clothing	9	16	10	10	13	17	12	13	6
Machinery and transport equipment	15	2	18	3	5	1	13	12	6
Chemicals	12	4	11	8	8	4	13	11	6
Others	40	42	41	52	29	39	34	38	54
Share of export of goods and non-factor services in GNP	15	18	14	29	15	27	16	22	27
Share of primary commodities in merchandise exports	82	94	59	93	82	99	73	88	95

Source: World Bank 1987

issues which bear upon the differences in economic performance, namely, the impact of exogenous shocks and the role of exchange rate policies.

3.5 THE COMPARATIVE IMPACT OF EXOGENOUS SHOCKS

In this section, we examine the assertion that vulnerability to external shocks is reduced by the openness of trade and financial regimes; and that the external shocks to which Latin American economies proved so vulnerable were, in fact, smaller than the shocks which hit the Asian economies. Our findings are to the contrary. While it is true that terms of trade shocks, *per se*, had a greater direct impact on the relatively open East Asian economies, that is not the end of the story. First, even excluding the oil-exporting countries, Asian economies received 'positive' as well as 'negative' shocks during the last two decades. In particular, they reaped the benefits of larger flows of workers' remittances from, and a larger volume of trade with, the booming Middle Eastern countries. These positive shocks are normally ignored by analysts looking at recent adjustment experience.

Second, just as the trade openness of Asian countries increased their exposure to trade shocks, the financial openness of Latin American economies increased their vulnerability to shocks originating in international financial markets. Moreover, while it is true that trade openness of the former countries reduced their vulnerability to financial shocks as well, it is also the case that the financial openness of the latter group actually *increased* their vulnerability to trade shocks. Indeed, Latin American countries were derailed by exogenous shocks mainly because of their open financial markets, rather than their closed trade regimes. The upshot is that once these additional aspects of the issue are taken into account, it becomes incorrect to say that the direct impact of external shocks on Asian economies was greater than that on Latin American ones.

The impact of an exogenous shock to an economy depends on the size of the shock and the structure of the economy. Thus, the larger the share of imports in the GDP of a country, the greater would be the impact on its real income of a decline in its terms of trade. Table 3.12 presents changes in the terms of trade for nineteen Latin American and Asian countries from the period 1975–8 to 1979–83. It shows a wide variation across countries—from Brazil, which suffered a 28.9 per cent decline in its terms of trade, to the oil-exporting countries which, despite the slippage of oil prices in 1982 and 1983, registered huge gains: in the case of Indonesia, a whopping 98.8 per cent!

On average, however, the terms of trade of Asian countries deteriorated much more than those of Latin American economies. It is also true, moreover, that because of their greater trade openness, the adverse impact of these shocks on the real incomes of East Asian countries was, on average,

Table 3.12 Terms of trade shock, 1979–1983

	% change ToT from 1975–78	Imports as % of GDP 1975–78	Real income effect of ToT change
	(a)	(b)	(c) = (ab) ÷ 100
Asia			
India	−13.4	6.8	−0.9
Indonesia	98.8	21.5	21.3
Korea	−6.4	34.7	−2.2
Malaysia	11.7	44.3	5.2
Pakistan	−6.7	20.9	−1.4
Philippines	−4.1	24.1	−1.0
Sri Lanka	−4.5	29.9	−1.4
Thailand	−17.0	24.7	−4.2
Median	−5.4	24.3	−1.2
Latin America			
Argentina	−8.2	8.6	−0.7
Bolivia	−9.4	24.1	−2.3
Brazil	−28.9	9.4	−2.7
Chile	−2.1	23.4	−0.5
Colombia	−12.8	14.7	−1.9
Ecuador	22.1	27.4	6.1
Mexico	28.7	9.8	2.8
Peru	30.8	18.7	5.8
Venezuela	42.4	32.5	13.8
Median	−2.1	18.7	−0.5

Source: World Bank Data Bank.

greater than either on South Asian or Latin American economies. For example, Indian terms of trade worsened by 13 per cent during this period, but the effect on real income was only 0.9 per cent of GDP; South Korea's terms of trade loss was only half the size of India's, but because of its much more open economy its effect on real income was more than twice that for India.

3.5.1 'Positive' trade shocks

The terms of trade deterioration is not the only trade shock to have affected Third World countries in recent years. Another exogenous shock, which had an important differential impact on the Asian and Latin American economies, derives from the regional distribution of changes in economic growth and world trade during the last two decades. In particular, the Middle Eastern market, which continued to expand during this period, was much more significant for many of the Asian countries than for Latin America.

There are two important channels by which the South Asian (India, Pakistan, and Sri Lanka) and South-East Asian countries have benefitted from the economic prosperity in the Middle East: (*a*) workers' remittances, and (*b*) the growth of merchandise and construction exports.

By 1975 there were 1.6 million migrants working in the Arab oil-producing countries, comprising as much as 17 per cent of the total labour force of these countries. Although most of the migrants came from the other Middle Eastern countries, a little over 20 per cent were from South and South-East Asia. It is estimated that by 1980, the number of migrants to the Middle Eastern oil-producing nations increased to 3 million, of whom more than a quarter came from South and South-East Asia (Talal 1984; Burki 1984; Singh 1985*a*; Banuri 1986).

In view of the size of the migration, the scale of the remittances and their impact on the balance of payments has been highly significant for a number of Asian countries. Workers' remittances, constituted a little over 28 per cent of the exports of goods and non-factor services in Pakistan in 1975, but by 1982 their share had increased to over 80 per cent, or four times the country's debt service requirement for the year. Similarly in India, workers' remittances as a proportion of exports increased from a little over 5 per cent in 1974 to nearly 15 per cent in 1978 and about 25 per cent in 1980. The corresponding figures for Sri Lanka are 1.4 per cent in 1974, 4.1 per cent in 1978, and 22 per cent in 1982. In Thailand, remittances constituted less than 1 per cent of exports in 1967 and over 10 per cent in 1983, while the increase in Thailand's debt service over this period was from 2.5 per cent of exports to 11.5 per cent.

Apart from workers' migration and remittances, the Asian economies were able to greatly expand their exports to the oil countries. Since 1973, the high-income Arab oil-producing countries (Oman, Libya, Saudi Arabia, Kuwait, and the United Arab Emirates) have been by far the fastest growing market in the world. Between 1973 and 1984 the imports of these countries increased at a rate of 18.3 per cent per annum; the corresponding growth rate of imports in the industrial market economies was 3.2 per cent, and in the middle-income developing countries less than 5 per cent (World Bank 1986). The proportion of high-income oil-exporting countries in Pakistan's total exports increased from only 4 per cent in 1965 to 22 per cent in 1983; India's share of exports to these countries increased from 2 to 7 per cent over the same period, while South Korea's share grew from almost zero in 1965 to 10 per cent in 1983 (World Bank 1985: table 12, pp. 196–7).

3.5.2 Capital market shocks

Be the above as it may, the fact is that Latin American as well as Asian countries managed to accommodate to the trade shocks of the 1970s without a noticeable impairment of their economic conditions. Such an impairment was brought about, rather, by a series of shocks which were unrelated to the trade regime *per se*. These began with the enormous increase in nominal and real interest rates on international debt, which followed the adoption of highly restrictive monetary policies in the United States and the other advanced countries. Measured as the London Interbank Offer Rate (LIBOR) on three-month US dollar deposits less the rate of change in the GDP deflator in the United States, the real interest rates increased from an average of only 0.5 per cent during 1947–78 to more than 7 per cent in 1981 and 1982, and 5 per cent in 1983. If the real interest rates are defined more appropriately in terms of differences between LIBOR and the rate of change of export prices of developing countries, the recorded increase in these rates is astounding. As Table 3.13 shows, the average real interest rate on developing country floating-rate debt increased from −11.8 per cent in 1977 to 15.9 per cent in 1983.

Table 3.13 Average real percentage interest rate on developing country floating rate debt, 1977–1983

1977	−11.8
1978	−7.4
1979	−9.7
1980	−6.0
1981	14.6
1982	16.7
1983	15.9

Source: Reisen 1985.

This rise in interest rates had a much greater effect on the economies of Latin American countries than on those in Asia. A larger proportion of the Latin American debt was of the floating rate variety. Further, the World Bank data on the average terms of new loans (e.g. maturity, the grace period, the grant element) during the period 1972–87 show that Latin American countries faced by far the worse loan conditions. Sachs (1985) suggests that with a few exceptions the impact of the rise in interest rates on the developing countries' economies was not particularly significant. He writes: 'At the peak, the measured US real interest rate rises by about 10 percentage points and is multiplied by a debt/GDP ratio of the order of 20 per cent, producing a peak annual loss of about 2 per cent of GDP and an average annual loss of about 1 per cent of GDP.' However, this is not a valid argument. Since as seen in Table 3.7 the median current account deficit in the Latin American countries was only about 3 per cent of GDP in the late 1970s, the impact of the increase in interest rates (whether measured in nominal or real terms) on the current balance of these economies was highly significant. The dynamic consequences (particularly in terms of capital flows) of an increase (or decrease) by nearly a third in the current account deficit for an economy constrained by the balance of payments cannot be exaggerated.

The issue also has an important bearing on the general question of the vulnerability of an economy to international fluctuations. If two countries have the same debt/GDP ratio, other things being equal, a rise in interest rates will have a more serious impact on the less rather than the more 'open' economy (where 'openness' is defined in terms of the share of exports or imports in GDP). This is because the less 'open' economy will be obliged to increase its exports or reduce its imports by a greater proportion than the more open economy to compensate for the increase in interest rates. Thus, compared with the Asian countries, the Latin American economies suffered far more from the interest rate shock not only because of the worse terms and conditions of their loans, but also because their economies were less 'open'.

There are two other exogenous shocks which need to be considered. First is the emergence of a large volume of capital flight in countries with relatively open financial markets. As noted in Section 3.3, capital flight was far more pronounced in Latin American countries and contributed greatly to the worsening of the debt crisis. Such capital movements were stimulated by the expectations of economic difficulties (particularly those relating to the balance of payments) created by trade or financial shocks. In other words, the financial openness of these countries, far from alleviating the problems created by external shocks, helped actually to exacerbate them and to increase the vulnerability of the economy. This issue is discussed in more detail in Section 3.6.

The second shock is what Williamson (1985) calls the 'contagion effect', whereby following the Mexican debt crisis in 1982, voluntary private capital flows to most Latin American countries were greatly reduced, if not stopped altogether. He rightly notes: 'South Korea got close to the brink in 1980 as a result of overexpansionary policies in 1979 and large external shocks; had it been in South America and therefore subject to contagion, it might well have succumbed' (ibid. 569). The important point is that because of the contagion effect, capital flows were reduced much more to the Latin American than to the Asian economies. This in turn worsened the balance of payment constraint in the Latin American countries to a greater extent and more suddenly than in the Asian economies. In that context, the effects in terms of lower economic growth and higher inflation in Latin America in the 1980s are not surprising.[12]

---

[12] For a discussion of the effects of the balance of payments constraint on all spheres, real and financial, of developing country economies, see Singh 1986b.

3.5.3 The case of Mexico

This point is best illustrated by considering the case of Mexico itself. The Mexican economy expanded rapidly during the oil boom years 1978–81. As Table 3.14 shows, the rate of growth of GDP during these four years was more than 8 per cent per annum. More detailed data indicate that even the non-oil GDP increased at the extraordinary rate of nearly 8 per cent per annum, at a time of significant deceleration in world economic growth (see Ros 1986; Barker and Brailovsky 1983; Singh 1985b). Instead of the increasing unemployment which most industrial countries experienced during this period, in Mexico half a million new jobs were being created each year on average, at a conservative estimate, and revised figures indicate that towards the end of the period nearly a million new jobs were being created annually. Similarly, investment in plant and equipment recovered strongly. From 1977 to 1980, gross fixed capital formation rose from less than 20 per cent of GDP to nearly 25 per cent.

However, as Tables 3.14 and 3.15 also suggest, the financial economy was not so robust. After a sharp fall from its 1977 level of 29 per cent to 17.5 per cent in 1978, the rate of inflation in 1980 was again 26.4 per cent and in 1981, 27.9 per cent. But the most important indicator of the deterioration of the financial economy was the continuing increase in the current account deficit, which by 1981 had reached a colossal figure of $11.7 billion, or 5.9 per cent of GDP (Table 3.15). This was despite the nearly 30-fold increase in oil revenues, which rose from $0.5 billion in 1976 to $14.4 billion in 1981. This disjuncture between the financial and the real economy was directly responsible for the economic crisis which followed in 1982.

There were three main reasons for the huge increase in the current account deficit during the years of the oil boom: (a) a massive increase in manufactured imports, which quadrupled in nominal value and tripled in terms of volume over the five years 1976 to 1981; (b) relatively poor performance of non-oil exports, in part due to the US and world recession; (c) interest payments on public debt increasing very rapidly (see Table 3.15). Of the three, (a) was an avoidable act of public policy while (b) and (c) were less so since they depended to a large extent on US and world economic activity and interest rates. The government's programme of liberalization of imports, which it vigorously pursued between 1977 and 1981, played a significant role in the surge of imports (see further Barker and Brailovsky 1983).

However, the important point is that up to 1981 Mexico had little difficulty in financing these increasingly large current deficits from foreign borrowings. Thus, from 1978 to 1981, while international bank loans to developing countries as a whole increased by 76 per cent, they rose by 146 per cent to Mexico, already a large debtor in 1978. To meet the Mexican government's

Table 3.14 Mexico: main economic indicators 1973–1985

	1973	1974	1976	1977	1978	1979	1980	1981	1982	1983	1984	1985
GDP, real growth rate, % pa	8.5	6.1	4.2	3.5	8.2	9.1	8.3	7.9	-0.5	-5.3	3.5	2.7
Inflation rate, % pa	12.1	23.9	15.7	29.0	17.5	18.1	26.4	27.9	59.0	101.9	65.5	57.7
Trade balance/GDP, %	-2.7	-4.2	-4.0	-2.5	-3.3	-4.2	-4.5	-6.0	-3.8	3.5	2.0	4.8
Current balance/GDP, %	-2.6	-4.1	-3.9	-2.4	-3.2	-4.1	-4.5	-5.9	-3.7	3.6	2.1	0.7
Total debt, US$b	9.0	11.9	20.5	31.1	35.7	42.8	57.1	77.9	85.8	93.7	97.3	97.4
of which short-term, US$b	0.0	0.0	0.0	5.5	4.9	8.0	16.2	25.0	26.1	10.1	7.4	5.4
Total debt/GDP, %	16.3	16.6	23.1	38.0	34.7	31.8	30.7	32.5	51.4	65.6	55.5	54.9
Debt service/exports, %	23.3	19.7	32.6	45.4	58.4	65.8	33.5	29.4	35.9	40.4	36.9	48.2
Terms of trade, index	99.9	107.4	110.9	101.9	104.6	114.8	147.6	158.0	154.6	107.5	103.3	...
Export volume, index	101.8	75.0	78.6	91.1	128.6	151.8	178.6	219.6	241.1	260.7	...	...
Exports/GDP, %	8.3	8.4	7.7	9.5	10.4	11.2	12.6	12.0	15.7	19.1	17.1	16.8
Imports/GDP, %	9.5	10.5	9.3	9.4	11.0	12.4	13.8	14.0	11.8	8.9	9.2	16.7

Source: Original data from the World Bank Data Bank; IMF 1987; *World Debt Tables 1986–7.*

Table 3.15 Mexico: current 1976–1981 (US$ billion)

	1976	1977	1978	1979	1980	1981
Balance of payments current account	−3.069	−1.623	−2.693	−4.856	−6.761	−11.7
Balance of goods and non-factor services	−1.190	0.360	−0.310	−1.542	−1.808	−4.1
Balance of factor payments	−1.879	−1.983	−2.383	−3.314	−4.953	−7.6
Memorandum						
Interest on external/public debt	1.266	1.542	2.023	2.888	3.958	5.5
Oil exports	0.543	1.029	1.799	3.861	10.305	14.4
Merchandise imports	5.427	5.150	7.376	11.380	17.174	23.1
% change in unit value in dollars of manufactured imports	7.4	8.0	10.5	12.7	15.2	17.0
% change in unit value in dollars of oil exports (dollars)	8.4	6.7	0.5	47.2	55.2	8.2

Sources: Sistema de Cuentas Nacionales de Mexico, SPP, *Informe Annual de Banco de Mexico*, various years.

increased demand for foreign loans to finance the current account deficit, the international banks accelerated their lending to Mexico in 1981, albeit with an increasing shortening of the term structure of the new loans (Ros 1986). In that year, the capital account of the balance of payments indicates that Mexico's net public short term liabilities rose by $12.7 billion (compared with $6 billion in 1980 and $1.7 billion in 1979). However in the crisis year of 1982 these capital flows were abruptly halted, and the capital account shows that Mexico's net public external short term liabilities actually decreased by $614 million.

Barker and Brailovksy (1983) rightly observe in this context:

Although the conditions for a balance of payments crisis were present, the extent to which it actually took place in 1982 was certainly out of proportion with the underlying disequilibria. These were hugely amplified by capital movements that, under the system of free exchange convertibility then prevailing, could not be brought under control, even when domestic interest rates were risen dramatically. The situation was made untenable when the international banking system imposed a freeze on borrowings by Mexico. In fact, this means that Mexico was forced to reduce in absolute terms the debt outstanding during the second half of 1982, a quite unprecedented action by international standards. This action, moreover, served no good purpose: it hindered the Mexican economy to an unnecessary extent and it endangered the international financial system. Were it not for these aggravating circumstances, the 1982 crisis could have had much less damaging effects on the Mexican economy, an economy that despite policy mistakes, ended this period (1976–82) with a strengthened productive potential after having created sizeable new resources and employed a growing proportion of its working population.

Following the Mexican crisis, serious 'contagious' interruptions in normal capital flows occurred in a number of other Latin American countries. As Fishlow's paper in this volume suggests, such capital supply shocks were much more significant for the Latin American than for the Asian economies and had a far greater impact on the former.

To summarize this discussion: while it is technically correct to say that external shocks had a greater impact on the 'open' East Asian economies than on the closed Latin American ones, a more careful examination of the evidence reveals this assertion to be meaningless in any sense which is relevant for the analysis of recent conditions. First, the 'positive' shocks to Asian economies are generally ignored in the literature. Second, the financially 'open' Latin American countries were hit much harder by shocks originating in financial markets; and the adjustment to *these* shocks were rendered much more difficult by the inward-oriented nature of their trade regimes. But here it seems more correct to say that the problem was the open nature of the financial regime rather than the closed nature of the trade regime.

3.6 EXPORTS, CAPITAL FLIGHT, AND THE EXCHANGE RATE

We now turn to the second part of the assertion by mainstream theorists, namely, that adjustment to export competitiveness and trade openness, which supposedly contributed to the success of East Asian countries in accommodating external shocks, derive directly from exchange rate and commercial policies. The argument is that the crisis in Latin American countries resulted from their inappropriate exchange rate policies, which affected both current and capital account transactions, and made adjustment more problematic. This argument has been made most forcefully by Jeffrey Sachs (1985), who singles out exchange rate changes as one of the most important determinants of the differential economic performance of the

Table 3.16 Volume of merchandise exports in Asia and Latin America, 1973–1979, 1979–1983 (*average annual rates of growth*, %)

	1973–9	1979–83
Asia		
China	. . .	. . .
India	7.4	1.6
Indonesia	2.1	–2.2
Korea	15.2	13.7
Malaysia	1.7	5.0
Pakistan	2.3	12.3
Philippines	7.4	–5.2
Sri Lanka	0.0	5.9
Taiwan	. . .	. . .
Thailand	8.6	6.4
Median	4.9	5.4
Latin America		
Argentina	10.9	0.0
Bolivia	–3.7	–3.0
Brazil	5.1	7.7
Chile	16.0	0.9
Colombia	3.2	–2.0
Ecuador	–3.8	–10.5
Mexico	6.9	14.5
Peru	15.7	–9.5
Venezuela	–6.3	–9.6
Median	3.2	0.0

Source: World Bank Data Bank.

Table 3.17 Exports of manufactures (SITC 5–8 less 68) by selected developing countries or territories, 1970–1980

Country or territory[a]	Annual growth rate[b]		Share in total (%)		
	1970–3	1973–80	1970	1973	1980
Korea	43.1	18.3	6.0	16.1	14.2
Hong Kong	19.9	25.2	18.5	12.0	11.9
Singapore	34.3	41.3	4.0	6.5	8.2
Brazil	35.9	33.4	3.4	6.1	6.8
India	17.2	10.0[c]	9.8	5.4	...
Mexico	20.2	...	3.7	2.5	...
Argentina	27.1	5.4	2.3	2.4	1.7
Malaysia	37.1	32.8	1.0	2.0	2.2
Kuwait	36.9	38.4	0.9	1.6	1.9
Thailand	50.7	36.8	0.3	1.2	1.5
Pakistan	9.6	22.7	3.8	1.2	1.1
Philippines	31.4	31.3	0.7	1.0	1.1
Other countries	25.2	...	45.6	42.0	...
All developing countries[d]	26.5	26.0	100.0	100.0	100.0

[a] Ranked by value of their exports of manufactures (SITC 5–8 less 68) in 1978.
[b] Compound growth rate.
[c] Annual growth rate in 1979 over 1978.
[d] Seventy countries.
Source: UNIDO (1984).

Asian and Latin American countries. The overvalued exchange rates of the Latin American economies, it is asserted, not only hampered their exports but were also responsible for the massive capital flights they suffered. Some evidence bearing on this issue will be briefly reviewed in this section.

The strong export performance of East Asian countries, as revealed in Tables 3.16 and 3.17, is quite well known. Table 3.16 provides information on the growth in the volume of merchandise exports of the Latin American and Asian countries during 1973–9 and 1979–83. In the first period, the Asian group increased its exports slightly faster on average than the Latin American countries; in the latter period, the Asian performance has been considerably better. Table 3.17, which gives UNIDO data on *manufactured* exports alone for selected developing countries over the period 1970–80, shows the strong performance of South Korea, Malaysia, the Philippines, and Thailand. However, there are some surprises. Over the decade as a whole, Brazilian manufactured exports expanded at much the same rate as the South Korean exports. Thus despite the lack of 'openness' of the Brazilian economy relative to South Korea's, Brazil's exporters did extremely well in the foreign markets. Similarly, during 1970–8, Mexico and Argentina's manufacturing exports grew faster than India's.

3.6.1 Exports and exchange rates

The essential question is to what extent, if any, the differential exporting records of the various countries can be explained in terms of their exchange rate policies. Is export success simply a function of the exchange rate, as is often implied in the orthodox literature, or does it depend on other factors too, which may be more important? The mainstream argument is not based on empirical evidence. There are few empirical studies of developing countries which compare the differential impact of exchange rate behaviour and other relevant factors (e.g. the growth of world demand on export performance). Moreover there is contrary evidence, particularly striking for the advanced countries, which is simply overlooked. It will be useful to examine this evidence.

Table 3.18 provides data on exchange rates, relative costs (as measured by labour costs per unit of output, converted to a common currency), and export performance (indicated by the share of manufactures in industrial country exports) for the leading advanced economies over the period 1956–76. The table shows perverse results as far as the relationship between these factors is concerned. Over the period 1956–76, the United Kingdom's exchange rate depreciated by nearly 50 per cent and its share of industrial country exports was halved. The currencies of West Germany and Japan appreciated significantly over this period and yet these countries greatly increased their export share. The relationship between relative costs and export share is also perverse for these countries, as well as for the United States and Italy. Such perverse results hold not only over the long period 1956–76, but also over a shorter period such as 1970–6.

There is a large literature which attempts to explain these observations in terms of the importance of investment and a host of non-price factors which influence a country's exporting performance (see e.g. Kaldor 1978; Stout 1979). It may perhaps be argued that such considerations do not apply to developing country manufacturing exports.[13] However, Brailovsky (1981a) carried out a similar exercise for a sample of both developing and developed countries and arrived at much the same results (see also Chapter 5). The developing countries included in his sample were Argentina, Brazil, Hong Kong, South Korea, Mexico, and Singapore. He found on the whole no relationship between real exchange rate changes and foreign market penetration for either the developed or the developing countries over the entire period 1960–77 or over four sub-periods.

[13] In view of the low price elasticity of primary commodities, there are good grounds for not expecting a significant positive relationship between currency depreciation and exports of these commodities; see Branson 1983.

Table 3.18 Index numbers of trade-weighted exchange rates and of unit labour costs in dollar terms and percentage export shares of manufactures (selected years 1956–1976)

	1956	1960	1965	1970	1975	1976
United Kingdom						
Exchange rate	100	106	105	89	68	59
Relative costs	100	110	109	101	101	94
Export share of manufactured goods	18.7	15.9	13.5	10.8	9.3	8.7
United States						
Exchange rate	100	106	105	108	87	94
Relative costs	100	104	85	80	51	55
Export share	25.5	21.7	20.5	18.5	17.7	17.3
West Germany						
Exchange rate	100	106	113	126	178	185
Relative costs	100	116	135	146	165	163
Export share	16.5	19.7	19.2	19.8	20.3	20.6
Japan						
Exchange rate	100	105	104	106	111	119
Relative costs	100	87	87	105	132	136
Export share	5.7	6.9	9.4	11.7	13.6	14.6
France						
Exchange rate	100	71	70	62	69	66
Relative costs	100	79	75	67	80	79
Export share	7.9	9.7	8.8	8.7	10.2	9.8
Italy						
Exchange rate	100	105	104	106	85	69
Relative costs	100	94	107	104	119	108
Export share	3.6	5.2	6.8	7.2	7.5	7.1

Note: Trade weighted exchange rates: For each country an index of average exchange rates was divided by a trade-weighted index of the average annual exchange rates of the other five countries, weighted by 1970 export.

Unit Labour costs: For each country, unit labour costs in dollars (manufacturing earnings divided by indices of trends in productivity) were divided by the weighted average of the unit labour costs of the other five countries, the weights in each case being determined by the export shares of each country in 1970.

Export shares of manufactures: Each country's share of the value of manufactured exports of major developed market economies, in US dollars. 'Special category' exports are excluded in the case of the US.

Source: Kaldor (1984).

Brailovsky notes that Singapore's real exchange rate appreciated over two periods; in one it gained and in the other it lost its share of world markets. It depreciated over the two remaining periods, but in one of these it had negative penetration. South Korea and Hong Kong had persistent large gains in their market shares, although in two out of four periods their real exchange rate appreciated. Similarly, Mexico's share in the world market decreased during 1964–8 although it maintained an almost constant exchange rate. In the next period, there was a small real appreciation of the peso yet substantial market penetration was achieved.

Let us consider the South Korean example further. Between 1974 and 1978, the volume of South Korean exports more than doubled. This was one of the most important factors in ensuring that South Korea's trade deficit, which had risen to 11.9 per cent of GDP in 1974 following the first oil shock, had practically vanished by 1977–8. However, this enormous increase in South Korean exports during this period could not simply be ascribed to 'getting the prices right'. On the contrary, over these years, South Korea's real exchange rate, corrected for inflation, had appreciated by nearly 20 per cent. Much more important to the country's export drive were two institutional mechanisms which had been established: the system of setting export targets and the practice of holding national trade-promoting meetings. As the World Bank noted, 'these two mechanisms helped translate political resolve into bureaucratic and corporative resolve. They also provided up-to-date information on export performance by firm, product and market and enabled the government to analyze the reasons for any discrepancies between targets and performance. The government then adjusted its export incentives and targets accordingly' (World Bank 1983: 68).

3.6.2 Exchange rates and capital flight

The alleged positive relationship between capital flight and currency overvaluation is also a more complex phenomenon. It is true that countries like Mexico, Venezuela, and Argentina suffered massive capital flights in the early 1980s. In economies where there are few exchange controls, currency depreciation—to the extent that it leads to wage–price increases and consequent financial instability—may encourage rather than discourage capital flight. This is what happened in Mexico when, in February 1982, because of the shortage of reserves, the government floated the currency instead of imposing exchange controls. At the time the peso/US dollar nominal exchange rate was 26 and the Mexican rate of inflation was about 28 per cent. It was argued at the time that because Mexico's inflation rate was higher than that of its trading partners (chiefly, the United States), the equilibrium exchange rate for the peso was 35. However, the currency soon overshot, to 50 pesos per dollar. This in turn led to wage–price increases, financial instability, capital flight, and further devaluation. By August 1982, the peso/dollar exchange rate had depreciated to 120, the rate of inflation had increased to nearly 100 per cent, and the differential between the Mexican and its trading partners' rate of inflation had widened further. It was at this point that the government decided to impose exchange controls; they did not totally stop the capital flight, but they greatly reduced it.

Under the new administration of President De La Madrid, who came into office at the end of 1982, the government accepted an IMF programme and embarked on orthodox economic and financial policies. These policies were showing clear evidence of failure even before the earthquake and fall in oil price. By 1985 the peso/dollar exchange rate had depreciated to 500, the rate of inflation at over 60 per cent was still much greater than the world rate of inflation, and the capital flight continued. Ros (1986) estimates that as a proportion of the net real private financial savings, the capital flight in 1983 and 1984 was greater than in 1981 and 1982.[14]

The important question is why the Mexican government did not impose exchange controls in 1980 or 1981 to forestall the financial crisis and capital flight.[15] The answer lies in the nature of the class bargain which had long prevailed in the Mexican polity. Just as the working class were able to recoup price rises with wage increases, albeit with a lag, it was the privilege of the bourgeoisie to have more or less free convertibility of currency. Whereas Mexico's upper classes had always accepted import controls, it required a major financial and political crisis for exchange controls to be introduced. However, in other developing countries (e.g. South Korea, India, and Brazil) exchange controls have long been accepted, and these countries had relatively little capital flights.

3.7 NOTES ON LARGE SEMI-INDUSTRIAL ECONOMIES IN ASIA AND LATIN AMERICA

The last two sections have criticized the mainstream argument that the degree of openness of an economy contributes to its welfare, and that such openness is determined mainly by exchange rate policies. In this section, we go on to argue that relative success in macroeconomic performance is ensured by a cautious attitude towards foreign borrowing, and reducing the country's exposure to world financial markets; in addition to effective action in pushing resources into technology-intensive or export sectors. A corollary is that

---

[14] Ros 1986 notes: 'since, from 1983 onwards, the change in the real value of the private sector holding of Mexican public debt has actually been negative and thus the whole of its *net* real savings has been invested abroad. At present, the latter are financing the current account deficit of the rest of the world (with respect to Mexico) as well as through the inter-mediation of foreign banks, the [nominal] borrowing from abroad by the Mexican public sector. This borrowing is, thus, a consequence of the need to balance the external accounts in the face of a major alteration in the asset composition of the private sector's net financial savings.'

[15] Exchange controls had been proposed throughout 1981 by economists at the Ministry of Oil and Industry to forestall an impending balance of payments crisis. At the time, these proposals were totally unacceptable.

liberalization policies of the type recommended by mainstream theorists have, more often than not, hurt economic prospects. This argument is developed through a somewhat more detailed examination of the experience of the largest Asian and Latin American economies: India, China, Brazil, and Mexico. These four countries account for the bulk of the Third World's industrial production. More significantly, they have for long followed rather different development strategies and economic policies.

In terms of absolute size, Brazil's manufacturing sector in 1980 was about twice as large as that of Mexico's or India's. UNIDO 1984 estimates that in absolute terms, China's manufacturing economy in 1980 was twice as large as that of Brazil's. Other relevant indicators, such as technology exports and the sophistication of the machine tools and capital goods industries, suggest that these countries were also among the most advanced in the Third World in terms of the quality of their industrial development (Singh 1984).

With respect to economic policy for the last four decades, India and China have long followed inward-oriented import substitution industrialization strategies; direct foreign investment has played a very small role in the Indian economy and hardly any in China. In contrast, foreign multinationals play a major role in the industrial economies of both the large Latin American countries (ibid.). Brazil had an inward-looking trade regime until the early 1960s, but then in 1964, following the military coup, it started a fundamental switch towards 'outward orientation' by encouraging exports and foreign investment (by instituting important changes in tariff structure, exchange rate, and export promotion policies).[16] The Mexican case is more mixed. Strong import substitution policies were implemented in the 1950s and 1960s, but in the late 1960s, it too initiated steps to give its trade regime an outward orientation. Imports began to be liberalized and various export promotion measures were instituted (Balassa 1981). The balance of payments crisis of 1974 led to a reversal of import liberalization measures, but with the coming of oil and the improvement of the balance of payments situation between 1977 and 1981 the government again embarked on strong import liberalization policies (Brailovsky 1981*b*).

It was noted in Section 3.3 that during the world economic slowdown of the 1980s, India and China have performed considerably better than Brazil or Mexico. As Table 3.2 showed, between 1980 and 1985 the two Asian countries have been able actually to improve on their long-term trend rates of growth, while the two large Latin American economies suffered a sharp break in their development momentum. How can the differences in the economic experience of these countries be explained?

[16] Krueger 1977, which is based on a study of trade regimes in a group of developing countries until 1973, regarded Brazil (along with South Korea) as an exemplary case of a switch towards outward orientation. Balassa 1981 also notes that in the mid-1960s, Brazil changed its policies towards outward orientation.

3.7.1 India

Consider first the case of India. In the wake of deceleration in world economic growth in the 1970s and 1980s, the Indian economy was subject to all the shocks which emanate from such world economic crisis. There was a sharp adverse movement in its terms of trade, the growth of export markets slowed down, it was exposed to higher real interest rates, and there was also (relative to the GDP) a reduction in capital inflows.[17] Table 3.19, which gives summary data on the Indian economy for the period 1972 to 1984, shows that India's terms of trade declined by 40 per cent between 1972 and 1976 and by 33 per cent between 1977 and 1979. This adverse movement in the 1970s was greater than that recorded for South Korea. Nevertheless, during 1977 to 1979 the country moved into a significant current account surplus: the debt service/export ratio in the 1980s, at a little over 9 per cent, was less than half that recorded in the early 1970s.

How did this successful economic adjustment come about? Singh 1985b refers to three medium-term factors. One, a decline in food imports made a substantial contribution to the balance of payments compared with the situation in the late 1960s and early 1970s. Two, there was an enormous increase in migrants' remittances as a consequence of the economic boom in the Middle East (see Table 3.19). Three, there was a rapid expansion of India's own oil production and impressive progress in oil-conservation measures. Between fiscal years 1980/1 and 1982/3 the volume of oil imports declined by 30 per cent as a result of increasing domestic production and conservation.

India's oil production programme and associated programmes of conservation and development of alternative energy sources required a major investment effort. This was financed by increasing domestic savings rather than by foreign borrowing. The domestic saving rate increased from 14 per cent of GDP over 1965–72 to 19 per cent over 1973–8 and nearly 25 per cent in 1984.

One of the most important reasons why India has been able to weather the world economic storms so well lies precisely in this factor: that the country did not borrow in the world capital markets in the 1970s. India had a very high credit standing and could easily have borrowed extensively from the international banks in the mid-1970s, but it was deliberate policy on the part of India's economic managers not to do so. India did obtain a structural loan from the IMF in 1981—a three-year extended arrangement. However, this was for the relatively small sum of $5 billion, not all of which was drawn; as a part of the arrangement with the IMF, there was also a relatively small

---

[17] The following discussions summarize the information contained in Singh 1985b, to which the reader is referred for a fuller analysis.

Table 3.19 India: main economic indicators 1973–1985

	1973	1974	1976	1977	1978	1979	1980	1981	1982	1983	1984	1985
GDP, real growth rate, % pa	3.6	0.2	1.2	8.3	6.6	-5.1	6.7	5.8	2.9	7.6	4.5	6.3
Inflation rate, % pa	20.8	26.8	-3.8	7.6	2.2	8.9	11.4	12.5	7.8	12.6	6.2	5.5
Trade balance/GDP, %	-1.1	-1.3	0.6	0.5	-0.8	-1.5	-3.2	-3.4	-3.2	-2.4	-2.5	-3.2
Current balance/GDP, %	-0.9	-1.0	1.3	1.7	0.2	-0.4	-1.5	-2.1	-1.7	-1.1	-1.4	-2.3
Total debt, US$billion	10.5	12.3	14.1	15.5	16.4	16.8	19.2	20.7	24.9	28.3	30.7	35.4
of which short-term,	0.0	0.0	0.0	0.4	0.7	0.7	0.9	1.2	1.8	1.6	1.7	1.5
Total debt/GDP, %	13.9	14.2	15.7	14.8	13.8	12.7	11.9	12.5	14.6	14.9	16.7	20.2
Debt service/exports, %	19.9	17.7	11.7	10.8	11.7	10.7	9.4	9.1	9.5	12.9	14.6	19.8
Terms of trade, index	85.1	61.4	60.7	76.2	72.2	52.7	60.1	58.0	58.0	58.6	56.0	...
Export volume, index	106.0	109.0	156.7	150.7	156.7	162.7	149.3	156.7	173.1	173.1	...	...
Exports/GDP, %	4.3	4.8	7.2	7.2	6.8	7.3	7.0	6.8	7.2	8.0	8.4	8.1
Imports/GDP, %	4.9	5.8	6.4	6.3	7.5	9.0	10.5	10.5	10.3	11.0	10.6	10.7
Workers remit/exports, %	5.4	5.6	9.9	12.3	14.4	14.8	24.5	20.4	21.5	19.6	16.7	17.3

Source: Original data from the World Bank Data Bank; IMF 1987; *World Debt Tables, 1986–7.*

amount of borrowing from the private capital market to cover specific investment projects. The total amount of such borrowing, multilateral as well as from private sources, has been minuscule compared with the large-scale foreign indebtedness of Mexico, Brazil, and South Korea.

The other main reason for India's successful economic record in the midst of the world economic crisis lies in the country's long-term economic and industrial strategy. This strategy, which India has followed more or less consistently over the last three decades, has led to an impressive build-up of the country's scientific and technical infrastructure, the training of high-level technical cadres, and a diversified capital goods industry.[18] It has brought about not only a deep development of the country's technical know-how, but also of 'know-why', to use the expressive phrase coined by Lall (1984). An important consequence of the development of these supply-side capabilities is that India did not need to borrow as much abroad to finance large investment projects as was the case with the other countries.[19]

3.7.2 China

China has a rather different relationship with the world economy from that of most other developing countries, including large economies like India. The main difference is that China has normally maintained a trade and current account surplus. Table 3.20 provides data on aggregate trade balances and the growth of Chinese exports and imports since 1970. The second row of the table also shows China's cumulative visible trade balance since 1950; in 1983, this stood at nearly $21 billion. As a consequence, in 1983 China had the seventh largest gold and foreign exchange reserves in the world. Its external debt is miniscule. In 1984, it stood at $6 billion, compared with foreign assets in that year of $26.9 billion and foreign exchange reserves of $22.1 billion.

Thus, the disruptions of the world economy during the last decade have had relatively little impact on the pace of Chinese economic expansion. Essentially, the Chinese economy has not been constrained by its balance of payments during this period. The central long-term factor responsible for this happy situation is that the Chinese over the last thirty years have built up their own industrial capacities and capabilities, which enable them to have sustained high rates of economic growth without being affected by the state of the world economy.

There are, however, two points about China's recent international economic relationships which deserve attention. First, Table 3.20 shows that in 1978, 1979, and 1980, China sustained deficits in her visible trade,

---

[18] There is a very large literature on these subjects; for a recent review and discussion of the main issues, see Lall 1982 and 1984.

[19] The argument here is in terms of supply-side capabilities. Had such capabilities not been available, the foreign exchange requirements of the investment programme would have been much greater.

Table 3.20 China: aggregate trade balances and growth of exports and imports, 1970–83 (US$ million)

	1970	1975	1976	1977	1978	1979	1980	1981	1982	1983
Visible trade balance										
Yearly balance, FOB	112	303	1,697	1,564	−161	−906	−305	3,547	6,868	5,584
Cumulative total since 1950[a]	1,260	2,985	4,682	6,264	6,103	5,197	4,892	8,439	15,307	20,891
Exports:										
Total, FOB	2,163	7,121	7,269	8,178	10,170	13,458	18,875	21,496	23,501	23,983
Real growth, % p.a.[b]		10.1	12.7	−1.9	23.9	17.6	21.4	...	...	xxx
Imports:										
Total, FOB	2,051	6,818	5,572	6,614	10,331	14,364	19,180	17,949	16,633	18,399
Real growth, % p.a.[b]		11.6	−4.4	32.3	51.0	21.0	14.2	...	...	...
Capital goods imports[c]										
Total	411	1,996	1,671	1,165	1,994	3,705	5,131	4,343	3,068	xxx
Real growth, % p.a.[b]		19.2	−11.1	−33.0	58.1	76.3	...	...	...	xxx

[a] Figures for 1970 and 1975 are calculated from data given in John L. Davie and Dean W. Carver, 'China's international trade and finance'. Joint Economic Committee, US Congress. *China Under the Four Modernizations*. Pt. 2 (Washington, DC: US Government Printing Office, 1982), p. 40.
[b] The price deflators are from *ibid.* 44.
[c] These cover machinery (SITC 71, 722–24), transport equipment (SITC 73), and precision instruments (SITC 861).

Sources: CIA, *China: International Trade Annual Statistical Supplement*, March 1984; and *Fourth Quarter, 1983*, March 1984, for 1970, 1975, and 1978–83; other earlier issues for 1976–7.

particularly in 1979 when the deficit was nearly $1 billion. There has been a remarkable turnaround since then, and in the 1980s the Chinese have achieved impressive surpluses on visible trade. As China also usually has a surplus on invisibles, in 1983 the current account surplus was of the order of $14 billion.

The main reason for the deficits in the late 1970s was the large rise in imports: as Table 3.20 indicates, imports increased in real terms by 32 per cent, 51 per cent, and 21 per cent in 1977, 1978 and 1979, respectively. Plant and technology imports for fertilizer, steel, and other industries played a major role in the rise of imports. Subsequently such imports were sharply curtailed, basically for reasons of domestic absorptive capacity. In addition to the reduction in the rate of growth of imports, the other main factors responsible for the large turnaround in trade balance since 1979 have been the rapid growth of manufactured exports and the oil exports.

The second point to note is that particularly since Chairman Mao's death, the Chinese have been making vigorous efforts to increase China's economic relations with the world in order to modernize various sectors of the Chinese economy. For this purpose, since the mid-1970s they have rapidly expanded their exports, and also their imports—especially of technology; they have also encouraged direct foreign investment in various forms, notably in oil exploration. Further, the Bank of China has been borrowing abroad in order to finance imports of plant and technology. However, unlike the East Europeans, who borrowed heavily for similar reasons in the late 1960s and in the 1970s and subsequently found themselves in serious difficulties when the world economic situation changed, the Chinese normally take a conservative and rather cautious approach to these foreign economic entanglements. The pace and degree of integration of China with the world economy seems to be firmly dictated by domestic industry's absorptive capacity.[20]

3.7.3 Brazil and Mexico

We shall now briefly examine the cases of Brazil and Mexico. As seen in Table 3.2 both countries were high-growth economies during the 1960s and 1970s and were able to maintain fast growth to 1980. However, in the 1980s both countries have been in serious economic crisis. The following points may be made to summarize the experience of Brazil and Mexico in the context of the crisis of the international economy during the 1970s and 1980s.[21]

First, both countries borrowed heavily on the international market to adjust their economies in the wake of the 1973 oil shock. It will be appreciated that the market signals were particularly favourable for such

[20] In 1985 there has been a large increase in imports reminiscent of the late 1970s. This is likely to lead before long to a corrective similar to that which occurred in the early 1980s.

[21] For a fuller discussion, see Singh 1985b and the reference contained therein.

borrowing: not only were private banks ready and able to lend, but real rates of interest during the period 1974–9 were negative.[22]

Secondly, it is important to emphasize that, contrary to what is often alleged, the foreign borrowings were used not for increasing consumption but for investment and structural change in the economy. In Brazil, gross domestic investment as a proportion of GDP increased from 25.8 per cent during the period 1965–72 to 28.1 per cent in 1973–9. In Mexico, the corresponding increase was from 21.3 per cent to 23.4 per cent (see Table 3.6). However, the latter figure understates the increase in the Mexican rate of investment since it includes the years 1975–7 when the economy was experiencing a recession. Gross fixed capital formation as a proportion of GDP rose in Mexico from 19.6 per cent in 1977 to 21.2 per cent in 1978, to 23.2 per cent in 1979 and 24.7 per cent in 1980. Similarly, gross national savings as a proportion of GDP increased from 16.03 per cent over 1960–70 to 16.8 per cent over 1970–6 and to 19.9 per cent in the period 1976–82 (see Singh 1985b).

Third, in addition to foreign borrowing, both countries sought greater integration with the world economy to cope with post-1973 world economic conditions. As shown by Table 3.16, Brazilian manufactured exports grew at a phenomenal rate of nearly 35 per cent per annum in the decade 1970–80, a rate almost equivalent to that of South Korea's. Mexico's total exports rose more than three-fold between 1976 and 1981 (because of the huge expansion of oil exports), and, as noted earlier, there was a determined effort to liberalize imports after 1977.

Fourthly, the main consequence of the very large foreign borrowing and the greater degrees of integration with the world economy was that when the world market conditions abruptly changed after 1980, both Mexico and Brazil were thrown into a deep and prolonged economic and social crisis. Under the present institutional parameters of the Mexican and Brazilian economies, the resolution of their crisis—in the sense of resumption of their normal trend rates of economic growth—depends crucially on international factors: the rate of growth of the world economy and world trade, world interest rates, the exchange rate for the US dollar, and the terms of trade for their primary commodities. All of these factors clearly lie outside their control as they are essentially determined by economic interactions among the United States and other OECD countries (see Singh 1984; Taylor 1982).

With respect to India and China, in contrast, it can be reasonably asserted that their rate of economic growth is essentially independent of the world rate of economic growth and depends instead on the internal dynamism and domestic factors in these economies.

---

[22] See IMF 1984; chart iv. 5, p. 67. The real interest rate is defined as LIBOR less rate of change of non-oil developing countries export unit values. The discussion in Section 3.4 is also relevant here.

3.8 CONCLUSION

The main conclusion of this chapter is that theories which attempt to explain the differential economic performance of the Asian and Latin American countries during the 1980s in terms of the greater openness of the Asian economies or their superior exchange rate policies do not fit the evidence. The far from open Asian countries like China and India were able to cope at least as effectively with the world economic recession as the more open East Asian economies. These theories also do not give adequate attention to the greater impact of the interest rate shock on the balance of payments position of the Latin American countries. Nor do they consider the full implications of the 'contagion effect', whereby normal capital flows to all Latin American countries were sharply curtailed as a consequence of Mexico's debt crisis in August 1982. We have argued here that the contraction of world economic activity is likely to have had a different impact on the markets of the two groups of countries including the market for migrant labour. We have also suggested that the relationship between the exchange rate, export performance, and capital flight is much more complex than the mainstream analyses of these issues envisage.

With respect to the question of economic vulnerability, we have argued that compared with India and China, the poor economic performance of Mexico and Brazil during the 1980s may be ascribed to their large foreign borrowings and their greater integration with the world economy, particularly with the international financial markets. However, it may be objected that despite similarly large borrowings relative to GDP and even greater integration with the world economy, the South Korean economy has continued to perform well in the 1980s. A main reason for this, we suggest, lies in an important structural difference: Brazil and Mexico had relatively much smaller exports/GDP ratios at the onset of the debt crisis than South Korea did. This made them much more vulnerable to interest rate and capital supply shocks and to financial disruption. In order to reduce their vulnerability to international economic fluctuations, countries with relatively low exports/GDP ratios, other things being equal, should also have correspondingly low debt/GDP ratios. This would help towards insulating them not only from financial market disruptions but also from trade fluctuations.

4

Economic Openness: Problems to the Century's End

Lance Taylor

How open a national economy should be to foreign goods and financial flows is an antique question—to a large extent the conflicting answers of mercantilists and anti-mercantilists are still with us after 300 years. For developing countries, controversy about openness to goods has always been present, but sharpened in the 1970s as eminent trade theorists turned to policy advice. Starting with the publication of a book called *Industry and Trade in Some Developing Countries*, by Little, Scitovsky, and Scott (1970), the notion that trade liberalization is an optimal development strategy has come to dominate the mainstream. Openness to international capital also has its defenders—most notably Cline (1984), who acknowledges the 1982 debt crisis but puts the best face possible upon it. Finally, the role that the developing world plays in the international system has gathered both attackers and admirers (or at least advocates of the potential advantages inherent in the poor countries' position). Consistent with the conservatism of the times, the latter group is more numerous now than it was some years ago.

One more essay on these topics is not going to end the debate. None the less, in wake of the debt crisis and the apparent failures of many liberalization attempts, it is appropriate to rethink the issues. The last reconaissance was by the late Carlos Diaz-Alejandro (1978), and amply reflected his scholarly breadth. He concluded that a case can be made for partly severing an economy's international links, with those to be subjected to the knife selected as much for political as economic reasons. On more narrowly technical grounds, partial delinking is also the recommendation here; criteria are suggested to single out connections bringing the least benefits or exacting the greatest costs.

Thinking about openness involves several levels of abstraction: empirical; theoretical in the sense of bourgeois economics; political; and ideological. Diaz-Alejandro walked tightropes across them all. The present review is less audacious, concentrating on empirical and theoretical economics *per se*. The central theme is that arguments for and against openness are meaningless outside a country's (and the world's) historical and institutional context, especially its dynamics of growth and change. However, at the present time, for many developing countries the arguments that follow seem decisive.

First, structuralist models of both commodity and capital flows suggest that openness or a hands-off policy in either market will not necessarily lead to faster growth or less costly adjustment to external shocks. These conclusions are at variance with much theoretical work in international economics, and are spelled out at length.

Second, empirical evidence implies that neither observed greater openness to trade nor absence of trade distortions is linked with higher growth or reduced external vulnerability.

Third, open capital markets have led in important recent cases to financial crises requiring painful macroeconomic adjustment and large burdens of foreign debt.

Fourth, these observations point to the advisability of selective international delinking: industrial and trade policies directed to growth in selected sectors, exchange controls, and veiled non-repayment of interest, and amortization on debt. On practical grounds, such steps are far easier for large economies than for smaller, more open ones, pointing to potential gains for international co-operation among countries of the South.

The reasoning behind these conclusions is set out mostly at the national level, with excursions into the global macroeconomics of South–North trade and debt relationships where they are required to set the stage. In what follows, sections deal with different components of the balance of payments as an organizational device. Section 4.1 takes up commodity and service trade, asking whether openness in the form of high proportions of trade (especially exports) in GDP or liberal policy accelerates growth. Data are presented which suggest that neither proportions nor policy strongly affects growth performance. Orthodox arguments to the contrary are then reviewed critically, and a structuralist model which sets out mechanisms through which commercial policy affects steady state growth is described. The model shows that 'liberal' policy, in the sense of equal incentives to all economic activities, is not optimal. The section closes with a related model which illustrates the difficulties of moving towards liberal trade policy in the short run.

The analysis is further developed with regard to short-term effects of external shocks in Section 4.2. It begins with a review of the global economic forces acting upon poor countries in the last two decades and draws upon a theoretical framework developed further in Section 4.3. How individual countries respond to shocks is illustrated with simple models—the problems arise from foreign exchange dearths and gluts, and risks inherent in unduly open capital markets. An empirical overview of developing country adjustment experience concludes the section, in an attempt to quantify the effects of external shocks on more or less open economic systems. Openness is shown to provide no very resilient cushion.

Although the main focus of the paper is on country-level experience, the first part of Section 4.3 provides necessary global background on the foreign debt position. Slow world-wide growth and secular 'revulsion' of the industrialized countries from lending to the Third World are argued to be likely prospects, making inward orientation of policy and non-repayment of debt increasingly attractive options. The section closes with an overview of how poor countries may choose to regulate their current and capital accounts in a non-bountiful medium run.

Morals from all these stories are drawn in Section 4.4, and the algebra of the planning model used in Section 4.1 appears in an appendix.

4.1 PERSPECTIVES ON TRADE FROM AN LDC

Evidence rarely carries the day in economics, since it is so easy to invent a theoretical twist to rationalize any inconvenient fact. None the less, knowledge of the quantitative aspects of international linkages is a prerequisite for sensible discussion. I begin with an empirical enquiry into how trade and trade policy affect growth at the country level. I then turn to the theorists' rather abstract arguments for openness in the long run, beginning with the views of those who are now middle-aged and passing on to those of somewhat more flexible younger colleagues. A more pragmatic model is proposed, which simply asks under what conditions the steady-state growth rate is likely to go up in response to commercial policy interventions. Short-term difficulties in rigging policy are discussed, using an import quota as an example, and the section closes with initial conclusions about trade.

4.1.1 The role of trade

Table 4.1, drawn from McCarthy, Taylor, and Talati (1987), shows average trade proportions of GDP for a sample of fifty developing countries in the period 1980–2 (with growth rates over the period 1964–82). The countries are classified into four groups by per capita GNP (below and above $1,000) and 'performance'. The latter is measured by whether a country lies above or below a regression line of growth rate on per capita GNP over 1964–82 (shown in Fig. 4.1), to take into account the fact that middle-income countries on the whole grew more rapidly than poorer ones during the 1960s and 1970s. The table combines data for trade in both merchandise and services; the primary source for the former is the United Nations; for the latter, the International Monetary Fund.

Several points relevant to the prospects of developing countries are apparent (and can be backed up by fuller econometric analysis):

1. *Trade proportions vary widely*. As is well known, countries with smaller populations typically have higher trade shares. Asian countries have larger shares of industrial exports, while African economies are specialized in

Table 4.1 Current account components as a percentage of GDP, 1980–1982

	Population (millions)	GDP growth rate (%) 1964–82	GDP per capita	Primary exports	Net oil exports	Industrial exports	Net service exports	Non-capital goods imports	Capital goods imports	Net commodity trade surplus	Current account (net of transfers)	Net transfers
Low income, low performance												
Madagascar*	9.2	1.4	320	9.94	-1.60	0.82	-7.34	-9.57	-6.19	-6.60	-13.94	1.06
Niger*	5.9	1.7	310	27.68	-6.62	0.62	-10.53	-17.26	-6.74	-1.80	-12.33	0.00
Central African Republic*	2.4	2.1	310	10.30	-0.18	3.66	-20.00	-7.60	-2.37	3.81	-16.19	10.00
Nicaragua	2.9	2.3	900	14.76	-6.98	1.91	-3.44	-21.32	-6.00	-17.63	-21.07	3.39
Senegal	6.0	2.5	440	9.92	-5.18	3.48	-0.22	-20.62	-6.59	-18.99	-19.21	3.80
Bangladesh	91.6	2.7	140	1.99	-1.53	4.00	-6.36	-11.03	-3.38	-9.95	-16.31	9.26
Burkina Faso	6.5	3.1	210	5.92	-4.10	0.86	-7.89	-18.68	-5.46	-21.46	-29.35	25.62
Ethiopia	32.6	3.2	140	8.63	-3.52	0.06	0.42	-8.40	-4.68	-7.49	-7.49	2.18
El Salvador	4.8	3.4	740	10.01	-4.91	7.36	5.78	-19.70	-3.18	-10.42	-4.64	1.54
India	705.7	3.6	250	1.87	-3.78	3.10	0.30	-3.55	-1.10	-3.46	-3.16	2.05
Togo	2.8	4.0	350	20.19	-3.80	3.65	3.60	-34.70	-9.22	-23.88	-20.28	8.47
Sudan	19.8	4.2	460	5.82	-2.43	0.05	-1.30	-9.91	-3.48	-9.95	-11.25	3.02
Honduras	4.0	4.2	670	26.14	-5.95	3.52	-5.43	-22.03	-9.32	-7.64	-13.07	0.95
Low income, high performance												
Tanzania	19.3	4.5	280	9.09	-4.90	1.51	-1.54	-8.41	-6.84	-9.55	-11.09	3.03
Sri Lanka	15.2	4.5	320	14.86	-8.13	8.24	-4.80	-22.52	-8.47	-16.02	-20.82	7.97
Pakistan	87.0	5.2	380	3.82	-4.93	5.36	-3.59	-9.71	-4.08	-9.54	-13.13	9.97
Morocco	21.6	5.2	820	9.60	-6.53	5.16	-6.17	-14.66	-5.25	-11.68	-17.85	6.82
Cameroon	8.9	5.4	850	9.85	4.93	1.20	-3.33	-12.73	-6.24	-2.99	-6.32	0.02
Malawi	6.5	5.5	210	19.36	-4.98	1.63	-6.95	-17.79	-8.22	-10.00	-16.95	5.26
Philippines	50.7	5.6	820	8.15	-6.16	4.24	-1.12	-8.23	-4.64	-6.64	-7.76	1.26
Egypt*	44.3	5.8	680	3.06	7.14	1.34	10.07	-21.29	-6.80	-16.55	-6.48	8.00
Kenya	18.1	6.5	390	10.07	-6.18	2.18	2.94	-15.00	-8.58	-17.51	-14.57	2.08
Thailand	48.5	7.1	890	13.54	-7.99	5.98	-2.21	-10.65	-5.90	-5.02	-7.23	1.90
Indonesia*	152.6	7.7	580	5.20	18.17	0.90	-12.09	-7.91	-5.20	11.16	-0.93	0.06

High income, low performance												
Jamaica	2.2	1.3	1,350	21.39	-16.00	12.40	-7.87	-24.81	-5.24	-12.23	-20.10	3.82
Chile	11.5	2.1	2,210	13.68	-3.21	3.04	-6.55	-10.17	-4.37	-1.03	-7.58	0.41
Uruguay	2.9	2.6	2,650	7.05	-4.40	4.62	-1.36	-7.44	-3.00	-3.17	-4.53	0.10
Argentina	28.6	2.8	2,520	5.77	-0.35	1.86	-4.15	-4.23	-2.43	0.62	-3.53	0.01
Peru	17.5	3.3	1,250	7.76	2.89	2.80	-5.48	-8.59	-4.25	0.61	-4.87	0.71
Spain	38.5	4.4	5,328	2.50	-6.28	8.08	2.32	-7.53	-2.50	-5.73	-3.41	0.92
Venezuela*	15.9	4.6	3,229	1.30	27.05	0.58	-7.70	-11.85	-5.74	11.34	3.64	-0.83
Trinidad and Tobago*	1.2	4.6	6,450	1.19	31.56	3.79	-2.00	-20.72	-11.09	4.73	2.73	-0.85
Portugal	9.9	5.0	2,490	4.08	-8.97	15.78	-3.25	-21.00	-8.55	-18.66	-21.91	12.11
Cyprus	0.6	5.1	3,740	10.35	-9.66	19.66	12.16	-36.39	-8.01	-24.05	-11.89	3.28
Greece	9.8	5.2	4,284	4.37	-4.86	7.10	3.27	-12.29	-6.56	-12.24	-8.97	0.81
High income, high performance												
Guatemala	7.7	5.3	1,130	11.44	-6.55	4.14	-0.04	-11.38	-3.26	-5.61	-5.65	1.22
Costa Rica	2.4	5.5	1,260	20.64	-6.27	8.71	-8.77	-21.59	-6.92	-5.43	-14.20	0.88
Turkey	47.5	5.5	1,330	4.71	-6.55	3.55	2.12	-4.95	-1.72	-6.40	-8.12	4.16
Colombia	27.0	5.5	1,470	6.61	-1.44	2.39	-0.62	-7.40	-4.36	-4.20	-4.82	0.52
Yugoslavia	22.7	5.6	2,840	2.98	-5.12	13.32	-2.44	-11.07	-5.41	-5.30	-7.74	6.44
Ivory Coast	8.8	6.0	1,140	23.31	-3.50	3.05	-11.30	-16.20	-5.25	1.86	-9.41	-7.28
Congo	1.7	6.0	1,180	2.05	45.63	3.61	-10.28	-15.90	-4.56	30.83	-9.45	0.00
Dominican Republic	5.8	6.5	1,400	9.77	-5.83	1.02	-3.87	-9.82	-3.23	-8.09	-11.96	2.70
Algeria*	20.3	6.5	2,200	0.53	37.27	0.07	-7.54	-16.96	-8.77	12.14	4.60	0.75
Tunisia*	6.7	6.8	1,370	3.40	6.06	13.69	6.84	-24.82	-9.74	-11.41	-4.57	4.62
Malaysia	14.5	7.0	1,840	26.08	5.78	10.80	-12.56	-23.10	-15.34	4.22	-8.34	-0.12
Brazil	122.7	7.0	2,310	4.42	-3.81	3.03	-4.31	-2.84	-1.49	-0.69	-5.00	0.04
Ecuador	8.9	7.6	1,210	5.74	10.04	0.57	-7.86	-8.03	-6.39	1.93	-5.93	0.12
South Korea	39.6	8.0	1,760	2.83	-11.56	35.35	-8.31	18.69	8.53	-0.60	-8.91	0.78
Jordan	3.5	9.4	1,860	7.85	-14.85	5.69	11.35	-45.14	-20.67	-67.12	-55.77	56.25

* Services trade shares for 1978–80.

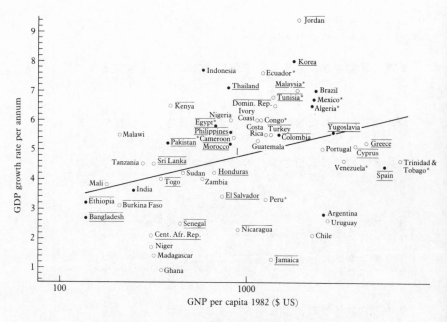

Fig. 4.1 GDP growth rate vs. GNP per capita

primary-product exports and are substantial net importers of services. From the four-way classification in the table, there is no obvious relationship between performance and overall openness to trade.

2. *The importance of primary exports diminishes with per capita income.* Poorer countries are more fettered by the commodity terms of trade than richer ones, a point pursued in Section 4.2. The mean ratios of industrial to primary trade by group are I, 0.45; II, 0.42; III, 1.29; IV, 1.80 (but 1.04 without South Korea, a distinct outlier in the sample). Industrial exports rise with per capita income, but independently of rates of output growth. This fact strikes the eye in Fig. 4.1, where countries with high shares of industrial exports for their size and income level are underlined. Note the scattering of observations above and below the growth rate/per capita GNP regression line.

3. *Export-led growth does not stand out.* As we have seen, the ratio of industrial to primary exports is not correlated with growth rates, in contrast to mainstream assertions, nor are overall export ratios higher in the high-performance economies. If shares of exports in GNP rose more rapidly with income in fast- than in slow-growing countries, then trade expansion might naturally be associated with good performance. From McCarthy, Taylor, and Talati 1987, the elasticities of the export share in GNP with respect to the growth in income ('share elasticity') by group are shown in Table 4.2.

Table 4.2 Elasticity of export/GNP ratio to income: grouped data

	All countries	Low performance countries			High performance countries		
		All	Low income	High income	All	Low income	High income
Primary	−0.18	−0.20	0.63	−1.16	−0.15	0.02	0.06
Industrial	0.34	0.30	0.36	−0.28	0.42	−0.08	0.00
Services	−0.08	−0.07	−0.49	−0.74	−0.04	0.34	0.07

Export-led growth, in the sense of a strong positive relationship between the share of exports in GNP and income (even in high income, high-performance countries) does not characterize our sample. Finally, in line with literature on the Dutch disease (Section 4.2.3) even the net oil exporters marked with stars in Fig. 4.1 are spread across the growth rate spectrum.

4. *Most developing countries are highly dependent on net service imports.* (This perhaps explains the resistance of the Third World to liberalization of trade in services in the Punta del Este GATT round scheduled for the late 1980s.) The exceptions are large exporters of tourism and/or labour to industrialized countries and the Persian Gulf. But more disaggregated data show that the gross service imports of these countries are large as well.

5. *With a few large, import-substituting exceptions (India, Brazil, etc.), almost all countries devote upwards of 5 per cent of GDP to capital goods imports.* Current account deficits (including all service transactions except transfers) typically exceed capital goods purchases from abroad so that, at least in the early 1980s, financial capital and transfer flows to poor countries exceeded their physical counterpart. The transfer component is shown in the final column of Table 4.1. Its magnitude varies widely across countries, in relation to the size of their emigrant labor forces and geopolitical position among other factors.

6. *Size bears some relationship to growth but capital inflows do not.* In Fig. 4.1, nations with populations exceeding 20 million are indicated by darkened circles and smaller countries with open ones. More large countries lie above the regression line than below. Recipients of above-normal capital inflows have an overbar. Many are slow growers, lying below the performance line. However, causation could as easily run from slow growth to high foreign transfers as the other way round.

7. *The countries in the sample largely engage in non-competitive merchandise trade, buying and selling commodities which do not loom large in domestic production and consumption activity.* Primary exports dominate in most countries. The mean GDP share of merchandise imports is 22 per cent in the entire sample, with primary products and intermediates making up 9.1 per

cent and capital goods 5.4 per cent. A large fraction of the remaining import categories will be non-competitive as well.

The central conclusion is that trade does not seem to be closely related to the way economies perform. Fast-growing countries are more or less open, have diverse patterns of specialization, and their success is not obviously led by exports, industrial or otherwise. However, it is also true that observed trade shares are 'output' variables, resulting from the general equilibrium of economic forces and policy choice. Could it be that eliminating distortions to trade—tariffs, subsidies, quotas, and the like—will lead to more rapid growth from the policy 'input' side?

4.1.2 Irrelevent distortions

Historically, there is no dearth of liberalization experiments to be examined. Indeed, they were the grist from which trade theorists milled their defence of liberal policy. Beginning with Little, Scitovsky, and Scott (1970), several rounds of country studies tried to sort out the effects of commercial policy changes. Despite the enthusiasm of the investigators, their results were none too strong. An early (and long-lasting) proponent of liberalization and co-director of one of the projects, Anne Krueger, was circumspect: 'while there are numerous microeconomic changes that accompany devaluation, liberalization, and altered [trade policy] bias, it was not possible to detect significant effects of these changes on growth performance' (Krueger 1978: 277). Later experiments with extreme liberalization, as under the military regimes in the 1970s in South America's Southern Cone or in Zaire and Mexico with IMF tutelage in the 1980s, suggest that such policies can disable an economy for years. Recent experience does not substantiate claims about liberalization's beneficial effects.

The case is not much stronger on the basis of cross-country data. Table 4.4 in Section 4.2.5 presents a list of 'open' and 'closed' economies based on Balassa (1985b). There, it is shown that differences in trade policy orientation had little to do with how successfully countries responded to the external shocks of the past decade. One can also ask if there is any relationship between orientation and the performance categories in Table 4.1. The contingency table goes as follows:

	Open	Closed
High performance	8	11
Low performance	2	7

Slowly growing economies partially escaped Balassa's gaze. But for the countries classified, it is clear that trade orientation is uncorrelated with performance. The point remains valid for plausible reassignments of country policy lines, as the reader can check out.

Another piece of evidence is a recent World Bank study, summarized with fanfare in the Bank's 1983 *World Development Report* and the *Economist* magazine. In the formal publication, Agarwala (1983) reports a negative relationship between growth in a sample of thirty-one developing countries in the late 1970s and a 'distortion index' based on seven indicators.

Agarwala's analysis can be criticized on several grounds. For example, his choice of period makes slow-growing Argentina, Chile, and Uruguay appear highly distorted, even though all were undergoing major liberalization experiments in the latter half of the decade. Even if we accept his data, however, later work by Aghazadeh and Evans (1985) shows that only two of Agarwala's index's indicators—real exchange rate appreciation and real wage growth in excess of productivity gains—bear a negative relationship with output growth. The other indicators—tariff distortions for agricultural and industrial products included—are unrelated. Aghazadeh and Evans argue that institutional variables such as military spending and planning capacity do influence growth. Since strongly trending real wages and exchange rates also reflect institutional factors such as open distributional conflict or the onset of Dutch disease, one can conclude that an economy's historical circumstances affect its performance but trade and other distortions do not play much of a role.

4.1.3 Trade theorists and development: the mainstream view

The data just reviewed suggest that trade patterns in developing countries have distinctive characteristics. First and foremost, the commodities they exchange internationally are non-competitive—exports are not consumed in large quantities at home, and imports are not produced. The implication is that trade theory's 'law of one price' will play a minor role in determining resource allocation. First, the the law itself will not apply in so far as large numbers of competitive traders for the same commodity do not exist both within and without a poor country's borders. Second, even if arbitrage occurs, it will not enforce competition among domestic producers. To put the point more succinctly, the share of effectively non-traded goods in the production basket of most developing countries is high. Chenery (1975) notes that development usually involves a secular shift from non-competitive towards competitive trade; as we shall see shortly, his observation has strong implications for policy in the medium run.

Another point to be stressed is that poor countries are strongly dependent on imports of capital goods. With very few exceptions (South Korea, India, Brazil) they have had no success in penetrating export markets for such commodities. Finally, size and history strongly influence a country's trading role—bigger economies are more self-sufficient, and many small and poor ones suffer from their inherited dependence on primary commodity trade.

Trade theory disdains such empirical regularities. Rather, it starts from the opposite position: a hypothetical open economy with tastes and technology uncontaminated by history and a preponderance of traded goods subject to the law of one price. Strictly speaking, the theorems demonstrate the static welfare benefits that accrue to consumers from liberalizing trade under such conditions; for advocacy purposes, these gains are supposed to manifest themselves in the form of faster growth. 'Old' arguments for the gains from trade are familiar, but since they have dominated development policy during the past decade they bear close review. 'New' trade theorists, though they accept many postulates from their elders, are less dogmatic about the costs of protection. Their perspective is taken up in Section 4.1.4. Both groups are oblivious to the evidence about the irrelevance of both trade and trade distortions to growth, as presented above, but then that is the strength of theory. Myriad other forces may simply be intervening to prevent the numbers from coming out right.

It is useful to start analysis of the role of trade with an old idea: Schumpeter's (1934) definition of development as a transition of the economy between states of circular flow. Circular flow might well involve output expansion, and when considered nowadays it is usually interpreted as some sort of steady growth. Since institutional rules may change between states of circular flow, Schumpeter's notion encompassed more than simple expansion, and bore some resemblance to a mode of production in Marx's terms. How does an economy switch from one circular flow or production mode to another involving different technology, changed social relations, and perhaps a higher rate of growth? This question has long been debated in terms of links between changes in the productive structure and international trade.

The first heirs of Schumpeter—Rosenstein-Rodan (1943) and Nurkse (1953)—adopted his metaphor in discussing vicious and virtuous circles of development. 'Balanced growth' for them was a change in the organization of production in which all sectors of the economy would participate in a massive expansionary burst. Hirschman (1958) and Streeten (1959) countered with a dose of imbalance to shock the system from low-level circular flow. In their view, the development process is characterized by the uneven advance of different sectors, disproportions and disequilibria, with inflationary and balance of payments tensions arising at different points. Instead of promotion of overall balance, investment strategies should be directed toward self-propulsion, correcting imbalances that arose at earlier stages and creating new ones. Some imbalances could arise in connection with the economy's international transactions and some not.

These theories are far from neoclassical since they do not focus on price signals or price-mediated general equilibrium. Nor are they congenial to mainstream development economics in the mid-1980s. However, they can be rephrased in neoclassical idiom, as in a subtle paper by Scitovsky (1954). He emphasized externalities such as economies of scale and imperfect tradability

of most goods that prevent price signals from leading the economy to even an
n-th best dynamically efficient point. For Walrasians who assert that price
reform is a guarantee for growth, Scitovsky brings an unwanted waft of
realism from within the camp.

Present-day neoclassicals obscure Scitovsky's institutional insights by
embellishment with optimizing agents and emphasis on market choice. Their
stress on trade liberalization is a response to the questions raised by Nurkse
and Rosenstein-Rodan, and tries to bring their balanced planning or Hirschman's unbalanced spontaneity within the fold of a Walrasian market game.

There are two fronts to the orthodox position. One stresses export-led
growth, and is taken up below. The other, closer to the Paretian core of
neoclassical thought, asserts that poor countries are inefficient because they
suffer from distortions or gaps between observed prices and some optimal
set. 'Getting prices right' becomes the neoclassical slogan, with special
emphasis on equating internal price ratios with those ruling in the markets of
the world. An immediate corollary is that there should be equal incentives for
exporters and import substituters, as in Bhagwati's (1986) formulation. We
will see in Section 4.1.5 that this suggestion is suboptimal in a realistic
growth model, but here we want to ask if it is worth pursuing even on the
trade theorists' own terms.

At first glance, the neoclassical appeal to the welfare improvements that
should result from relative price realignment does not look promising.
Walrasian circular flow presupposes full employment and a near approach to
Pareto efficiency. The 'surpluses' (for producers, consumers, or whomever)
that result from removing distortions under such circumstances are measured
by the famous little triangles in the demand–supply diagram. Such welfare
gains are trivial in magnitude, as Harberger (1959) noted to his chagrin back
in the era of balanced growth.

The implication of small calculable welfare losses from distortions is that
neoclassicals are forced to a position like Schumpeter's. The economy can
leap forward from one circular flow to another under appropriate incentives—
specifically, those that result from getting prices right. The international
marketplace has the right stuff, and internal relative prices should be steered
toward external ones. Calculations of effective rates of protection and
domestic resource costs can map the route. The propaganda for such policies
is usually couched in terms of the gains to be realized from trade. But the
Harberger problem of triviality remains. Moreover, as already noted, the
theoretical basis for the neoclassical case is artificial, if factor availability,
technologies, or demand patterns are determined by the patterns of
specialization evolving in historical time. Given the weakness of its visible
foundation on the gains from trade, the true support of the neoclassical case
can only be Schumpeterian.

Does that pillar hold? The cautions raised by Scitovsky become relevant here. He showed in an otherwise purely Walrasian context that if economies of scale are important and if commodities are not competitively traded (in the sense of having ample import supplies and export demand at the same well-defined international prices), then price signals will not lead to optimal tradable, as well as being time- and recourse-consuming in practice. Since Common sense suggests that Scitovsky's conditions apply. Economies of scale are rife in industry, and I have already noted that for most commodities in developing countries, non-competitive trade is the rule. In particular, as Pack and Westphal (1986) argue, mastery of technology is largely non-tradable, as well as being time- and resource-consuming in practice. Since technical innovation and transfer are required for productivity gains and are also closely tied to capital accumulation, price-guided investment decisions will neither maximize welfare in the standard neoclassical model nor lead to jumps between circular flows. Schumpeter's entrepreneurs were supposed to choose their innovations on the basis of benefit–cost calculations at market prices, but that turns out not to be advantageous on social grounds. His theory is not damaged (and possibly improved) if price signals are replaced by 'vision'. But then, the question is whether an environment in which national prices are equated to international ones enhances clairvoyance in a non-convex, uncertain world. We come to an impasse, at least as far as theory is concerned.

The ambiguity is not resolved by facts, as we have seen in Section 4.1.2. Nor is the case stronger for export-led growth, the other component of the mainstream cure. A theoretical problem is why more rapid export expansion should stimulate output at all. If, as neoclassicals suppose, the economy is at full employment, faster growth of one source of demand can only lead to slower growth of another. If investment suffers, for example, overall capacity expanion may be slowed in the medium run. In demand-driven models, more exports may accelerate growth, as noted by Hobson (1902) in his theory of imperialism. Moreover, export expansion does not run into a balance of payments restriction, as might other exogenous injections of demand (from investment or public expenditure).

However, simple demand expansion or the use of extra exports to break the trade constraint does not seem to be what neoclassicals have in mind. Rather, they argue that by enhancing competition with the world, opening the economy through exports leads to greater enterprise efficiency and faster technical progress. The price mechanism is said to be involved, though the details are rarely spelt out.

Given this lack of theoretical clarity, most arguments for export-led growth are presented along empirical lines. Indeed, showing a positive regression coefficient of output growth on export growth has become a thriving cottage industry in recent years (see e.g. Balassa 1985a). From the national accounts, the output growth rate can be expressed as an average of growth rates of the components of final demand (consumption, investment, exports, etc.), with the weights being shares of output. The export coefficient in regression studies often takes a value like an export share. It can be beefed up by making export growth 'explain' the residual from the standard decomposition of the output growth rate into a weighted average of primary input growth rates (Feder 1983). The results from regressing one trending variable on another are statistically significant but the rationale is hardly convincing. McCarthy, Taylor, and Talati (1987) run the regression the other way—export shares disaggregated by type on output growth, with per capita GNP, population, and other variables as controls. As we saw in Section 4.1.1, they find no strong relationships, aside from a tendency of low-income countries to specialize more in primary exports than richer ones. Their further test of export-led growth by trends in shares of total exports or some categories as per capita income rises in fast-growing countries also fails. From a fancier statistical point of view, exports can be shown *not* to temporally lead or 'Granger cause' output expansion in LDCs (Jung and Marshall 1985).

A more reasonable approach is to ask, along with Pack and Westphal (1986), whether a strong export orientation fits naturally into a planning framework. South Korean experience suggests that export targets are easy to verify, and ease communication between exporters and policy-makers who push exporters. But the Korean system is highly *dirigiste* (as in most other countries that have favored export-led growth), and price signals do not play a central role in the process of taking investment decisions. Productivity growth, as a definitional matter, is high in Korea, but more as a result of a long history of industrialization, high work norms coming from both labour's own motivation and an effectively interventionist state (unions report to the Central Intelligence Agency), aggressive macro policy, and centralized pressures on exporters to perform than of getting prices 'right'.

The conclusion would seem to be that exports may play a role in speeding growth by producing foreign exchange, adding to aggregate demand, and fitting into the planning process, but there is no guarantee that they will do so. Like the argument about benefits from removing trade distortions, the neoclassical case for export promotion runs into an empirical cul-de-sac.

4.1.4. New theories of trade

Little–Scitovsky–Scott, Krueger, Bhagwati, and epigones all operate on the basis of Heckscher–Ohlin trade theory—the Aeschylean version. Over the past decade, however, revisionist trade models have sprouted up. To the non-initiate's eye, the recent work seems to provide a clear rationale for policy intervention even though its authors argue to the contrary. It makes sense to sort out why they are not likely to be right.

The basic theoretical line is product diversification, following Linder

(1961). Trade, at least in final goods, depends on similarity of taste in the partner countries. The formal models divide the economy into a competitive, homogeneous (H) sector and a diversified (D) sector in which monopolistic competition prevails. Mark-up pricing rules, with each firm producing a single design under increasing returns. The mark-up depends on the elasticity of substitution between designs. Countries with similar factor endowments typically interchange D-products.

Superficially such theories seem to make liberalization desirable, since increased trade in D-goods brings both greater variety and decreasing costs. However, the transition towards a liberalized regime may be difficult, if firms in the home country must shut down. Indeed, in a small country, protection may be beneficial if the closest substitutes to home designs come from abroad (Lancaster 1984). Tariffs raise profits at home, but entry into the industry follows. Domestic competition and economies of scale may lead in the long run to *lower* domestic prices, encouraging the export of D-goods.

Further implications are drawn by Stewart (1984). First, if demand for D-goods rises with income, the South's dependence on the North for its supply will lead to trade gap problems of the type traditionally emphasized by the structuralist school (see Section 4.2). Second, if development of designs is costly, they will conform to the larger economy's (or Northern) tastes, for both consumer and capital goods. Northern technology may prove too capital-intensive for Southern needs, leading to the LDCs' 'structural technological heterogeneity', long ago emphasized by Prebisch (1952). Finally, expanded variety and price reductions can go hand-in-hand with greater South–South trade. However, Stewart rightly points out that realizing these potential advantages requires institutional change. In the North it was associated with market liberalization and the rise of transnational corporations which broke the tendency of trade to organize within national boundaries. In the South, such innovations are still lacking.

Arguments for liberal policy in the 'new' trade theories are traditional. Thus, as early as 1962, Eastman and Stykolt argued that protection of D-goods may lead all firms to raise prices and profits, causing in turn excessive entry. The outcome would be a congeries of small firms wiping up extra profits through efficiency reductions due to unutilized economies of scale. This sort of problem has some versimilitude in the developing world, but it can be overcome by licensing policy. Appropriate state intervention can also obviate Bhagwati's (1969) argument that industrial policy based on import quotas is even worse on economic efficiency grounds than tariffs. His story is that a quota creates a 'rent' leading under monopolistic competition to a higher domestic price and lower output than a tariff which allows the same level of imports. Quantitative production and export targets have helped successful industries around this temptation in Brazil, Korea, and other corners of the world. The key question is which sectors are likely to be successful in keeping up investment and making productivity gains (thus meriting protection) in the long run.

The following section presents some suggestions along these lines in model form. However, sensible authors correctly emphasize that historical processes are involved; thus, Amsden (1986) chronicles the redirection of labour-intensive Japanese exports from initial developing country markets towards developed countries over time. Learning in LDC markets is a plausible dynamic vehicle for Japanese market diversification. Similarly, Westphal (1981) and Krugman (1984) observe that if exports are a final objective, then import protection for the relevant commodities may be necessary to secure an adequate market for the initial production at a satisfactory rate of return. Quantitative restrictions may be preferable to tariffs since they secure the market. Dumping should perhaps be encouraged, and selectivity of sectors to be granted protection is surely necessary. Restating the Eastman–Stykolt argument to fit LDC institutional realities, Ocampo (1986) points out that free trade is unlikely to be undesirable, if 'the private sector tends to spread resources in an excessively diversified manner, without being able to accumulate in an industry the level necessary to start a process of cumulative causation'.

4.1.5 Planning trade interventions in the long run

The message to this point is that neither openness nor trade liberalization fosters income growth; the empirical and even theoretical linkages are simply not observed. Why serious scholars believed that openness to trade favoured growth is a bit of a mystery—the bias of mainstream economists in favour of competition (whether or not it can practically apply) and their lack of comprehension of the developmentalist state in 'success' cases like Korea and Brazil may have played some role. Also, neoclassical analysis has strong imperialistic tendencies. The problem is that like many empires, when it expands into a new area it tends to overlay quaint cultural artefacts (Schumpeter, Rosenstein-Rodan, Hirschman, etc.) with its own way of looking at the world.

Is there any way that earlier insights can be recovered? If non-liberal interventions to make growth cumulate are possible, how should their prospects be judged? The answers to such questions depend to a large extent on institutions. Designing effective schemes to stimulate entrepreneurial forces has never been a strong suit of the economics profession—at best the theory points the directions in which incentives may run. A simple model is sketched here (and set out formally in the Appendix) to illustrate how growth with interventions may proceed, assuming that investors respond to profit stimuli. They might respond better to more explicit state-administered carrots and sticks, but we ignore those possibilities here. Hughes and Singh in Ch. 3 give a more general view.

Causality in the model runs from the side of demand. If there is more demand pressure on a sector, either its sales rise (when there is excess capacity) or its product price goes up. Either way, the sector's profits increase and are assumed to stimulate investment. Feedbacks through the general equilibrium system affect profitability in other sectors in the short run, and the overall rate of growth over time. Emphasis in this section is placed on steady-state growth rates; short-term macro adjustments are dealt with later in the chapter.

From the data presented in Section 4.1.1, it makes sense to set up an illustrative model with three sectors—home goods, an import-substitution industry, and exports. All capital goods are treated as imported, largely to save notation. Non-intermediate imports in imperfect competition with home goods, along the lines of the last section, are not considered here, although they could easily be added for countries where they are relevant to policy choice (mainly, the NICS—the middle-income, newly industrializing countries).

Once installed in a sector, capital stock stays put. Let X stand for home goods output, J for import substitutes, and E for exports; the corresponding capital stocks are K_x, K_j, and K_e respectively. Resource allocation across the economy is desribed by the two ratios $\lambda_j = K_j/K_x$ and $\lambda_e = K_e/K_x$. We assume that the X-sector has mark-up pricing and a horizontal supply curve within the relevant range, and that the J-sector has a horizontal or rising supply curve. Export supply is determined by available capital, and the world market price declines as export volume goes up. Home goods production (and perhaps that of exports as well) depends on intermediate inputs that are either imported or produced at home; foreign and national intermediates are imperfect substitutes. All these assumptions about market structure could be modified without changing the tenor of the results.

Capital stock growth in each sector requires investment, which responds to rates of profit. In home goods, treated as the economy's central sector, the capital stock growth rate g_x rises as a function of the profit rate r_x, along the lines of most theories of investment demand. A simple, easily generalizable hypothesis is that growth of capital stock in the import substitution sector, g_j, responds to the differential profit rate $r_j - r_x$; the rationale is that investors need an extra incentive to enter non-standard activities like import substitution. A similar assumption applies to investment in the export sector.

Causality in the model is straightforward. A steady-state equilibrium has $g_j = g_e = g_x$, i.e. equal growth rates in all sectors. The steady state is characterized by constant capital stock ratios λ_i ($i = j$ or e), since the growth rate of each (denoted by a 'hat') is $\hat{\lambda}_i = g_i - g_x$. At long-run equilibrium $\hat{\lambda}_j = \hat{\lambda}_e = 0$. The state has two policy instruments—a tariff on intermediate imports (at rate σ) and a subsidy for exports (at rate ξ). We want to know how the long-run growth rate responds to policy changes via adjustments in the λ_j. The mediating variables are the profit rates, which determine investment demand. How are they affected by movements in λ_j, λ_e, σ, and ξ? The answers go as follows.

In the export sector, more capital increases supply, which drives down the external price. Per unit of capital, profits fall: $\delta r_e/\delta\lambda_e < 0$. If export demand has a greater than unitary elasticity, total revenue rises with λ_e. Part will be directed toward home goods, so that $\delta r_x/\delta\lambda_e > 0$. However, world demand may be inelastic, in which case $\delta r_x/\delta\lambda_e < 0$. An increase in the export subsidy rate ξ directly or indirectly raises both rates of profit.

In the import-substitution sector, an increase in λ_j reduces the profit rate at constant revenue: $\delta r_j/\delta\lambda_j < 0$. If the supply curve is horizontal, profits in the home goods sector do not depend on capital in import substitution, and are unaffected: $\delta r_x/\delta\lambda_j = 0$. However, more capital shifts a rising supply curve outward, cutting home goods costs: $\delta r_x/\delta\lambda_j > 0$. An increased tariff on imported intermediates which compete with the home-produced kind raises overall costs in the X-sector: $\delta r_x/\delta\sigma < 0$. On the other hand, import-substituters' profits go up: $\delta r_j/\delta\sigma > 0$. If the export sector also uses the intermediate, then $\delta r_e/\delta\sigma < 0$.

Algebraically, changes in the steady-state growth rate decompose independently into responses to σ and ξ (if cross-sector linkages are ignored, e.g. the effect of σ on r_e). Fig 4.2 illustrates what happens when the import tariff is increased. To understand the initial slopes of the schedules, note that

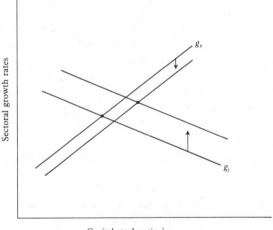

Fig. 4.2 Response of the steady-state growth rate and import substitution capital stock ratio to an increase in the import tariff σ. More capital is allocated toward import substitution, and the growth rate rises if increased investment demand from higher profitability in the sector offsets a lower profit rate and reduced investment demand in home goods

with an upward-sloping intermediate commodity supply curve, r_x responds positively to λ_j. Capital stock growth in the sector rises with the higher profit rate, as shown by the g_x schedule in the figure. Growth of the import substitution industry is stimulated by r_j (which declines with λ_j) and held back by a higher r_x. Hence the growth rate g_j is a decreasing function of λ_j, as shown. Steady-state equilibrium resides at the intersection of the two schedules. It is easily seen to be stable, since for example an increase in λ_j from its equilibrium value raises g_x, reduces g_j, and makes $\lambda_j < 0$. Around the equilibrium, we want to ask how λ_j and the growth rate adjust to changes in the tariff rate σ.

To see what happens, first note that a higher tariff cuts profits in home goods, so the g_x schedule shifts downward. Import substitution is stimulated, so g_j shifts up. From the figure, it is clear that resources migrate towards import substitution, as λ_j rises in the new equilibrium, but the growth rate may adjust either way. It tends to rise with more responsive import substitution investment (a big shift in the g_j schedule), and if the intermediate supply curve slopes strongly upward (more capital shifts the curve outward and reduces home goods costs). The outcome in the long run depends on cumulative effects from short-term profitability changes through the investment demand functions.

The story for a higher export subsidy is similar. The growth rate may fall if world export demand is sufficiently inelastic, but will go up otherwise. If the cross-sector negative effect of an import tariff on exporters' profitability is introduced, r_e and g_e will fall with an increase in σ. In the three-sector system involving λ_j and λ_e as state variables, the outcome could be slower growth.

To summarize, the discussion shows that long-run growth can respond with either sign to changes in commercial policy. In the specification sketched out here, it is likely to slow down with increased tariffs if domestic supply of import substitutes is quite elastic and/or if the export sector uses intermediate inputs intensively. Slowdowns in response to export subsidies may occur if world demand for national products is price-inelastic. When the growth rate accelerates in response to policy changes, its responses to changes in tariffs and subsidies will differ. Real devaluation—or equiproportionate changes in the 'forces' of tariffs $(1 + \sigma)$ and subsidies $(1 - \xi)$—will not affect growth as strongly as individually designed sectoral policies.

These results show that a liberal, equalized incentives policy stance will not maximize growth. This conclusion would be strengthened if scale economies and non-price-mediated intersectoral linkages were brought into the specification. More positively, the model provides a basis for computing effects on growth of policy changes in a practical format. The procedure could be readily quantified to explore likely effects of potential interventions on growth.

4.1.6 Relaxing import quotas

The foregoing discussion suggests that attempts to guide resource allocation through trade policy changes can have substantial effects in the long run. But rigging policy to generate beneficial results is a non-trivial task.

The same observation applies to policy moves in the conjuncture. They require administrative effort, and must be designed to be institutionally feasible in a world of conflicting interest groups and seekers for rents. In this context, the macroeconomic implications of changes in directed policies, such as export subsidies, and import tariffs and quotas deserve to be explored. Since quotas are widely applied in practice, in this section we work through a simple model to show how relaxing them can be counterproductive in the short run.

Import quotas are complicated analytically. Their macroeconomic ramifications have not been widely discussed, although there is an enormous literature in trade theory damning them on rent-seeking and efficiency-loss grounds—Bhagwati's (1969) elegant statement of the argument was noted in Section 4.1.4. In development economics, the trade theorists who took up policy advice in the 1970s stressed the allegedly beneficial effects of lifting quotas. None the less, in Krueger's (1978) well-known survey of country experience, only four of twenty-two episodes of devaluation-*cum*-liberalization ('phase III liberalization', in her terminology) did not result in a fall in output, faster inflation, or renewed balance of payments problems. It makes sense to ask why such responses occurred.

Recent papers on quota liberalization include Ocampo 1985 and Barbone 1985. The former emphasizes direct effects of quota changes on domestic absorption, while the latter works through a quota rent story *à la* Bhagwati 1969 and Krueger 1974. We follow Barbone here for compactness of exposition—his model is close to that of the preceding section and the Appendix. Two market-clearing processes are involved. The level of output of domestic 'industrial' goods is determined by demand, while its price follows from a mark-up on wage and intermediate input costs. The internal price of intermediate goods required by the industrial sector varies to equate demand and supply. Intermediates are either produced at home or imported subject to a quota.

On the supply side of the market for intermediate goods, assume that the import quota is set at level $\bar{J}$. For simplicity, let domestically produced and imported intermediates substitute perfectly. Then if the internal price of intermediates is P_j and the border price is $eP_j^\star$ (e is the nominal exchange rate and $P_j^\star$ the world price of intermediates), people with access to imports get a total 'rent' $(P_j - eP_j^\star)\bar{J}$ from internal resales resulting from their control of quotas.

Suppose that, in an attempt at liberalization, import quota $\bar{J}$ is increased.

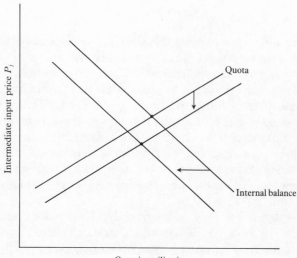

Capacity utilization u

Fig. 4.3 Effects of quota liberalization for intermediate imports. Initially, a greater quota generates increased rental income for import license-holders, leading potential saving to rise and the output level consistent with internal balance to decline. Simultaneously, excess supply in the intermediate goods market makes the price P_j fall. The outcome involves a lower P_j and a reduced level of activity unless P_j goes down sharply due to a low elasticity of domestic supply. Contraction could also be offset by a high elasticity of exports to a lower domestic price level resulting from cheaper intermediate input costs

Comparative statistics appear in Fig. 4.3. The slopes of the curves can be explained as follows. Higher capacity utilization in the industrial sector increases demand for the intermediate and causes its price to rise along the quota schedule. At the same time, a higher price P_j generates incomes for quota-holders and import substituting entrepreneurs, raising available saving. To maintain macro equilibrium with investment fixed, less saving from mark-ups on commodity production is required. Hence P_j and capacity utilization u trade off inversely along the internal balance line. A higher domestic price for a key intermediate input dampens aggregate demand.

The effects of raising the import quota $\bar{J}$ are shown by the shifts in the curves. In the internal market at the initial price P_j, aggregate demand falls since higher *ex ante* saving comes from a greater volume of quota rents. At the same time, the intermediate price P_j falls due to excess supply. Both changes lead to a lower P_j, but the net effect on aggregate demand is unclear. Capacity utilization u will decline unless P_j falls sharply, leading to lower final prices, an increased real wage, and a strong export response. Expansion requires a *low* supply elasticity to import substitution (so that a slight decline in sales volume leads to a big price drop) or a high elasticity of export demand. There is no particular reason to expect these conditions to apply. In other words, quota liberalization can easily prove contractionary in the short run. Rational economics ministers with typically short time horizons would have every reason not to pursue such a policy change. The same point carries over to many other liberalizing moves. In the longer run, as the model of Section 4.1.5 emphasizes, growth may be the victim.

4.1.7 Initial summary about trade

The conclusions from the initial review of trade-related issues are the following:

1. The case for a positive association between trade liberalization and economic performance as measured by growth is *prima facie* difficult to make, and is not supported by cross-sectional or time-series evidence.

2. Arguments are not much stronger for export-led growth. A few fast-growing countries have had rapid export expansion, but the correlation does not extend to the group of developing economies as a whole.

3. The model of Section 4.1.5 shows that probable directions of effects on growth of policy changes can be discussed formally. The signs of growth rate responses make economic sense, but depend on technical and institutional details of the economy at hand. In practical terms, finding 'right' prices or policy interventions is a non-trivial exercise, let alone imposing them on a functioning economic system. Short- to medium-run repercussions may be counter-productive, as illustrated in the macroeconomic example presented in Section 4.1.6.

4. Economic decision-making in the 'success' cases is highly *dirigiste*; perhaps in recognition of such difficulties. One can further argue that rapid growth is a major component in their process of political legitimation. Planners in South Korea, for example, have *not* used international prices as the keystone for investment decisions.

On the basis of the foregoing arguments, it is fair to say that in the mid-1980s the trade liberalization strategy is intellectually moribund, kept alive by life support from the World Bank and International Monetary Fund. But that does not mean trade policy issues have gone away. They may be clarified by the new micro theories being developed, as reviewed in Section 4.1.4. Models like the one in Section 4.1.5 could be implemented numerically to help trade and industrial planning. And in broader perspective, the implications of Chenery's (1975) suggestion that the process of development is characterized by a shift from non-competitive (unsubstitutable imports of intermediates and capital goods, primary product exports) to competitive trade should be explored. The issues are urgent; what has been lacking are sensible ways to address them.

4.2 EXTERNAL SHOCKS: THE CURRENT ACCOUNT

The next step is to consider current account adjustment: how economies respond to unexpected changes in either trading relationships or capital movements. Since all poor countries were affected by global macroeconomic conditions over the past two decades, we begin with a brief historical overview. Illustrative models are presented of the macroeconomic implications at the country level of foreign exchange dearths and gluts, and of the risks inherent in unduly open capital markets. A review of developing country adjustment experience concludes the section, focusing on the question of how painful external shocks are likely to be in more or less open national systems.

4.2.1 Global macroeconomics

An impressive growth performance in the developing world was rudely interrupted in the early 1980s. More generally, the global economic balance of forces has shifted markedly over the past quarter of a century. These events can be organized in terms of a simple macro model based upon the patterns of developing country trade noted in Section 4.1.1. The key factors are the dependence of poor countries on imports of intermediates and capital goods to support production and investment, respectively. Their primary export specialization, further, renders them vulnerable to terms of trade fluctuations and other external shocks.

The situation in the not too distant past was more favourable than it is today. In the two decades between 1960 and 1980, the developing countries made impressive economic progress. As shown in Table 4.3 developing market economies grew at 5.2 per cent per year between 1961 and 1973, and a still solid 3.8 per cent between 1974 and 1980. These rates were above those of the developed market economies in the same periods, and substantially higher than the historical speed of expansion of the now-industrialized countries.

This achievement has been put in jeopardy by the world recession that began in 1980. As Table 4.3 shows, the story of the 1980s is slow or negative growth tempered by a mild recovery in 1982-4. The few bright spots since 1985 include India and China among the poorer countries, East Asian middle-income economies, and Brazil. For the rest of the Third World, the recent record has been bleak.

At root, the poor growth performance of the developing countries is caused by the economic slump of the industrialized world. Their main short-run problems are:

1. Reduction in world demand for primary products stemming from slow growth in the OECD economies.

2. A fall in prices for these commodities which is deeper and more

Table 4.3 Population GDP per Capita, and GDP Growth Rates by Major World Regions

	Population (millions)	GDP per capita 1980	Growth in GDP (%)						
			1961–1973	1974–1980	1981	1982	1983	1984	1985
Developing market economies	2,160	546	5.2	3.8	1.3	0.4	0.2	3.3	3.8
Africa	440	459	6.1	4.3	-0.2	-0.6	-0.5	2.1	3.9
East and South Asia	1,248	251	4.8	6.0	6.6	3.5	5.5	5.7	7.3
West Asia	124	1,593	7.3	5.1	-3.5	-4.6	-1.3	1.2	-1.8
Western hemisphere	349	1,343	4.8	6.0	0.7	-1.4	-2.6	2.6	3.4
Developed market economies	763	6,347	4.9	3.2	1.4	-0.2	2.5	4.6	3.6
Ivory Coast	8	322	7.6	6.7	1.4	-3.8	-4.2	-2.2	12.6
Kenya	16	420	7.1	4.8	3.9	1.6	3.8	0.9	4.5
Sudan	19	410	0.9	9.0	3.2	4.2	-2.1	-2.4	-10.2
Zambia	6	560	3.9	0.3	6.2	-2.8	-2.0	-1.3	5.0
Egypt	40	1,001	4.7	9.4	7.8	5.9	5.4	5.2	1.9
Turkey	45	1,470	6.2	4.6	4.4	5.0	3.7	5.8	4.2
Sri Lanka	15	270	4.2	4.8	5.8	5.1	5.0	5.0	5.3
India	673	240	3.6	4.1	5.8	2.9	7.7	4.5	5.1
Bangladesh	89	130	2.0	6.1	5.9	1.1	2.9	4.5	4.0
Thailand	47	670	8.0	7.5	6.3	4.1	5.9	6.0	6.9
South Korea	38	1,520	9.0	8.6	6.9	5.5	9.5	7.9	5.7
China	977	290	7.1	5.4	4.9	7.7	9.6	14.0	12.3
Brazil	119	2,050	6.9	6.8	-1.6	0.1	-3.2	4.5	8.3
Mexico	70	2,090	7.7	6.2	7.9	-0.5	-5.3	3.5	4.2
Peru	17	930	4.5	2.4	3.9	0.4	-10.9	4.8	3.1
Jamaica	2	1,040	4.9	-2.6	2.5	1.0	2.0	-0.4	-5.0

Source: United Nations, World Bank.

sustained than simple demand contraction would predict. There may be a secular shift away from the use of many materials in production (Larson, Ross, and Williams 1986) which could signal a long downward trend in poor countries' terms of trade.

3. An increase in foreign payment obligations for amortization and interest on outstanding debt, made especially acute by extremely high interest on floating rate debt since 1980. As discussed further in Section 4.3.1, related longer-term handicaps include a reduction in foreign aid and the revulsion of the private banking sector from loans to the Third World since 1982.

These three factors have played havoc with the current account deficits of the non-oil developing countries, which rose to around $100 billion in 1980–1, but fell back to $50 billion or less thereafter. On *trade* account, after interest and other factor payments are subtracted from the current deficit, poor countries were running a historically unprecedented surplus of $15 billion by 1984. These changes after 1982 are directly related to the slow growth rates shown in Table 4.3. We shall see below that a time-tested method to improve the external account is to reduce the internal level of economic activity— exactly what economies constrained by the non-availability of foreign exchange have done. They have also made extreme efforts to increase the exportability of their products and reduce import coefficients. As discussed further in Section 4.2.5, a study sponsored by the United Nations shows that in the period 1978–81/2, twelve of fourteen countries that suffered adverse external shocks pushed up their export market shares. Expressed as a ratio of the absolute dollar value increase to GNP, the mean (median) export improvement was 3.0 (2.9) per cent—a remarkable achievement (Helleiner 1986). Eight of the countries also reduced import ratios. However, there was a generalized reduction in gross capital formation in the sample countries after the second set of world-wide economic shocks in the late 1970s. Such a decrease in investment did not occur after the first oil shock in 1973, as the solid growth rates of the developing countries until 1980 testify. Further improvements in 'tradability' and adequate growth will be impossible unless the investment cuts are restored. The problem is that although the surest way to improve the current account by economic contraction is to limit import-intensive capital formation, a vicious circle appears: cutting investment to improve the current account in the short run makes potential foreign exchange shortfalls more severe in the future. Many economies are on this self-destructive treadmill.

4.2.2 External strangulation

It makes sense to trace through the processes of macroeconomic adjustment in more detail. There are characteristic patterns of short- and medium-run response, which can be modelled along the lines laid out in Sections 4.1.5 and

4.1.6. Scenarios for achieving demand–supply balance at the macro level are sketched here and in the following two sections. Longer-term issues are taken up below.

The simplest way to think of a shock to the balance of payments is as a transfer to or from a country. Whether flowing in or out, transfers create adjustment problems. We begin with the one prevalent at the moment: 'External strangulation' from combined adverse movements in the current and capital accounts.

The label was coined by the United Nations Economic Commission for Latin America in the 1960s to describe the state of economies in which growth and/or output is limited by a shortage of foreign exchange. The malady is widespread in the 1980s after the debt crisis and stagnation of foreign aid—finance ministers and central bankers must scramble for every penny. We shall now consider some of the symptoms of strangulation, on both the real and financial sides of the economy.

Suppose that the trade surplus t (measured per unit of home goods capital) is specified exogenously, say from a strict limit by bankers on the amounts that can be borrowed externally. Fixing t imposes a restriction on the macro-system—what variable adjusts? In practice, several possibilities arise.

One mode of adjustment is via inflation. Tight bounds on the use of foreign resources create bottlenecks and lead to inflationary pressures. If key inputs into non-traded sectors (energy sources for example) are restricted, then price increases may be triggered along the lines of Fig. 4.5 (below) at the same time as output is held down. If aggregate demand responds negatively to inflation, contraction will be so much the worse. A foreign resource inflow can ease the situation, as discussed by Taylor (1987a).

A second policy option is to cut back public or private consumption via fiscal spending reductions or tax increases. The level of output declines, reducing intermediate import requirements and improving the trade balance.

A third option is to sacrifice public investment. As discussed above, this move became more frequent as the external shocks for the developing world deepened over time. We can illustrate the implications in a one-sector model in which output, unless externally strangled, would adjust to the level of aggregate demand. If there is an external constraint, then state investment per unit of home goods capital (call it z) becomes an endogenous variable in the short run.

The simplest way to tell the story is by decomposing macro adjustment into a demand injection and a saving response. Components of the injection are public spending on current and capital account (the latter is z) and private investment. In line with accelerator theories or the model of Section 4.1.5, private capital formation is stimulated by higher capacity utilization u. Also, since questions of investment finance are important in the current context, we assume that a fraction $1 - \theta$ of capital goods must be imported. The rest (typically, the construction part of investment) is made in the home goods sector.

Saving comes from wage and profit incomes—its total is an increasing function of u. Exports, for present purposes, are best treated as a negative element of saving (consistent with the notion that an export surplus is equivalent to negative 'foreign saving'). Macro balance occurs when the injection and saving are equal, as shown in Fig. 4.4. If capacity utilization is the adjustment variable, the equilibrium will be stable when demand responds less strongly to increased capacity utilization than saving supply. This requirement is satisfied by the schedules in Fig. 4.4. The curves for total imports in the diagram show that a given import bill is made up of capital goods and intermediates to support production—if one component rises, the other must fall.

If there is no foreign trade constraint, output expansion in the model is driven in the direction of the arrows by increased demand from government current spending or capital formation. Capacity utilization increases along the saving schedule and total imports rise. If imports must be curtailed due to a foreign exchange bottleneck, the schedules shift the other way. Government investment turns into an endogenous variable, and its reduction permits the demand injection locus to shift downward. Along the lines of the classic two-gap paper by Chenery and Bruno (1962), one can show that $dj/dt < -1$—

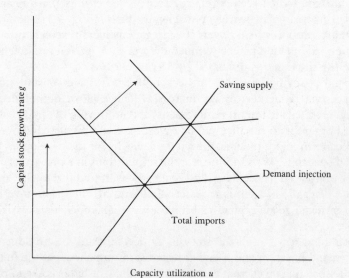

Fig. 4.4 Macro adjustment involving trade. A demand injection increases capacity utilization and the growth rate if total imports can increase. In another causal pattern, a cut in imports can force less demand by curtailing government capital formation (the schedules move opposite to the arrows)

that an increase in the trade surplus forces a greater than one-for-one reduction in government investment. The reason is that the import content of capital formation is the fraction $1 - \theta$. Cutting foreign resources forces investment to be cut by even more. (For the algebra see Taylor 1983 or Bacha 1984.)

On the financial side of the economy, the easiest analytical way to deal with external strangulation is to assume that $\hat{F}^\star$, the growth rate of the state's foreign obligations (assumed to dominate borrowing) is predetermined. Ignoring reserve changes, the trade surplus per unit of capital stock will be proportional to $i^\star - \hat{F}^\star$, where $i^\star$ is the interest rate on debt. For many developing countries in the 1980s $i^\star > \hat{F}^\star$, so that they have to run positive trade balances. Also, for a given government fiscal deficit, reduced foreign credit inflow forces state borrowing within the country to go up. This is the financial side of the transfer problem. To pay interest on foreign debt the country has to run a trade surplus. To 'finance' the external surplus, the government has to resort to extensive internal borrowing. Two exchanges enter the transfer, not just one.

To measure the full effects of the transfer, one also has to take macroeconomic adjustment into account. The fiscal deficit may not stay constant, for example. The argument in connection with Fig. 4.4 suggests that a higher trade surplus t makes government investment z decline more than one-for-one. Hence, a reduction in $\hat{F}^\star$ would make growth slow down enough to permit the internal public sector borrowing requirement to fall!

This conclusion perhaps shows that results from models should not be taken too literally. As noted above, what happens in the real world is that a binding trade constraint can be met by many devices: forced import substitution, reduction of inventories, policy changes such as imposition of quotas, even finding oil. All these moves plus reduced public capital formation help the economy reach a higher level of t, and all will have different implications for fiscal spending. The cut in investment is the one that will affect the borrowing requirement most. In the mid-1980s, countries like Korea and Brazil have pursued export promotion and import substitution so aggressively in the wake of the debt crisis that they seem to have a structural trade surplus. For such economies, finding sources of domestic borrowing to meet the excess of $i^\star$ over $\hat{F}^\star$ becomes a major issue. Elsewhere, less fortunate countries have cut government investment z so drastically that recourse to domestic credit is minimized. The real blessing for them would be faster growth of external debt (or lower interest rates), a reduction in their required trade surpluses, and the possibility to grow again.

4.2.3 Foreign exchange bonanzas

Given the dire straits of externally strangled countries, an ample supply of foreign exchange might be taken as a blessing. Regrettably, such may not be the case. Readily available foreign resources can lead to exchange appreciation and to declines in both export diversity and internal economic activity as competitive imports flood in. The phenomenon has been rediscovered by academics in recent years (it was first noted by the Australian economist J. E. Cairns in connection with that country's gold boom in the middle of the last century), and has given rise to a large literature on the 'Dutch disease'. Countries which borrowed massively in the 1970s were not immune to its effects.

The initial symptoms are easy to trace in Fig. 4.4. Import capacity shifts outward, and a corresponding demand injection is not difficult to (over-) achieve. Capacity utilization and the growth rate will initially rise. However, resource limitations may begin to bind. One common bottle-neck centres around goods whose supply within the country cannot easily be supplemented by imports—non-tradables and semi-tradables.

We can illustrate the problem using a model like the one in Section 4.1.6. Assume that imported intermediate inputs to domestic industry are limited in supply (say, by a quota) or are unavailable. Supply of domestically produced intermediates rises with their price P_j, but the curve may be shifted by wage

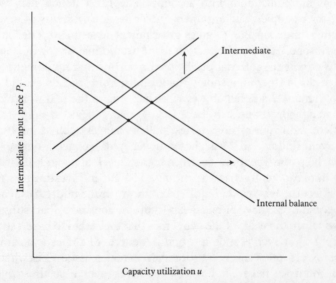

Fig. 4.5 Demand pressure against a non-traded intermediate good. An outward shift of the internal balance locus from extra demand leads to a higher intermediate price, with the increase being greater the more inelastic is the supply of the intermediate good and the steeper is the corresponding schedule. The upward shift of the intermediate locus could result from difficulty in obtaining required imported inputs when there is external strangulation. A higher intermediate price and potential inflation are the outcomes

increases or shortage of essential imported inputs. Comparative statics are in Fig. 4.5 where the slopes of the schedules have the same rationales as in Fig. 4.3.

As mentioned in the last section, lack of essential imports can squeeze home goods supply, shifting the intermediate locus upward. The price P_j rises (perhaps setting off inflation, as discussed shortly), and activity drops off. A foreign exchange bonanza has different effects. Not all the extra dollars can be spent abroad, and demand for nationally produced goods will rise. The internal balance schedule shifts outward, and P_j goes up. The higher cost of the intermediate good is passed along into final goods prices, and the real wage falls.

Both the upward shift of the intermediate locus (from strangulation) and the rightward shift of the internal balance locus (from a bonanza) are inflationary. The reason is that the reduced real wage just noted is likely to feed into an inflation from conflicting claims. With their real purchasing power cut back, workers bid up money wages. These are passed through a mark-up into higher prices, and a spiral can be set off. It will be more acute if the economy is highly inflation-indexed, as many developing countries were in the 1970s. The inflation will also be worse when increasing intermediate goods supply is difficult because investment projects of great size and/or long gestation are required.

If inflation were the only problem caused by the bonanza, it would be tolerable. However, there is often little incentive to devalue or adopt a crawling peg; after all, foreign exchange appears not to be a problem. The outcome is real appreciation. At best, lagging exports and reverse import substitution may result; at worst, unstable dynamic processes like the one illustrated in Fig. 4.7 below can be set off, imperiling prospects for growth in the medium run. Unless sensible policy measures like promotion of non-traditional exports, import controls, and sterilization of some part of the 'free' foreign inflows are pursued, outcomes can after a time be painful—especially after the bonanza ebbs. Wealth is a blessing, but one has to ponder how to use it well.

4.2.4 Opening capital markets

Just as current account liberalization can lead to unfavourable short-run developments, liberalizing capital controls can also be destabilizing. The effects may be insidious, since they initially look beneficial but can lead to near disaster in the medium run.

Experiments in the Southern Cone of South America in the late 1970s combined open capital markets with a slower rate of exchange depreciation meant to reduce 'inflationary expectations'. The unhappy story of resulting financial instability has been recounted by Diaz-Alejandro (1981) and Frenkel (1983); the model sketched here roughly follows Frenkel's.

Assume that nationals hold three assets—loans to domestic firms which carry an interest rate i; bank deposits at zero interest; and foreign assets with a return of $i^\star + \hat{e}\ (= R)$ where $i^\star$ is the world interest rate and $\hat{e}$ is the pre-announced rate of nominal exchange depreciation. In the financial market, a credible reduction in $\hat{e}$ switches asset demand from foreign holdings to deposits. Hence, the interest rate must rise to maintain the level of loans to firms. However, there are strong general equilibrium off-sets, as illustrated in Fig. 4.6. In that diagram, which relates i with foreign holdings $Y^\star$, the interest rate schedule slopes upward since an increase in $Y^\star$ represents a capital outflow. It must be met by a reduction in bank reserves and tighter domestic credit. In the foreign asset market, an increase in i makes holdings abroad less attractive, and $Y^\star$ declines along the corresponding curve.

Now consider a decrease in R, the foreign return. There are portfolio substitution and asset composition effects of opposite sign. As noted above, lower foreign returns tend to increase the cost of credit to firms, in a substitution response (the interest rate locus shifts upward). Second, asset portfolios shift away from holdings abroad. The resulting capital inflow adds to the stock of bank reserves. The money supply rises, and i declines in a leftward shift of the foreign asset schedule. The latter adjustment is more important in Fig. 4.6, and in practice.

The conclusion is that, other factors being equal, a slower crawl in liberalized capital markets may be associated with reduced interest rates and

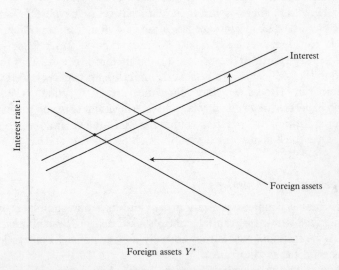

Fig. 4.6 Adjustment in asset markets to a fall in the return to holding foreign assets induced by a slower rate of exchange depreciation. A substitution response would tend to increase domestic interest rates. However, bank foreign reserves increase as the public trades in foreign currency, the money supply expands, and interest rates can fall

economic expansion; faster nominal depreciation could cause desired portfolios to shift toward foreign holdings, draining reserves and creating tighter money. The other factors will of course include the state of confidence in the regime, with political and economic uncertainty leading to capital flight.

Diaz-Alejandro (1981) makes clear that in the Southern Cone the initial slow-down of the crawling peg brought foreign exchange euphoria to the region. Reducing the return to foreign assets stimulated the domestic economy, making foreign holdings less attractive still. There was positive feedback of the initial reduction of the return to holding foreign assets into itself—a classic symptom of financial instability.

A model is easy to set up in terms of changes in the foreign asset return R and the economy's total foreign assets $\mathcal{J}^\star$ ($= Y^\star +$ bank foreign exchange reserves $R^\star$). Consider how the rate of increase R and $\mathcal{J}^\star$ respond to changes in the levels of the two variables:

$\delta\dot{R}/\delta R > 0$:   An initial downward jump in R from slowing the crawl increases visible national reserves $R^\star$, cuts interest rates and stimulates growth. National assets look even more attractive and R falls more, making the partial derivative positive.

$\delta\dot{R}/\delta\mathcal{J}^\star < 0$:   Higher foreign assets from any source also make R fall.

$\delta\dot{\mathcal{J}}^\star/\delta R < 0$:   An increase in R pulls the public towards foreign holdings, reducing domestic activity by driving up interest rates and increasing the trade surplus. The country's total foreign claims rise, or $\dot{\mathcal{J}}^\star$ goes up.

$\delta\dot{\mathcal{J}}^\star/\delta\mathcal{J}^\star < 0$:   Higher foreign assets lead to more reserves $R^\star$ and monetary expansion. The trade balance worsens so that $\dot{\mathcal{J}}^\star < 0$.

The positive own-derivative $\delta\dot{R}/\delta R$ can underlie a crisis linking the financial and real sides of the economy, along the historical–institutional lines set out by Minsky (1982) and Kindleberger (1978), and in a model by Taylor and O'Connell (1985). A phase diagram appears in Fig. 4.7, where potential instability is signalled by the fact that R goes up (or down) when it is already above (or below) that return locus along with $\dot{R} = 0$. Slowing a crawling peg makes R jump down from an initial steady stage. Foreign assets $\mathcal{J}^\star$ begin to fall immediately from a reduced trade surplus due to higher activity. However, R continues to decline for a time until the drop in $\mathcal{J}^\star$ (signalled by a widening trade deficit and over-expansion at home) begins to frighten investors. The return to foreign assets begins to rise as the trajectory crosses the return schedule. The central bank starts losing reserves, reversing the process in Fig. 4.7. The likely outcome is national economic stagnation before foreign asset stocks start to rebuild through a trade surplus. In

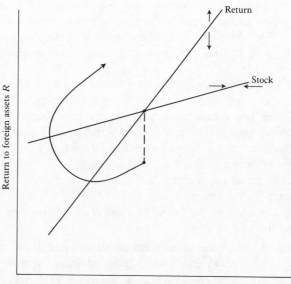

Fig. 4.7 Potentially unstable dynamics of the return to foreign assets. An initial downward jump from a slower crawl sets up a process with declining asset stocks from an increased trade gap and (after a period of decrease) a rise in the return. The outcomes are capital flight, decreased foreign reserves in the banking system, and domestic stagnation.

practice, the agony is often cut short (or made more acute) by a maxi-devaluation before the trajectory reaches the stock schedule along which $\dot{J}^\star$ equals zero. At that point, speculators are rewarded and currency may start to flow home.

This sad story repeats itself with some frequency in the Third World. There is no certain way to avoid its repetition as long as attractive asset markets exist abroad. However, controls on capital movements can temper destabilizing flows while a sensible crawling peg policy helps keep foreign and domestic asset returns (not to mention profits for exporters or import substituters) stable relative to each other over time. Steady asset market signals reduce the likelihood of the unstable dynamics of Fig. 4.7. Opening capital markets and dramatically altering returns—the recipe applied by Southern Cone monetarists of the 1970s—may make instability much more likely. Also, exchange controls are difficult to re-establish, once dismantled. Attempts to set up controls are underway in all countries that suffered capital flight, but their successful imposition will take a long time. The wealthy scan accustomed financial horizons in making portfolio choice. Once they start looking abroad, it may take years of good returns and barriers to capital outflow to make them shift their gaze largely towards domestic assets.

4.2.5 Strangulation and openness

Macro adjustment to balance of payments shocks in the developing world combines elements of external strangulation and foreign exchange bonanzas with instabilities rooted in open capital markets. Recounting the histories of scores of countries to back up this generalization is impossible here, but on the other hand we can use the models to throw light on the recent past.

Countries subject to bonanzas and capital market instabilities were in the minority, so we take them up below. Regarding strangulation, several recent studies use a broadly similar methodology of 'differentiating the balance of payments' to try to quantify its causes and effects. In line with the discussion in Section 4.2.1, the sources of balance of payments deterioration usually emphasized are foreign interest rate increases, adverse shifts in terms of trade, and the slow-down in world trade that occurred over the late 1970s and early 1980s.

The responses of afflicted countries can be decomposed in terms of Fig. 4.4. Reductions in consumption and investment shift the demand injection schedule downward, export increases shift saving supply downward and permit total imports to rise, and import substitution permits a lower total import level for given capacity utilization and growth. None of the studies fully link external shocks with macro adjustment as in Fig. 4.4, but implicitly that is their goal.

Table 4.4 presents the results of one decomposition exercise, reported by Helleiner (1986) and with methodology due to Edmar Bacha. The numbers are percentage shares of actual GNP; adverse shocks are positive and responses which offset the shock are negative. Thus, Chile had an external shock of 16.3 per cent of GNP in 1973–8. It further worsened its balance of payments 0.5 per cent by increasing investment, improved it 2.9 per cent by cutting consumption, and so on. To Helleiner's results we have added a further breakdown of countries by whether their overall policy was 'inward-oriented' or 'outward-oriented'. As already noted in Section 4.1.2, such classifications are treacherous. None the less they are widely discussed, and for this reason I include one. The policy orientation split is based on Balassa (1985b) as supplemented by Balassa and McCarthy (1984) and personal judgement, and is allegedly relevant for the mid-1970s. It also bears noting that the countries in the table are mostly middle-income and fairly large; data that would permit for the smaller, poorer countries that were probably more severely affected by external events were simply not available.

The first point that stands out in the numbers is that to restrain import demand countries increasingly cut back investment in 1978–82 as opposed to 1973–8; the potentially unfavourable effects on future growth have already been noted in Section 4.2.1.

Second, most countries in the sample at least partially offset the shocks by

Table 4.4 Responses to external shocks as shares of GNP

	1973–8					1978–82				
		Domestic contraction		Trade improvement			Domestic contraction		Trade improvement	
Country	Shock	Investment	Consumption	Exports	Imports	Shock	Investment	Consumption	Exports	Imports
Outward-oriented										
Chile	16.3	0.5	-2.9	-9.3	2.1	3.8	-1.3	1.7	-5.0	2.6
Costa Rica	-2.8					-14.1				
Indonesia	-6.8									
Korea	8.2	3.4	-2.6	-19.8	11.4	9.2	-2.2	0.7	-7.2	-0.2
Pakistan	3.1	-0.2	0.2	2.4	0.9	7.6	-0.1	-0.1	-2.9	-2.3
Sri Lanka	-3.0					65.9	5.7	-10.1	-11.4	-42.1
Thailand	10.6	0.8	-1.4	-4.4	-3.2	9.5	-1.7	0.4	-8.8	-3.2
Uruguay	11.3	1.6	-2.4	-6.8	1.0	0.7	0.2	0.1	-2.0	2.3
Inward-oriented										
Argentina	1.9	0.1	-0.4	-2.5	0.2	-0.9	-0.4	-0.0	-1.7	-1.1
Brazil	1.2	-0.2	0.4	0.5	-1.5	4.4	0.6	0.1	1.8	0.8
Colombia	-0.9					3.7				
Dominican Republic	5.5	0.3	0.2	-0.2	1.2	4.6	-1.0	1.1	-0.8	-4.5
Egypt	14.9	1.8	-4.0	-5.0	2.1	-0.9				
India	1.4	0.1	-0.2	-1.5	-0.1	1.5	0.0	0.1	-0.8	2.4
Ivory Coast	-3.7									
Mexico	0.2	0.1	-0.1	-1.0	0.2	-0.9				
Morocco	4.4	1.6	0.6	4.8	1.3					
Peru	3.2	-1.1	-0.1	-1.7	-6.5	-1.6				
Philippines	7.3	1.7	-0.8	-0.1	1.3	4.8	-0.3	0.2	-2.9	0.2
Sudan	3.8	0.5	1.2	5.0	-2.4	-1.3				
Tanzania	-3.6					8.9	0.4	-2.6	-5.4	-5.2
Turkey	3.0	0.5	-0.4	1.8	-3.7	4.7	-0.5	0.2	-3.6	1.4
Venezuela	-11.7					-13.2				
Zaire	5.8	-2.5	-6.9	11.2	-12.5					
Zambia	29.9	-6.1	2.0	5.0	-12.9	10.0	-6.3	8.7	8.6	-14.2

Sources: Decompositions of shocks from Helleiner 1986; country classification based on Balassa 1985a and Balassa and McCarthy 1984.

Table 4.5 Summary of responses to external shocks by policy orientation

| | 1973–8 | | | | | 1978–82 | | | | |
| | | Domestic contraction | | Trade improvement | | | Domestic contraction | | Trade improvement | |
	Shock	Investment	Consumption	Exports	Imports	Shock	Investment	Consumption	Exports	Imports
Outward-oriented										
Mean	9.9	1.2	-1.8	-7.6	2.4	16.1	0.1	-1.2	-6.2	-7.1
Median	10.6	0.8	-2.4	-6.8	1.0	9.3	-0.7	0.2	-6.1	-1.1
Inward-oriented										
Mean	6.3	-0.0	-1.0	1.3	-2.6	4.7	-0.9	1.0	-0.6	-2.5
Median	3.8	0.1	-0.1	-0.1	0.2	4.7	-0.4	0.2	-0.8	-0.5

Source: Table 4.4 summary relates to five outward-oriented countries in 1973–8 and six in 1978–2; and to thirteen inward-oriented countries in 1973–8 and eight in 1978–82.

improving their trade performance, raising export penetration in world markets and/or cutting import shares in GNP. Very broadly speaking, trade improvements outweighed domestic contraction as the main adjustment mechanism for both groups of countries, especially in the latter period.

Third, as can be seen from the adjustment data for the two groups presented in summary form in Table 4.5, shocks were greater as a share of GNP in the outward-oriented group, perhaps not surprising in so far as their initial trade shares were higher (presumably this was one of Balassa's criteria for classification). The improvement in trade relative to the improvement to GNP was also higher than those of the inward-oriented group. However, if one considers ratios of trade improvements to shocks, the outward-oriented countries were *not* substantially more successful in promoting trade. Their record on maintaining investment demand was not better either, when one discounts Sri Lanka's success in keeping the externally financed Mahaveli irrigation project underway during the latter period. We have already seen in Section 4.1.2 that presence or absence of trade distortions does not influence growth. The results in Table 4.5 further suggest that outward orientation (which is at least highly correlated with absence of distortions in the eyes of the orthodox) is no buffer against external shocks. Relative to GNP, the shocks themselves may be greater; relative to the size of the shock, trade improvement may be no stronger with an outwardly than an inwardly oriented policy stance. This point is developed more fully in terms of the historical experience of specific countries by Alan Hughes and Ajit Singh in Chapter 3 of this volume.

Finally, it bears repeating that the large economies are over-represented in Table 4.4. The only countries with populations markedly less than the convenient cut-off point of 20 million are Chile, Costa Rica, Dominican Republic, Ivory Coast, Peru, Sri Lanka, Uruguay, Venezuela, and Zambia. Their external shocks were large relative to GNP, reflecting the difficulties inherent in a small economy's unavoidable openness when the external environment turns harsh.

4.2.6 Further aspects of adjustment

Beyond countries' efforts to deal with acute foreign exchange shortages, several other aspects of the adjustment process are worth noting.

First, the major debtors in some ways enjoyed a foreign exchange bonanza, and reacted as the model of Section 4.2.3 predicts. They enjoyed rapid, debt-led growth associated with exchange rate appreciation, and faced a difficult readjustment process in the 1980s. Before even their versatile economies recovered, major debtors like Korea and Brazil had spells of slow growth.

Second, the adjustment was more difficult for large debtors with open capital markets. They suffered capital flights of billions of dollars—Mexico lost $26.5 billion, Venezuela $22 billion, and Argentina $19.2 billion, according to the World Bank's 1985 *World Development Report*. By contrast, exchange losses in Brazil, Colombia, and Korea, which have traditionally maintained functioning (if imperfect) controls on the capital market, were far smaller. For the open countries, the dynamic sequence is roughly described by Fig. 4.7—euphoria and capital inflows in the 1970s followed by massive outflows thereafter.

Third, as Hughes and Singh point out in Chapter 3, India and China have traditionally followed conservative foreign borrowing practices; China also had massive reserves until it started dabbling with import-led growth in 1984 and 1985. Both giant nations rode out the crises well. South-East Asian countries on the whole borrowed more prudently than did those of Latin America, and this aspect of not being completely open made their position in the 1980s less difficult.

Finally, with regard to inflation, fifteen of twenty-six economies receiving adverse shocks in 1979–82 saw their inflations accelerate; eight had rates which stayed essentially stable (within a range of 2 per cent per year), and three experienced declines (Balassa and McCarthy 1984). Though the period was one of inflation world-wide, the accelerations in many cases were large, suggesting that the mechanisms discussed in Section 4.2.2 were at work. Favourable external shocks were associated with faster inflation in three of five countries, including Mexico which had a classic bonanza.

4.3 CAPITAL MARKETS AND DEBT

Openness in capital markets was intimately related to the exponential growth of foreign debt in many developing countries before 1982. This section briefly takes up the implications of this unfortunate past for country policy in future years.

Three stylized observations about the debt accumulation process are worth making at the outset:

1. The share of debt from public sources in GNP declined for many middle-income countries (especially in Latin America) that 'graduated' from foreign assistance programs in the 1970s. However, in smaller, poorer countries, obligations to foreign, public creditors rose sharply. A hidden feature of the debt crisis is that many of the poorest countries of the world have extremely high obligations (as shares of GNP and of exports) to both public and private creditors. Some of the major recipients of public loans are in Asia and the Western hemisphere, but in the 1970s the African countries rapidly caught up. Their situation became more difficult in the 1980s, as overseas development assistance and other official credits stagnated in current dollars and fell in real terms. According to World Bank data, overseas development assistance from OECD countries and other official capital flows

in *current* dollars were 1980, \$32.6 billion; 1981, 32.1; 1982, 35.1; 1983, 32.5; 1984, 32.2. Flows from OPEC countries fell from \$9.7 billion in 1980 to \$5.8 billion in 1982 to \$3.3 billion in 1987. This slow-down in foreign aid efforts marked a significant reversal in a trend of growth that began in the 1950s.

2. Debt from private sources increased rapidly for most countries. The South Asian region lagged in this process, but the ratio of private credit to GNP rose sharply elsewhere, especially in Africa and the Latin American–Caribbean zone. Ratios of private debt to GNP or exports are higher for many smaller countries than for the major debtors (Brazil, Mexico, Korea, etc.). The same is true of interest obligations, since all developing economies pay floating, current interest rates on the bulk of their private debt.

3. These observations suggest that countries which borrowed heavily from private sources fall broadly into two groups. At one extreme, some small, open economies took enough credit to raise their debt–GNP ratios by large increments. Such increases are especially notable in African and Western hemisphere countries hit hard by external shocks. For most of the poorer economies, recourse to foreign debt is best seen as an attempt to cushion the decade's adverse developments in trade.

Larger borrowers in absolute magnitude had smaller increases in their private debt shares of GNP. One can argue that their borrowing was of a more discretionary nature as well: they were offered large loans, and chose to take them. Some of the larger Asian economies and a few from Africa either were more prudent or did not get as much access to Eurodollar credits. They started out with lower private debt ratios and increased them less.

Without losing sight of these problems, it makes sense to place the debt issue of the 1980s against a long-term bcakground, to enquire whether secular or merely conjectural forces underlay the crisis that began in 1982. The natural time of reference is the 'long' nineteenth century that culminated in the First World War. During that period, foreign capital flows originated largely in Britain, France, and (later) Germany. Developed economies were the major debtors, with annual inflows ranging up to 10 per cent of GNP, and one-half of capital formation in peak years in Canada, Australia, and the Scandinavian countries. Poorer nations, many still colonies, also received some international investment. By 1914, Latin American, African, and Asian countries accounted for 43 per cent of outstanding foreign capital (Kuznets 1966).

Flows diminished drastically in the decades between the wars, including the depression years. In 1913 prices, international capital movements in the early 1900s were on the order of a billion dollars per year. On average, annual flows dropped to \$100–200 million between 1920 and 1940, and then recovered to about \$3 billion (\$7 billion in current dollars) in the late 1950s. By that time the United States had emerged as the major creditor.

There were also changes in forms of finance. In the nineteenth century, long-term bonds originating in London and Paris were the chosen vehicle. Private bondholders predominated, and the issues were usually tied to investment projects in recipient countries—to this day, trolley-cars in Rio de Janeiro are called *bondis* in honor of a long-forgotten British loan. After 1945 there was a shift toward direct foreign investment and (especially) official donations and loans, which accounted for over one-half of annual flows in the late 1950s.

The process of bond finance was by no means tranquil. Numerous scholars have detected cycles of capital flows to different parts of the world, with a time period of decades. For example, Kindleberger (1985) observes that 'the bond market experienced spurts of lending—for Latin America in the 1820s, the United States in the 1830s, for Latin America again in the 1850s, Canada from 1900 to 1913, Latin America and Australia (plus Germany) in the 1920s—but . . . foreign lending to a particular area died away between spurts . . . it is perhaps fair to say that after a boom in lending to LDCs followed by default, *European capital markets lost interest for roughly 30 years before lending again* (emphasis mine).

If the historical patterns holds, the current 'revulsion' from bank-mediated private lending to developing economies may persist for a decade or so before credit flows begin another upswing (though of course individual countries may get access to capital markets in the meantime—again consistent with historical experience). The situation is also more complex than in the nineteenth century because syndicated Eurocurrency (predominantly Euro-dollar) credits bear floating as opposed to fixed interest rates. Specifically, the London Interbank Offered Rate, or LIBOR, rules the developing country market for loans. After a spell of being low or negative in the middle of the decade, real interest rates rose sharply after 1979. How much of the increase was due to restrictive OECD monetary policy and how much to revulsion is not clear. If revulsion was the key factor, the shrinkage of loans in the 1980s bodes ill for developing country borrowing for the rest of this century.

4.3.2 The infeasible transfer

As the situation stands now, poor countries are making net transfers to the North by running trade surpluses to pay interest and retire some small portion of their obligations. Proposals beyond number for changing this situation have been floated, but not one has been put into practice beyond 'muddling through'. The policy stasis seems unlikely to budge. On the other hand, many feel that large transfers from the poor countries will not persist. If they do, two conditions must be satisfied.

First, the South must agree to divert $50–60 billion Northward on a permanent basis to meet interest obligations alone; the North must accept strong currencies *vis-à-vis* the South and deindustrializing payments deficits.

Neither action is politically attractive. Second, the fiscal–financial counter-parts to the permanent transfer would involve internal fiscal surpluses in the South, deficits in the North, and secure international price relationships to allow the payments to be made. Again, stability of such arrangements is not in the cards.

If flow transfers break down, what other options are available? Historically, large outstanding obligations between countries have in many cases not been met. Debt has been liquidated in four ways. The first is by financial recycling (Kindleberger 1984). Examples are the Thiers *rente* and the Dawes–Young plans for recycling reparations payments after the Franco-Prussian War and the First World War, respectively. New financial vehicles have been proposed along these lines, but without enough detail about what sources of new credit may be tapped to refinance developing-country paper. The seemingly permanent Japanese and German trade surpluses are one possibility (Okita, Jayawardena, and Sengupta 1986), but how channels would be cleared to direct them toward developing countries is not apparent.

The three remaining options are: repudiation (broadly construed along the lines laid out in Section 4.3.3); inflation of the currency in which the debt is denominated; and overall cancellation of obligations in the aftermath of war. All hope desperately that the last alternative will not arise. Discreetly veiled repudiation appears to be underway, and as the United States swings into a net debtor position it will find exchange depreciation and inflation with appropriately controlled interest rates to be increasingly appealing options. With their dollar-denominated obligations, LDCs would gain from an American inflationary gambit. The dislocations of wealth and income flows that all these possibilities present will become acute unless the world economic scenario is extremely favourable or serious steps are taken toward recycling. Meanwhile, poor countries would be well advised to postpone payments and concentrate on internally oriented development at the national or regional level. Otherwise they may find it impossible to maintain any sort of acceptable growth between now and the century's end.

4.3.3 Debt management at the country level

It is not obvious what a country faced with large external liabilities is supposed to do. Its overall debt burden may be on the order of 10–20 per cent of GDP. At 10 per cent interest, the required transfers abroad, disregarding amortization, are 1–2 per cent of GDP. These figures should be compared to the commodity trade data for developing countries in Table 4.1. Typical trade *deficits* there are 10 per cent of GDP, yet meeting debt obligations in the absence of other resource inflows calls for trade surpluses. The obvious question is whether resources will flow to developing countries to enable them on paper to roll over their liabilities. If not—if interest and repayment obligations really bind—can they achieve the degree of resource reallocation required to pay? Recall from Section 4.2.2 that at least two major allocational shifts are involved—a trade surplus has to be arranged, and an internal transfer from the private to public sectors has to be organized to permit the latter to meet its sovereign debts.

As just argued, a sensible view is that poor nations will not meet their payments on debt in the absence of new transfers from the industrialized world. The trade pattern for the past 200 years has involved deficits for poor countries and surpluses for rich. This rule seems unlikely to break down, but if it does not the debt will not be paid. The mutual obligations of debtors and creditors are, after all, nothing but a set of conventions, functional only so long as both parties choose to stay in the game. In the present conjuncture, the conventions can readily fail. Standard economic theory is useless under the circumstances, since it is designed to deal with anything but abnormal events. On common-sense grounds, however, a half-dozen points can be raised for policy consideration at the national level.

First, debt repudiation is obviously an option. The term can be applied, albeit imprecisely, to several kinds of policy moves. Partial repayment of some obligations (possibly with magnitudes linked to export receipts, etc.) is one example. The repayments could be varied by type of creditor—public or private, short-term or long-term. Costs and benefits differ with the various options.

Second, regarding short-term debt, the usual view is that it is largely used for trade finance. When its imports and exports are large relative to GNP, a country may be loath to repudiate foreign debt if this would cut off trade credits. A highly neoclassical counter-argument can be mounted on reasoning like that underlying the Coase (1960) theorem: if there is money to be made from trade and its finance, someone (probably from Switzerland) will provide the required services. The experience of South Africa and (then) Rhodesia under trade sanctions suggests the argument has force. Even North Korea—a socialist country that defaulted long ago and refuses to come to terms with bankers—seems to find trading relationships tolerable on the basis of cash. More recently, Peru has opted not to meet full obligations on its long-term debt but meets short-term obligations scrupulously. The country's trade credits have not dried up.

Third, regarding type of creditor, the obvious question is what future benefits may be forthcoming from each one. Cross-default clauses apply to loans from private banks—if one syndicated Eurocurrency credit goes into default, the others are called as well. This institutional fact leads countries to deal with banks as a group; outcomes in the mid-1980s were a few 'multi-year rescheduling agreements' at not very favourable terms. The International Monetary Fund and (to a lesser extent) the World Bank acted as interlocutors in the negotiations. There seems no pressing institutional need for them to continue do so, as countries and groups of banks become more familiar with dealing directly. Indeed, given their current policy biases, the absence of the Bank and Fund in these discussions might further a poor country's cause.

Fourth, IMF and World Bank loans involve conditionality—demand contraction of the usual monetarist variety applied by the Fund and exhortations by the Bank to get prices right. Historically, acceptance of Fund conditionality has been a 'seal of approval' to get loans from commercial banks. However, if new private bank credits are unlikely to materialize (the revulsion thesis developed above), then the Fund's approval is not useful; its own loans are not very large. Hence, more independently minded developing countries may find it convenient not to deal with the Fund (nor repay what they owe it?) while they strike their own deals with private banks. The resources provided by the World Bank are massive—one can put up with the attached preaching if the institution lets its funds go to useful purposes. Also, the bank has historically not been averse to rolling over delinquent credits in cases of need.

Fifth, since developing country loans trade among private banks at discount, the banks themselves do not anticipate complete repayment. What has not yet occurred are explicit write-downs of LDC loans, in part because of difficulties created by American regulatory practices. Changes of the relevant legislation on the side of the United States would be helpful, and might ease the recognition that few developing countries are in a position to pay full value on their debt in the foreseeable future. Otherwise, partial repayment schemes à la Peru, large build-ups of arrears as in the case of many African nations, and other modes of not meeting foreign obligations will continue to spread.

Sixth, debt from public sources is often renegotiated at international gatherings, e.g. loan consortia for specific countries or sessions of the Paris Club. For a specific country, meeting its official obligations will bring benefits if new money is likely to be forthcoming. Small, poor countries probably have no choice but to pay: richer ones which have 'graduated' from the aid process have every incentive to string the proceedings along forever.

The gist of the above arguments is that in the mid-1980s it makes sense for poor countries to take a careful look at what they gain from meeting all the burden of their debts. The trend seems to be towards operating on the basis that they do not necessarily have all to be paid. How such a choice would affect the global macro system is of course a relevant question, but the answers are extremely obscure.

4.4 MORALS FOR POLICY LINES

To begin with global macroeconomic analysis, it seems clear from Section 4.2 that a medium-term foreign trade stimulus to developing country growth from OECD expansion and changes in other variables such as interest rates and the dollar exchange is a chancy prospect. Nor are capital flows likely to surge if a revulsion on the part of rentiers from LDC lending is occurring, as argued in Section 4.3.1. Finally, the arguments of Sections 4.1 and 4.2 suggest that there were no great benefits (plus some loss) in following open trade and capital market strategies in developing countries, even in the retrospectively well-favoured decades of the 1960s and 1970s. What does all this say about policy prospects in the future?

The obvious moral is that development strategies oriented internally may be a wise choice towards the century's end. However, such a path is not easy to follow. Arranging appropriate sectoral policies is difficult at the abstract level, as Section 4.1.5 shows, and even harder in practice. Nor are short-run and long-run implications of policy moves of similar magnitude, let alone direction (Section 4.1.6). When problems of implementation in a typical developing country are factored into the equation, one may despair of any action except 'hands off'. None the less, bearing in mind the failures of extreme liberalization attempts in recent years, the inwardly oriented resource allocation strategy seems the least risky, especially for large countries.

As far as capital account transactions are concerned, historical experience provides justification for limitations—inevitably imperfect but none the less of some impact—on private capital movements (Section 2.4). Regarding sovereign debt, the best guess is that in the long run it will not be paid. Some points applicable to countries attempting to put a cap on the burden are set out in Section 4.3.3. Pending an inevitable global solution—recycling, inflation, or cancellation—veiled repudiation seems to be the order of the day. Repayment by a continual transfer from South to North of around a $100 billion dollars per year is not on the cards, but on the 'revulsion' hypothesis, neither are major flows the other way in the next decade or so. We are driven on capital account towards a situation of relatively balanced trade and inwardly oriented strategy.

The key question is, what does 'inwardly' mean? For India and China—large, closed economies—the issue is almost academic. In a smaller nation, more openness becomes inevitable. The constraint may bind at a population of (say) 20 million—surely no less. Integration of the myriad small countries of the South into regional systems (as opposed to global exploitation) becomes a vital issue. South–South trade may provide some help, but it is not likely to be a complete solution. The main losers from a less dynamic global system in the late 1980s and 1990s will be the small, poor economies. Finding ways to ease their plight may be a major international problem.

APPENDIX:
TRADE POLICY AND GROWTH

As discussed in the text, there is no reason to argue for liberalizing trade policy in the sense of providing equal incentives for all production activities when growth and income distribution are major economic objectives. Rather, trade and industrial strategy should be designed to fit the structure and institutions of the economy at hand. A simple Kaleckian model is laid out here to illustrate these points. The specification follows Boutros-Ghali 1980, and conclusions similar to the ones here are derived in a more neoclassical framework in Buffie 1986.

There are three sectors: home goods, an industry producing intermediate inputs in competition with imports, and exports. Each sector has fixed capital stock (or production capacity) in the short run, and an independent investment demand. We assume excess capacity and mark-up pricing in the home goods and intermediate input sectors, while exports use all that sector's available capital stock. The main thrust of our dynamic results will go through under alternative specifications.

The home goods output level is X, with price P_x given by

$$P_x = (1 + \tau_x)(wb_x + \tilde{P}_j a), \tag{A.1}$$

where τ_x is the mark-up rate (assumed constant), w is the wage, b_x is the X-sector's labour–output ratio, and a is the input–output coefficient for intermediates. The price $\tilde{P}_j$ is for an aggregate intermediate product made up of domestically produced and imported goods. Details on its composition appear shortly.

Let K_x be the home goods capital stock. In line with the North–South trade models discussed in the text, we assume (without much loss of generality) that all capital goods must be imported. The sector's profit rate r_x is given by mark-up income divided by the value of the capital stock, or

$$r_x = \frac{\tau_x (wb_x + \tilde{P}_j a) X}{eP_k^\star K_x} = \frac{\tau_x}{1 + \tau_x} \frac{P_x}{eP_k^\star} u_x. \tag{A.2}$$

In the denominator after the first equality, e is the nominal exchange rate and $P_k^\star$ is the world price of capital goods (assumed to be importable tariff-free). After the second equality, u_x stands for the output–capital ratio (or 'capacity utilization') X/K_x. The ratio $\tau_x/(1 + \tau_x)$ is easily shown to be the share of mark-up income in output; the profit rate is the profit share times the output–capital ratio (scaled by the home goods/capital goods relative price). Profit rates like r_x influence sectoral investment demands and the steady state growth rate in our dynamic specification. We show how r_x is determined after discussing the other sectors.

Intermediate inputs come either from domestic industry at price P_j or from imports at price $e(1 + \sigma)P_j^\star$, where $P_j^\star$ is the world price and σ is the tariff for such goods. Domestic and imported intermediates are assumed to be imperfect substitutes. The usual way of describing such a situation is to let the two sorts of goods combine to form an aggregate product $\tilde{j}$ which is demanded by the home goods sector according to the rule $\tilde{j} = aX$. If imports and national goods trade off to form $\tilde{j}$ with a constant elasticity of substitution (the production function is CES), then its price $\tilde{P}_j$ will also be a CES function of the input prices

$$\tilde{P}_j = \tilde{P}_j \left[P_j, e \left(1 + \sigma \right) P_j^\star \right]. \tag{A.3}$$

Explicit functional forms for aggregates like $\tilde{y}$ and $\tilde{P}_j$ are readily available in the literature (e.g. Taylor 1979: app. D).

Demand levels for domestic and imported intermediates ($\tilde{y}$ and M, respectively) are given by the equations

$$\tilde{y} = \alpha_j \left(P_j / \tilde{P}_j \right) a X \tag{A.4}$$

and

$$M = \alpha_m \left[e \left(1 + \sigma \right) P_j^\star / \tilde{P}_j \right] a X, \tag{A.5}$$

where the input coefficients α_j and α_m decline as their arguments (or relative cost ratios) rise. For example, a higher tariff σ will increase the aggregate $\tilde{P}_j$ from (A.3), but less than proportionately. The cost ratio in (A.5) will go up, while the one in (A.4) will decline. Hence, α_m will fall and α_j will rise as import substitution occurs. Since $\tilde{P}_j$ rises, the cost of production of home goods goes up, and so does the output price P_x, from (A.1). The overall cost decomposition for intermediates can be written as

$$\tilde{P}_j = P_j \alpha_j + e \left(1 + \sigma \right) P_j^\star \alpha_m, \tag{A.6}$$

an expression that will be useful below.

As with home goods, we assume that pricing in the intermediate sector follows a mark-up rule

$$P_j = \left(1 + \tau_j \right) w b_j, \tag{A.7}$$

where τ_j is the mark-up rate and b_j the sector's labour–output ratio (it uses no intermediates itself). For the most part we assume a constant mark-up or horizontal supply curve for intermediates, though the effects on growth of a rising supply curve are taken up below. After some manipulation, the sector's profit rate r_j can be expressed as

$$r_j = \frac{\tau_j \, w b_j \, \tilde{y}}{e P_k^\star K_j} = \frac{\tau_j \, w b_j \, a \alpha_j}{\tau \lambda_j \, P_x} \frac{1 + \tau_x}{\tau_x} r_x. \tag{A.8}$$

K_j after the first equality is the intermediate sector's capital stock; after the second one it appears relative to home goods capital, i.e. K_j / K_x as λ_j. The profit rate in intermediate production is proportional to the one in home goods, since demand for intermediates is proportional to the X-sector's output level.

Exports are produced using only capital stock K_e (with implications of what happens when the technology requires intermediates discussed below). The sector operates at full capacity, so its output E, is given by

$$E = \phi_e K_e, \tag{A.9}$$

where ϕ_e is the technically fixed output–capital ratio. (Such ratios in the other two sectors fluctuate according to demand.) The export profit rate r_e is

$$r_e = \frac{\left(P_e - w b_e \right) E}{e P_k^\star K_e} = \frac{\left(P_e - w b_e \right)}{e P_k^\star} \phi_e, \tag{A.10}$$

where P_e is the domestic price of exports, and b_e the labour–output ratio.

The country is assumed to face less than fully elastic demand for its exports—P_e

falls as E rises. For ease in setting up steady states, assume that world demand for 'our' exports is scaled to the size of the national economy as measured by K_x,

$$\frac{E}{K_x} = \varepsilon_0 + \varepsilon_1 \frac{eP_e^\star}{P_e(1 - \xi)}.$$ (A.11)

In this expression, the price of exports placed abroad is $(1 - \xi)P_e/e$, where ξ is the rate of export subsidy. If this price rises relative to $P_e^\star$, the world price of foreign 'similars', exports fall. The demand function has an elasticity exceeding unity if the constant ε_0 is negative.

If $\lambda_e = K_e/K_x$, then $E/K_x = \lambda_e\phi_e$, and the demand function in (A.11) can be inverted to give

$$P_e = \frac{\varepsilon_1 eP_e^\star}{(1 - \xi)(\lambda_e\phi_e - \varepsilon_0)}$$ (A.12)

This formula shows that when λ_e rises as more capital resources are devoted to exports, the price P_e and profit rate r_e fall. An increased subsidy rate ξ gives opposite results.

So far, we have derived expressions for the profit rates r_j and r_e in intermediate and export production, which in turn will affect these sectors' investment demand. For home goods, profitability is determined by domestic demand. Suppose that all consumer goods are produced at home (a convenient simplification that does not do excessive violence to the facts). Let all wage income go for consumption, while a fraction s of profits (regardless of sector of origin) is saved. Then if government consumption is G, the condition that excess demand for home goods should equal zero can be written as

$$P_x G + w(b_x X + b_j \mathcal{J} + b_e E) + (1 - s)[\tau_x(wb_x + \bar{P}_j a)X + \tau_j wb_j \mathcal{J} \quad \text{(A.13)}$$
$$+ (P_e - wb_e)E] - P_x X = 0.$$

To convert (A.13) to an expression for the profit rate r_x, we can add and subtract $P_j aX$ to the left side, note from (A.6) that

$$\bar{P}_j aX - P_j \mathcal{J} = e(1 + \sigma)P_j^\star a \, \alpha_m X,$$

and divide every term by $P_x K_x$. Then after much shuffling, we arrive at the equation

$$qP_k^\star [s + q(1 + \sigma)P_j^\star \alpha_m \frac{1 + \tau_x}{\tau_x}] r_x = \gamma - sqP_k^\star \lambda_j r_j \quad \text{(A.14)}$$

$$+ q\lambda_e [\frac{\varepsilon_1 P_e^\star \theta_e}{(1 - \xi)(\theta_e\lambda_e - \varepsilon_0)} - sP_k^\star r_e],$$

where $q = e/P_x$ is the real exchange rate, $\gamma = G/X_k$, and expressions for r_j and r_e appear in (A.8) and (A.10) respectively. This equation is a Keynes–Kalecki multiplier, with r_x measuring the home goods activity level and rising in response to demand injections from government spending or exports. The variables that affect r_x in (A.14) are the capital stock ratios λ_e and λ_j, the export subsidy ξ, and the intermediate import tariff σ. We want to find the signs of the corresponding multipliers.

With regard to the intermediate capital stock ratio λ_j, note from (A.8) that it cancels out in the second term after the equals sign in (A.14). Hence, $\delta r_x/\delta\lambda_j = 0$—intermediates have a horizontal supply curve, so that total capital in the sector is irrelevant to profitability in home goods production. A more neoclassical specification with a rising intermediate supply curve would make τ_j go up in response to a lower λ_j (less capital drives up the mark-up). From (A.8), r_j would decline more than proportionally to an increase in λ_j, and from (A.14) r_x would go up: $\delta r_x/\delta\lambda_j > 0$. We consider both kinds of supply curve in the discussion of steady state growth paths which follows. With either, $\delta r_j/\delta\lambda_j < 0$.

As noted above, an increase in the tariff rate drives up the price of intermediates. The impact can be gauged from the coefficient of r_x in (A.14) when r_j is replaced from (A.8). The coefficient becomes

$$qP_k{}^\star\left[s + q\,\frac{1 + \tau_x}{\tau_x}\,a\,\frac{s\tau_j\,wb_j\,a_j}{P_x} + (1 + \sigma)\,P_j{}^\star a_m\right].$$

Here, an increase in σ reduces q, drives up P_x, reduces a_m, and increases a_j and the term $(1 + \sigma)$. With plausible intermediate input ratios and CES parameters, the positive effects dominate and the coefficient rises. Hence, to maintain equality in (A.14), r_x must fall: $\delta r_x/\delta\sigma < 0$. By driving up input costs, tariffs on intermediates make home goods production less profitable. On the other hand, the increase in a_j is likely to divert enough demand towards domestic production to make $\mathcal{J}$-sector returns rise: $\delta r_j/\delta\sigma > 0$.

Turning to the export sector, recall that an increase in the capital stock ratio makes the price level P_e and profit rate r_e fall. An increase in the subsidy rate has opposite effects. We have $\delta r_e/\delta\lambda_e < 0$ and $\delta r_e/\delta\xi > 0$. The term involving λ_e in (A.14) can be written as

$$(\theta_e/e)\left[(1 - s)\,P_e + swb_e\right]\lambda_e,$$

using (A.12) for P_e. When $\varepsilon_0 < 0$ and export demand is more than unit elastic, it is easy to see that the whole expression increases with λ_e; even with $\varepsilon_0 > 0$, the term swb_e can make the derivative positive. If the export commodity is 'industrial', with fairly elastic world demand, it is likely that income from extra export revenue will stimulate the domestic economy ($\delta r_x/\delta\lambda_e > 0$). However, if the main exports are price-inelastic primary products, increasing their output might cut revenue enough to be counter-productive ($\delta r_x/\delta\lambda_e < 0$). An increased subsidy is helpful in either case ($\delta r_x/\delta\xi > 0$).

The overall conclusions are that in the short to medium run, an increased import tariff (export subsidy) rate will increase the profit rate in the import substitution (export) sector. The home goods profit rate will go up with the export subsidy and decline with the import tariff. A higher capital stock ratio (sector capital divided by home goods capital) will reduce the sector's profit rate and can affect the home goods profit rate in several ways—it may stay unchanged if the supply curve of domestic intermediates is horizontal, or fall if world demand for exports is sufficiently price-inelastic. The next step is to relate these changes to investment demands and growth rates of the different sectors.

We assume the economy is 'large' in the sense that home goods is its major sector. Along standard neo-Keynesian lines, investment by home goods producers should respond to the profit rate. If we let g_i stand for I_i/K_i—the ratio of investment to capital or the capital stock growth rate—in each sector, the home goods investment demand function is

$$g_x = g_0 + \phi_x r_x,$$ (A.15)

where ϕ_x is a response coefficient.

Investors in the other sectors compare their profit rates to r_x, the 'base' rate in the economy, in making investment decisions. Hence we have

$$g_j = g_0 + \phi_j (r_j - r_x)$$ (A.16)

for the import substitution sector, and

$$g_e = g_0 + \phi_e (r_e - r_x)$$ (A.17)

for exporters. When either sector's profit rate rises above the base rate, its investment demand is stimulated.

To see the implications of this investment demand specification, we can consider accumulation in the import-substituting sector. The growth rate of its capital stock ratio $\hat{\lambda}_j$, is $\lambda_j.036 \, g_i - g_x$. Substitution from (A.15) and (A.16) gives

$$\hat{\lambda}_j = (\phi_j + \phi_x) (\varrho_j \, r_j - r_x),$$ (A.18)

where

$$\varrho_j = \phi_j /(\phi_j + \phi_x).$$

By definition, the economy is at a steady state when $\hat{\lambda}_j = 0$, or $g_j = g_x$. At steady state, profit rates are *not* equalized, since import substituting industries require extra incentives to keep up investment, $r_j = r_x/\varrho_j > r_x$.

The question we want to ask is whether or not a tariff increase will stimulate overall growth. Around an initial steady state, we can linearize the growth equation as

$$\hat{d\lambda}_j = (\varrho_j \, \frac{\delta r_j}{\delta \lambda_j} - \frac{\delta r_x}{\delta \lambda_j}) \, d\lambda_j + (\varrho_j \frac{\delta r_j}{\delta \sigma} - \frac{\delta r_x}{\delta \sigma}) d\sigma.$$ (A.19)

From the first term, the steady state is stable, since $\delta r_j/\delta \lambda_j < 0$ and $\delta r_x/\delta \lambda_j > 0$, i.e. if λ_j is shocked upward from equilibrium, λ_j becomes negative and returns to its original level. Setting the right side of (A.19) to zero gives a solution for λ_j as a function of σ at steady state, as illustrated in Fig. 4.2 in the text.

An increase in λ_j reduces the import substitution profit rate r_j and increases (or leaves unchanged) r_x. Investment demand in home goods thus rises with λ_j, while investment in import substitution declines, as illustrated by the g_x and g_j schedules in the figure. A higher tariff rate stimulates g_j and cuts back on g_x. The outcomes are a higher capital stock ratio λ_j in the new steady state, and a change of uncertain sign in the growth rate. If home goods profitability is severally penalized by higher intermediate import costs, steady state growth could be slowed. An analytical expression for the change in r_x (and for g_x from (A.15)) can be derived by solving (A.19) for $\delta \lambda_j /\delta \sigma$, and plugging the result into the total differential expression for dr_x. One finds that r_x rises in response to a higher σ when

$$\frac{\delta r_j}{\delta \sigma} \frac{\delta r_x}{\delta \lambda_j} - \frac{\delta r_x}{\delta \sigma} \frac{\delta r_j}{\delta \lambda_j} > 0.$$ (A.20)

There is a negative response if the supply curve of domestically produced intermediates is horizontal, since $\delta r_x/\delta\lambda_j = 0$ under such circumstances. With a rising supply curve, the steady state growth rate can go up—the increase in λ_j across steady states cuts back on input costs and makes home goods production more profitable.

Without going through the details, it is clear that similar results apply with regard to an export subsidy. The condition for an increased steady-state growth rate in response to a higher subsidy is

$$\frac{\delta r_e}{\delta\xi}\frac{\delta r_x}{\delta\lambda_e} - \frac{\delta r_x}{\delta\xi}\frac{\delta r_e}{\delta\lambda_e} > 0. \tag{A.21}$$

The whole second term here is positive ($\delta r_x/\xi > 0$ and $\delta r_e/\delta\lambda_e < 0$), so the sign depends on the first term. Sufficiently inelastic foreign demand could make $\delta r_x/\delta\lambda_e$ negative enough to slow the steady-state growth rate; otherwise, it will rise when ξ is increased. Also note that cross-effects between sectors can be introduced. For example, if the export industry uses intermediate inputs, then r_e would fall with an increase in σ. In the two-variable growth rate system involving λ_j and λ_e as state variables, the outcome could be slower long-term growth.

5

Some Reflections on Comparative Latin American Economic Performance and Policy

Albert Fishlow

5.1 INTRODUCTION

There is an increasingly pervasive view that Latin American post-war development has been badly flawed. The prominent success of the export-led expansion of several Asian countries, and especially Korea and Taiwan, weighs heavily in this assessment. That comparative example of the benefits of outward orientation is, moreover, strong support for the corollary proposition that the principal cause for Latin American failure is the continuing import substitution bias of the region.

Angus Maddison relates the two. 'The economic growth performance of Latin America since 1973 has been abysmal . . . there has . . . been a certain continuity in economic policy attitudes since the 1930's, and the liberal international order which was created by OECD countries and has influenced policy in Asia has left them virtually untouched' (Maddison 1985; 53).

Balassa and associates go further. They emphasize that external shocks in the region were not disproportionate and use the troubled Latin American adjustment to the debt crisis to emphasize three more fundamental deficiencies: inward orientation, lack of appropriate incentives to savings and investment, and the excessive role of the state. They prescribe remedies emphasizing trade liberalization and reliance on market signals (Balassa *et al.* 1986).

Jeffrey Sachs, in another influential comparative analysis, likewise rejects differential economic shocks and debt exposure, but also government involvement, to conclude that 'the more important differences seem to centre on exchange rate management and on the trade regime. Latin American and Asian borrowers have differed not only in the amounts borrowed, but also in the uses to which the loans were applied. Simply put, the Latin American countries did not use the foreign borrowing to develop a resource base in tradable goods, especially export industries, adequate for future debt servicing' (Sachs 1985: 525). His focus then shifts to the political determinants of inadequate Latin American policies, with the largest role explained by greater rural influence in Asia relative to Latin America.

In this chapter, I shall take up three issues that figure centrally in this analysis of the deteriorating Latin American position. First, I shall argue that the 'dismal' Latin American performance has been exaggerated. Two factors contribute to this phenomenon: the selectivity of comparisons of the whole region against the very best Asian performers; and the inclusion of the post-1980 period, when Latin American income absolutely declined. The relative severity of the external shock, moreover, is not to be discounted as an important reason for less satisfactory Latin American performance. Second, faulty exchange rate management and trade policy is not as key to lagging performance as has been stressed. In fact, during the critical period when Latin America registered the largest decline relative to its trend value, exchange rate policies in the region were aggressively favourable to exports. The earlier commitment to overvaluation as an instrument of import substitution industrialization, and consequent loss of export share, had largely gone by the 1970s. Export volume increases after 1979 were greater relative to Asia than they had been previously.

Third, the political constraints underlying Latin American policy response and development strategy extend beyond the urban–rural distinctions stressed by Sachs. Political imperatives weaken the interventionist Latin American state, limiting its autonomy and diminishing its capacity to react to the debt crisis, even as they strengthen the Asian state. Simple deregulation and privatization, however, are not first-best solutions; reconstructing a developmental state is.

5.2 LATIN AMERICAN ECONOMIC PERFORMANCE

Table 5.1 sets out some performance characteristics for Latin American and East Asian and South Asian countries. Growth rates, inflation, and debt are the objects of interest. What is clear is the much steeper fall off in Latin American growth rates over the period. From a very small disadvantage relative to the East Asian countries in 1965–73, the margin widens in the 1970s with the first oil shock. But the real difference emerges after 1980 and the debt crisis, with an absolute decline in Latin American product. The gap in this later period is, for the weighted average, 6.2 percentage points. Without giving special attention to the depths of this Latin American depression after 1980, growth rate differentials calculated over longer periods miss much of the point. Indeed, Latin America hardly has a 'dismal' record over the period 1965–80, and it is one that markedly improves on the 1950–65 results.

Of equal significance, moreover, is the disparity apparent among the Latin American countries in rates of product growth. Argentina, Chile, and Peru are consistently poor performers, before and after 1980; on the other side,

Table 5.1 Comparative economic performance

	GDP growth rates			Inflation			EDT/GNP			Debt service/exports		
	1960–70	1970–80	1980–85	1960–70	1970–80	1980–85	1973	1983	1985	1973	1983	1985
Latin America												
Argentina	4.2	2.2	-1.4	21.7	130.8	342.8	0.17	0.68	0.80	0.28	0.44	…
Brazil	5.4	8.4	1.3	46.1	36.7	147.7	0.15	0.48	0.51	0.23	0.54	0.35
Chile	4.5	2.4	-1.1	33.2	185.6	19.3	0.31	1.03	1.42	0.12	0.55	0.44
Colombia	5.1	5.9	1.9	11.9	22.0	22.5	0.23	0.28	0.43	0.20	0.38	0.33
Mexico	7.2	5.2	0.8	3.6	19.3	62.2	0.16	0.61	0.58	0.34	0.43	0.48
Peru	4.9	3.0	1.6	10.4	30.7	98.6	0.14	0.73	0.88	0.29	0.34	0.16
Venezuela	6.0	5.0	1.6	1.3	12.1	9.2	0.28	0.46	0.66	0.18	0.29	…
Median	5.1	5.0	1.1	11.9	30.7	62.2	0.17	0.61	0.66	0.23	0.43	0.35
Weighted average	5.7	5.8	0.4	24.7	47.9	277.7	0.18	0.56	0.61	0.26	0.46	0.31
East Asia												
Indonesia	3.9	7.6	3.5	…	20.5	10.7	0.36	0.29	0.43	0.07	0.13	0.25
Korea	8.6	9.5	7.9	17.4	19.8	6.0	0.35	0.55	0.58	0.19	0.21	0.21
Malaysia	6.5	7.8	5.5	-0.3	7.5	3.1	0.10	0.39	0.62	0.03	0.06	0.27
Philippines	5.1	6.3	-0.5	5.8	13.2	19.3	0.18	0.40	0.81	0.19	0.22	0.19
Taiwan	9.8	5.4	6.2	3.5	12.2	3.3	0.11	0.14	0.08	0.04	0.05	0.04
Thailand	8.4	7.2	5.1	1.8	9.9	3.2	0.09	0.25	0.47	0.13	0.21	0.25
Median	7.4	7.7	5.3	3.5	11.5	4.6	0.18	0.34	0.52	0.10	0.17	0.23
Weighted average	6.9	8.0	4.9	7.8	14.8	7.7	0.23	0.34	0.25	0.12	0.15	0.30
South Asia												
Bangladesh	3.7	3.9	3.6	3.7	16.9	11.5	0.06	0.38	0.43	0.02	0.15	0.17
India	3.4	3.6	5.2	7.1	8.5	7.8	0.14	0.11	0.19	0.20	0.10	0.13
Pakistan	6.7	4.7	6.0	3.3	13.5	8.1	0.66	0.31	0.38	0.15	0.28	0.30
Sri Lanka	4.6	4.1	5.1	1.8	12.6	14.7	0.22	0.44	0.62	0.13	0.12	0.15
Median	4.1	4.0	5.1	3.5	13.0	9.8	0.18	0.34	0.40	0.14	0.13	0.16
Weighted average	3.9	3.7	5.2	6.2	9.6	8.3	0.19	0.15	0.24	0.18	0.12	0.16

Source: World Bank 1982, 1987 for growth rates and inflation: *World Debt Tables 1986–7* for debt and debt service. Weights are average of 1973 and 1983 GNP.

Brazil, Colombia, and Mexico fare rather better. The heterogeneity is such that until 1980, the differences in simple averages between Latin America and East Asia are not statistically significant. Put another way, the better-performing Latin American countries might be mistaken for East Asian countries. One must therefore be careful in one's generalizations: indeed, if the smaller Latin American and Asian countries were included, more variability would be apparent.

Higher inflation clearly differentiates Latin America from East Asia and South Asia, but again with an increasing intensity. Latin America's proclivity to inflation is not as pronounced until the countries must cope with the oil price shocks and significant balance of payments adjustment. The very relative price changes required, including devaluation, are readily turned into accelerating inflation through formal or informal indexing arrangements that characterize high inflation economies. Prominently included among such relative prices is the real interest rate as the public sector uses internal debt to acquire resources to meet external debt service. But then inflation has a strong inertial component, and its absolute level is a misleading index of internal distortion and misallocation. Conventional monetary and fiscal restraint do not work effectively to reduce this kind of inflation. This incompatibility became an essential sticking point in the implementation of IMF stabilization programs in many of the countries in the region.

The uniformity that emerges from Table 5.1, and which underlies these other measures of economic performance, is Latin America's much greater reliance on indebtedness in the 1970s. Colombia largely but not wholly excepted, the other countries embraced debt to a much greater extent than anywhere else in the world. The weighted debt/GNP ratio tripled between 1973 and 1983, and the already higher debt service/export ratio almost doubled. South Asian conservatism, and ineligibility for bank loans, equally comes through. So does the mixed East Asian response: note in particular the very great difference in the Korean and Taiwanese reliance on external finance.

When the Latin American countries were given the opportunity of availing themselves of increased bank lending in the 1970s, they substantially did so. Initially, virtually all countries borrowed to adjust to higher oil prices. Mexico and Peru were not yet net oil exporters; Venezuela initially did not borrow, but rather deposited its surplus abroad. Such borrowing decisions conformed to market signals: world real interest rates were low and even negative, particularly with respect to export price indexes. They also conformed to structural limitations to immediate realignment of the domestic economy; time was needed to adjust. Finally, debt was consistent with a politics of continuity rather than abrupt dislocation, a continuity which especially appealed to governments seeking to legitimize their power (see Fishlow 1985a, 1986).

For the larger countries, Mexico and Brazil especially, this access to external saving became habit-forming. Reduced resource transfer as later borrowing was negated by reverse debt service was an important factor in increasing demand for loans. As interest payments rose with accumulated debt, still more debt could guarantee a transfer of real resources, underwriting high levels of investment and high growth rates. To accommodate to the bank preference for public guarantees, state enterprises were increasingly the issuers of debt. The public sector correspondingly assumed an expanded role as an integral part of the reliance on foreign saving.

On the whole, the strategy worked. Later failure obscures the general contemporary evaluation that the massive flow was justified. During this period of the 1970s investment ratios for the Latin American borrowers increased and growth rates continued high. Analysis of consumption functions show that the marginal propensity to save out of external borrowing was on the whole the same as, or greater than, domestic income.[1] At the margin, therefore, there was an expected substitution for domestic saving. But there seems to have been no difference in this respect between Indonesia and Korea, on the one hand, and Brazil and Mexico, on the other.

Nor do the Asian countries seem to have been spared mistakes in public investment. In Korea, there was much criticism of the support for domestic import substitution in the heavy and chemical industries. 'A massive investment program in these industries financed largely by foreign loans and central bank credit was put in effect in 1973 and pursued vigorously until 1979. To the dismay of policymakers who had conceived this industrial restructuring, the development strategy ran into a host of financing, engineering, quality, and marketing difficulties (Park 1986: 1028).

What complicated later Latin American performance were three factors. The first was exaggerated borrowing, which began to become evident in 1979–80. It was of two types. Argentina and Chile increasingly relied upon external loans to implement their international monetarist anti-inflation and trade liberalization policies; overvaluation was now an instrument of non-structuralists and depended upon capital inflow to sustain it. In addition, Mexico and Venezuela, beneficiaries of the second rise in oil prices, abused easy access to credit. Mexico borrowed to take on an ambitious expenditure programme to support accelerated growth; Venezuela indulged in expanded public spending even while private investment was contracting. In all four countries, balance of payments adjustment was no longer the motivating consideration. It is not accidental that capital flight soon emerged as a major offset to new debt in all except Chile. Excess borrowing could not be absorbed through an increase in imports; capital outflows equilibrated. If there is a case for loan pushing, it is to be found in these countries.

[1] For estimates of consumption out of national product and foreign capital, see Fishlow 1985b: 105–6.

Second, even in the absence of external shocks, asymmetric Latin American opening to the international economy was already worrisome in 1978. Debt had expanded much more rapidly than exports. Note in Table 5.1 that the Latin American countries had started in 1973 from much higher debt-service—export ratios than the Asian countries. By 1978, that indicator had increased some 40 per cent. There was danger in such reliance on capital inflow by economies that were so closed; it would have taken an enormous effort to reallocate resources to service the accumulated debt even if the international economic environment had not deteriorated. It was not only the inward style of Latin American development that is to be faulted, but even more its combination with external borrowing. Third, massive external shocks intervened after 1980 and proved the Latin American vulnerability. They are highlighted in Table 5.2. Four effects are measured against a standard of continuity of the international economy. First is the terms of trade effect, derived by comparing the evolution of export and import prices in the period 1977–9 with the 1981–3 years. Second is the rise in real interest rates between the two periods. Third is the impact of reduced OECD growth on the export volume of developing countries. Fourth is the shift in willingness of commercial banks to lend, measured as the change in the ratio of normal capital flow relative to gross product. Note that I consider the impairment of capital market access as a shock, as it was, rather than as a means of adjustment.[2] Two principal conclusions derive from Table 5.2. The first is that, Colombia excepted, the interest rate and capital supply effects had a relatively greater effect on the Latin American economies than terms of trade and recession effects. The reason is straightforward: the former depend on the debt/GNP ratio, the latter on the export/GNP ratio. The more open East Asian economies were buffeted by deteriorating conditions of trade, while the Latin American countries, because of their reliance on debt, were more sensitive to changes in financial markets. But, for that very reason, financial markets remained open to East Asian countries to compensate for the trade shock and facilitate adjustment. That was not true for Latin America. Countries had relied on the capital market, not trade, in order to adjust to the first shock. Now, on the occasion of the second, there was no longer a choice.

That explains why the conventional measurement of shocks relative to

---

[2] These effects derive from a straightforward analysis of the sources of changes in the balance of payments: $\Delta BP = P_x \Delta X + X \Delta P_x - M \Delta P_m - D \Delta i + Cap$; where the terms have their usual meanings. Excluded are changes in imports as a consequence of internal adjustment; changes in debt, because they are multiplied by interest rates, makes only a small contribution.

Sachs considers only interest and terms of trade effects, excluding the recession effect. Balassa (1984), in his decompositions, allows for the impact of recession on export volume, but by hypothesizing a constant market share rather than an income elasticity. Neither allow for the exogenous shock associated with a shift in the supply of capital. Balassa rather considers the capital account exclusively as a means of adjustment. But if the effect comes from the supply side and is exogenous, the logical treatment is to classify it as a shock.

Table 5.2 The impact of external shocks, 1981–1983

	Import and export prices[a]	Interest rates[b]	OECD recession[c]	Capital supply[d]	Total[e]	Total[f]
			(Ratio to GNP)			(Ratio to exports)
Latin America						
Argentina	0.006	−0.025	−0.009	−0.047	−0.075	−0.64
Brazil	−0.044	−0.022	−0.005	−0.022	−0.093	−1.37
Chile	−0.097	−0.034	−0.016	−0.026	−0.173	−0.80
Colombia	−0.057	−0.004	−0.012	0.023	−0.050	−0.31
Mexico	0.018	−0.035	−0.008	−0.020	−0.045	−0.42
Peru	−0.001	−0.039	−0.017	0.027	−0.030	−0.13
Venezuela	0.131	−0.034	−0.020	−0.162	−0.085	−0.31
East Asia						
Indonesia	0.141	−0.012	−0.018	0.021	0.132	0.53
Korea	−0.068	−0.027	−0.022	−0.011	−0.128	−0.43
Malaysia	−0.047	0	−0.038	0.112	0.027	0.05
Philippines	−0.076	−0.012	−0.014	−0.027	−0.129	−0.70
Taiwan	−0.154	−0.004	−0.038	0.014	−0.182	−0.35
Thailand	−0.087	−0.007	−0.016	−0.004	−0.114	−0.52

Sources: Import and Export Prices: Economic Commission for Latin America; IMF.
Interest Rates: *World Debt Tables*; OECD.
OECD Growth Rates and Capital Flows: IMF, ADB.
[a] Price effect: percentage change in export price index times export/income ratio 1977–9 minus percentage change in import price index times import/income ratio 1977–9.
[b] Interest rate effect: change in nominal implicit interest rate on medium- and long-term debt, adjusted for change in US wholesale price index, between 1977–9 and 1981–3 times net debt/GNP ratio in 1980. (Net debt in dollars divided by World Bank estimates of GNP in *World Development Report, 1982*.)
[c] OECD recession effect: change in OECD growth rate between 1977–9 and 1981–3 times imported volume elasticity of 1.5, averaged over three-year period, times export/income ratio, 1977–9.
[d] Capital supply effect: ratio of capital inflow, exclusive of exceptional financing and adjusted for net errors and omissions, to income in 1981–3 minus ratio in 1977–9.
[e] Sum of all effects.
[f] Sum of effects relative to GNP times export/GNP ratio, 1977–9.

GNP, which shows the Asian countries as having suffered badly, is misleading. This is the second and critical point. If the deterioration in the balance of payments—and that is what the shocks measure—must be adjusted by the trade account, then growth consequences will be shown much more accurately by the ratio of the shocks to exports. It is easy to see why. Let the sum of the shocks be ΔBP, and allow change in the balance of payments to be compensated by changes in imports. Then dividing by Y, and allowing the marginal import ratio to be equal to the average (and the export ratio), we can write that the implied growth required to accommodate to the shocks is equal to the conventional ratio to GNP multiplied by the inverse of the export/product ratio: $\Delta Y/Y = (\Delta BP/Y)(Y/X)$.[3] In other words, for closed economies the impact on growth of a given decline in real income is much larger. This simply reflects the fact that for closed economies it will require much larger changes in income to produce the same decline in imports. It was thus easier for the Asian economies to adjust because of their greater trade, even without taking into account the greater possibility of using export expansion rather than import contraction. When the total shock is related to exports rather than to gross product, almost all the Latin American countries (as well as the Philippines) clearly emerge as equivalent or more serious victims of the deteriorating international economy. The relative size of the export shocks, moreover, turns out to be more informative about the consequences for reduced growth in the 1981–3 period than the size of the GNP shocks does. While the relationship between changes in growth between 1970–80 and 1980–3 and the size of the shock relative to gross product is statistically insignificant, the export shock enters significantly even after a regional dummy is included.[4]

Above all else, it was the need to attend immediately to the imbalance in the external accounts that was so catastrophic for Latin American performance. Countries borrowed too much relative to their short-term capacity to adjust to variability in the external environment. When the crisis came, imports had to be disproportionately reduced, at the expense of output and income growth. Between 1981 and 1983, imports declined by $40 billion, and more than 40 per cent in volume terms; in comparison, the output decline of 4 per cent reflects a significant dampening of the potential impact.

5.3 TRADE POLICIES AND PERFORMANCE

The discussion so far has elaborated on the special problems of the Latin American countries in the early 1980s that derived from their asymmetric

---

[3] The derivation is straightforward: $\Delta BP = \Delta M$. Dividing by ΔY, $\Delta BP/\Delta Y = \Delta M/\Delta Y$. Let the marginal propensity equal the average and exports equal imports. Then $\Delta BP/\Delta Y = X/Y$.

[4] The relevant regressions (with t-statistics in parentheses) are:

$$G = -2.44 - 3.27D + 4.26GS; \quad R^2 = 0.54$$
$$\quad\quad (3.41)\quad (3.82)\quad\quad (0.81)$$

$$G = -2.36 - 2.60D + 1.89XS; \quad R^2 = 0.64$$
$$\quad\quad (4.95)\quad (3.09)\quad\quad (1.91)$$

where G is the difference in the rates of growth between 1970–80 and 1980–3; D is a dummy variable for the Latin American region; GS is the ratio of the total shock relative to income; and XS is the ratio relative to exports. Data are from Tables 5.1 and 5.2.

integration into the world economy, which made them vulnerable to the international downturn beginning in 1981. This section will examine the other side of the high regional debt/export ratio: lagging trade performance. I shall argue that better Latin American trade policies did yield improved results during the 1970s, and that strenuous efforts were made in the 1980s to follow the prescription of real devaluation to ease adjustment. Export volume in fact expanded, but not enough to take much of the burden from import contraction.

Latin American reliance on import substitution as a route to industrialization reached its peak in the 1950s when import ratios were sharply lowered and trade policies were consciously biased against exports. Overvaluation taxed the primary export sector and simultaneously distributed the proceeds to producers of manufactured goods able to import capital goods and other inputs cheaply. But by the early 1960s that model had outlived its effectiveness. Balance of payments problems and accelerating inflation signalled reinforcing external and internal disequilibrium. Both dependency theorists and orthodox economists found the trade policies wanting. Even the larger capital inflow facilitated by the Alliance for Progress could not avert economic crisis and political upheaval in many countries.

From the mid-1960s on, Latin American countries grappled with the need to modify their policies, just as did many of the East Asian countries. The solution was found in crawling pegs, export subsidies, dual exchange rates, duty free zones, public investment, and a variety of other means to reduce the bias against export activities, particularly those of non-traditional products. While not as spectacular as the emergence of the Asian NICs Latin American export performance also improved through the 1960s and permitted more rapid product growth. But there was a fundamental difference in outlook about the export market that continues to this day. For Latin America, already industrialized and with higher income and wages, the export market was never conceived as the basis for growth of the manufacturing sector; its function was to supply needed foreign exchange, and there was still heavy dependence on resource-based exports. For Asian NICs, the foreign market oriented domestic investment in industry, first in labour-intensive goods compatible with low wages and later in others. Exports were the instrument of industrialization.

In the 1970s, despite Latin America's greater dependence upon borrowing, the new attention to exports was sustained. While middle-income developing countries on average experienced slower export growth over 1970–80 than over 1960–70, for every one of the principal Latin American countries except

An alternative functional form, allowing for a differential slope for each region, again does better for the impact relative to exports, although the slope for the East Asian countries is then statistically insignificant. There is virtually no difference in the percentage of variance explained between the constant and slope regional effects.

Venezuela and Colombia, export growth accelerated (see World Bank 1982; App. table 8, pp. 124–5). Under the pressure of the crisis of the early 1980s, an even greater effort was made. Between 1980 and 1983, Mexico increased its export volume at a rate exceeding that of Korea and Taiwan; in addition, Argentina, Brazil, and Chile bettered the performance of Indonesia, Malaysia, Thailand, and the Philippines (IMF 1985). Unfortunately, with adverse price movements, that effort translated into too little revenue, too late. Export unit values for the Western hemisphere have declined 26 per cent from 1980 to 1987, compared to 18 per cent for Asia, and less for Korea and Taiwan whose exports are more industrialized.

Table 5.3 provides a decomposition of export changes between 1962–4 and 1980–2 for a number of countries. It divides the observed change in dollar exports, deflated by two-digit SITC deflators, into three sources: world trade growth, compositional effects calculated by positing a constant market share within each category, and a residual competitive effect associated with changing market shares.[5]

There are three major points to be gleaned from the calculations. First, the exceptional performances of Korea, Taiwan, and Malaysia in increasing market shares in both periods is evident (but Brazil is not very far behind). Second, the switch in the contribution of competitiveness between the two periods is shared by all countries except India and Pakistan. Argentina and Mexico move away from large reductions in market share to achieve gains just like Indonesia, the Philippines, and Thailand. Third, compositional effects are uniformly negative for the Latin American countries. Taiwan and Korea are unique in benefiting from their increasing share of industrial exports in total trade; other East Asian countries also suffer the consequences of a large share of slow-growing and resource-based exports. Few countries could avoid the record slide in the terms of trade in the 1980s, even with an unbiased trade policy.

Latin America's better trade results were on the whole associated with better exchange rate management. Sachs's evidence of real exchange rate change between 1976–8 and 1979–81, shows little difference between Latin America (excluding Argentina) and Asia (see Sachs 1985: table 6, p. 41).[6] Instead of being a policy instrument used to accomplish an internal sectoral transfer of real resources or as a means of holding down internal inflation, the

---

[5] The decomposition of the change in trade, in contant dollars, is $q = s\Delta Q + (\Sigma s_i \, \Delta Q_i - s\Delta Q) + (\Sigma Q_i \, \Delta s_i)$ where 'Σ' is the summation operator; s refers to export shares, the subscript i to SITC class, and Q to world exports. The first term measures the contribution of world trade growth, the second the effect of commodity composition, and the third the result of increasing competitiveness.

[6] Sachs's conclusion is different, but seems to lean more on the black market premia that the real exchange rates, particularly when the Southern Cone is excluded. But these measure the severity of the crisis, not the misalignment of rates. Brazil, about to experience an export boom, has the largest margin; Venezuela, frankly overvalued, the smallest.

Table 5.3 Decomposition of trade changes

Country/source of charge	1962–4 to 1970–2		1970–2 to 1980–2	
	$ million[a]	%	$ million[a]	%
Latin America				
Argentina				
World trade growth	1439.2	567.3	1190.5	113.4
Composition[b]	–717.7	–282.9	–225.8	–21.5
Competitiveness	–467.8	–184.4	85.3	8.1
Total	253.7	100.0	1050.1	100.0
Brazil				
World trade growth	1463.7	98.2	2064.4	68.7
Composition[b]	–758.0	–50.9	–483.1	–16.1
Competitiveness	784.6	52.7	1424.0	47.4
Total	1490.2	100.0	3005.3	100.0
Chile[c]				
World trade growth	. . .	. . .	192.7	43.7
Composition[b]	. . .	. . .	–54.6	–12.4
Competitiveness	. . .	. . .	302.5	68.7
Total	. . .	. . .	440.5	100.0
Mexico				
World trade growth	1439.2	502.0	1190.5	97.9
Composition[b]	–717.7	–250.3	–225.8	–18.6
Competitiveness	–467.8	–163.2	85.3	7.0
Total	286.7	100.0	1216.0	100.0
East Asia				
Indonesia[d]				
World trade growth	734.7	169.1	819.1	46.7
Composition[b]	–296.5	–68.2	–503.9	–28.8
Competitiveness	–3.7	–0.9	1437.1	82.0
Total	434.6	100.0	1752.3	100.0
Korea				
World trade growth	95.1	9.4	767.9	12.7
Composition[b]	–19.1	–1.9	36.2	0.6
Competitiveness	935.8	92.5	5262.7	86.7
Total	1011.7	100.0	6066.8	100.0
Malaysia[e]				
World trade growth	580.3	101.6	886.1	48.9
Composition[b]	–305.0	–53.4	–396.9	–21.9
Competitiveness	296.1	51.8	1323.6	73.0
Total	571.4	100.0	1812.9	100.0

Table 5.3 (*continued*)

Country/source of charge	1962–4 to 1970–2		1970–2 to 1980–2	
	$ million[a]	%	$ million[a]	%
Philippines				
World trade growth	737.1	269.1	709.5	144.6
Composition[b]	–387.7	–141.5	–273.6	–55.8
Competitiveness	–75.5	–27.6	54.8	11.2
Total	273.9	100.0	490.6	100.0
Taiwan				
World trade growth	354.0	20.1	1470.6	26.0
Composition[b]	–66.1	–3.8	110.3	2.0
Competitiveness	1474.7	83.7	4072.1	72.0
Total	1762.6	100.0	5652.9	100.0
Thailand				
World trade growth	531.0	330.4	485.7	32.7
Composition[b]	–290.9	–181.0	–136.7	–9.2
Competitiveness	–79.4	–49.4	1137.0	76.5
Total	160.7	100.0	1486.0	100.0
South Asia				
India				
World trade growth	1749.1	656.3	1380.3	306.2
Composition[b]	–318.6	–119.5	–48.0	–10.6
Competitiveness	–1164.0	–436.8	–881.5	–195.5
Total	266.5	100.0	450.8	100.0
Pakistan[f]				
World trade growth	412.2	217.1	438.0	179.7
Composition[b]	–150.7	–79.4	–137.5	–56.4
Competitiveness	–71.6	–37.7	–56.8	–23.3
Total	189.9	100.0	243.7	100.0

Source: UN, *International Trade Statistics Yearbooks; Statistical Yearbook of the Republic of China*; and *Trade of China*.
[a] 1970 dollars, deflated by unit values using SITC one-digit categories.
[b] Six categories were used: SITC 0 + 1; 2 + 4; 3; 5; 6 + 8 – 68; 7.
[c] No data for 1963–4, 1982.
[d] SITC 68 for 1964 using 1963 ratios.
[e] Data for 1962–4 are for 1964 only.
[f] First period is 1963/4–1970/1; second period is 1972–1980/2, using data for West Pakistan only.

exchange rate's primary function was to measure the relative profitability of exports and import substitutes compared to non-tradables. This was a function not performed in isolation from other government policies, including not only trade restrictions and subsidies but also public investment.

Paradoxically, the liberal, international monetarist strategy of some of the Southern Cone countries was clearly retrograde in returning to conscious overvaluation at the expense of misallocation of resources. More restrictionist Brazil prevented capital flow from prejudicing the productive structure and had larger export and industrial growth.

While recognizing the importance of a better exchange rate policy, it is important not to exaggerate the influence of such market signals in isolation. In earlier work, I referred to the lack of any association between observed export volume changes and exchange rate imperfections for a cross-section of developing countries in the decade 1970–80.[7] The World Bank's 1986 *World Development Report* now cites new evidence for the period 1960–83, but it too does not seem to stand up very well to close scrutiny. Working with that data set, I find that exchange rate misalignment and exchange rate variability provide a limited explanation of export performance; in addition, the results are very sensitive to sample definition. Thus, the variance in export growth explained by exchange rate misalignment is always substantially below the explanation of per capita growth; adjusted R^2 for the former (for the twenty-four country Bank sample) is 0.39; for the latter, 0.12, with coefficients on exchange rate variabilty and misalignment both statistically insignificant. Introducing the investment ratio in the regressions leads to its domination of exchange rate misalignment, both in statistical significance and quantitative importance. Finally, simple exclusion of South Korea from the sample is sufficient to deprive exchange rate misalignment of its explanatory power. This reality is a far cry from the Bank's confident conclusion: 'a 10 percent increase in the misalignment of the real exchange rate was associated with a GDP growth that was 0.5 percentage points lower and an export growth that was 1.8 percentage points lower than would have prevailed without the increase in misalignment (World Bank 1986: 31–2).[8]

Further evidence is available in Table 5.4. It provides the results of a regression analysis relating deviations from 'normal' export shares (i.e. adjusted for country population and income level), to deviations from purchasing-parity exchange rates and their variance over time as well as to the share of manufactures in total exports, for Asian and Latin American countries. The cross-section results for three dates, 1962/4, 1970/2 and 1980/2, are presented in Table 5.4. Exchange rate misalignment is measured relative to 1970–2 purchasing power parity for the early and intermediate periods, and relative to 1984 (after devaluations) for the later period. These cross-section regressions are supplemented by consideration of changes between successive panels in Table 5.4; changes in real wages are now introduced as an additional variable.

[7] See Fishlow 1985c: 139–41, which also critically examines the hypothesis of export-led growth.

[8] My statistical analysis uses the data from the *World Development Report* background study by Cavallo *et al.* 'Real Exchange Rate Behavior and Economic Performance in LDCs'.

Table 5.4 Regression results (*t*-values in parentheses)

Cross-section

Period[a]	No. of observations[b]	Independent variables			$\bar{R}^2$
		Exchange rate deviation (%)	SD/Exchange rate deviations	Share of manufactured exports	
Pooled	47	−0.079 (1.23)	−0.406 (1.23)	0.042 (0.35)	0.01
Early	15	−0.140 (1.70)	−0.094 (0.26)	0.012 (0.04)	0.00
Intermediate	16	−0.080 (0.88)	−0.180 (0.25)	0.030 (0.15)	−0.16
Late	16	−0.115 (0.26)	−1.430 (1.06)	0.096 (0.40)	−0.02

Changes between cross-sections

Period[a]	No. of observations[c]	Independent variables				Change in $\bar{R}^2$
		Change in exchange rate deviations	Change in SD	Change in share of manufactured exports	Change in real wage	
Pooled	23	−0.072 (0.24)	−0.263 (1.14)	−1.17 (0.56)	3.56 (1.14)	0.02
Early–Intermediate	10	0.354 (1.57)	0.107 (0.10)	−3.18 (2.81)	−9.11 (1.65)	0.35
Intermediate–Late	13	−1.340 (1.37)	−0.465 (0.85)	−0.12 (0.09)	8.78 (2.19)	0.16

Source: See text.
[a] Early period is average of 1962–4; intermediate, 1970–2; late, 1980–2.
[b] Country panel includes Argentina, Brazil, Chile, Colombia, Ecuador, Mexico, Peru, Uruguay, Venezuela, India, Indonesia, Korea, Malaysia, Pakistan, Philippines, Thailand. (NB: no data for Indonesia in early period.)
[c] Panel as above less Uruguay (early), Venezuela (early), Indonesia, Malaysia, Thailand.

The tabulated results in Table 5.4 affirm that although average exchange rate deviations are of the correct sign, they are not statistically significant in explaining the differences in export orientation. Nor is the variability in the deviations, reflecting lack of continuity of policy; and nor is concentration on the export of industrial products. These findings are replicated for all three periods as well as for the pooled results, and are thus not an aberration. Some of the difference with other studies is due to the use of export shares already corrected for the influence of population and income. If the issue is the effect of exchange rate policy upon trade orientation, this method seems preferable to using export growth as the dependent variable.

Results are not much better in the analysis of changes reported in Table 5.4. There the principal novelty is the reversal in role of real wages. In the 1962/4–1970/2 interval, there is some indication that more slowly growing real wages contribute to greater than normal export share: cheap labour contributes to competitiveness. But in the second period there is a positive association. Above-average productivity gains make favourable trade performance and rising real wages compatible. Looking for exchange rates to lower labour costs rather than higher investment and increased efficiency may be the wrong way to go about policy.

The point of Table 5.4 is that sweeping generalizations about the importance of exchange rate policy do not come through clearly and uniformly in the data. Productive structures matter in the determination of comparative cost, and so do other policies, including non-market interventions. While Korea pegged the won to the dollar in the mid 1970s, its exchange rate appreciated by 13 per cent because internal prices rose more than in partner countries; export volume none the less expanded by 23 per cent a year. In the same period, 1975–8, Peru's real exchange rate depreciated by almost 70 per cent; export volume did increase, but by a lesser 15 per cent a year. The more specialized a producer, and more dependent on primary commodities, the lesser the effect of exchange rates on the supply and demand sides.

After the large real devaluation in the United States has triggered only a limited trade response, it is perhaps less difficult to sustain the point that exchange rates are not all-determining. The undeniable competitiveness of the East Asian NICs does not imply that aggressive exchange rate policy was solely responsible. Indeed, the absence of a tight relationship between exchange rates and performance partially contributes to the Latin American tendency to use the instrument for other purposes: if there was an automatic effect, positive and negative, then there would be greater discipline.

There is no doubt that East Asia has been more outward oriented than Latin America and has relied to a much greater extent on export demand to stimulate its industrialization. It is not the only route to accelerated growth, however. Note from Table 5.1 that South Asian countries emerge after 1980 with the highest growth rate, without being export-led. They escape the adverse turn in the world economy that even leads to perceptible deterioration in the East Asian performance. Others in this volume argue this variety of options forcefully; I have briefly addressed the desirabilty of an export-adequate growth strategy in *South*, January 1987.

In the end, the question of development centres on the right blend of intervention and market forces. To understand why Latin America has not been equally adept in sustaining economic growth in recent years requires focus upon the role of the state and the political constraints upon its activities.

5.4 THE ROLE OF THE STATE

Development economics, until recently, has largely been about the limits of the market and the need for policy intervention. Externalities and discontinuities caused private and social rates of return to diverge and required conscious public redress. Different perspectives on development strategies generalized about where the divergences were greatest and what kinds of policies might be most effective: social overhead investment, industrialization, education, agricultural technology, etc.

In the last decade, there has been a reversal in opinion. Liberalism and the virtues of the market are now in vogue. Just when political scientists are bringing the state back in, economists are urging strict limits upon public sector activity. They do so on the basis of the East Asian success and Latin American failure. Balassa and associates are clear: 'a central factor that gave impetus . . . to the severity of the economic and social crisis of the 1980s was the pervasive and rapidly expanding role of the state in most of Latin America' (Balassa *et al.* 1986: 24). And economists also counsel restraint on the basis of new theories. The conventional Smithian propositions about the virtues of the invisible hand and the distortions caused by intervention have been supplemented by important additions of three kinds.

One is the additional misallocation attendant upon rent-seeking. Intervention creates a surplus; individual agents will spend resources to get their hands on it, as well as to change the rules. As a first approximation, unproductive activity will equal the real cost of the distortion, doubling the economic loss and imposing a high penalty upon active state policy. These costs of intervention are associated with the public choice literature of James Buchanan and Gordon Tullock (see e.g., Buchanan and Tullock 1962), as extended and applied to trade and development by Krueger, Bhagwati, Srinivasan, and others.[9]

The second line of attack upon government intervention is its susceptibility to favour distribution rather than growth. Mancur Olson has emphasized how the free-rider problem contributes to institutional distortion. The costs of organizing small, self-interested groups are lower, and their potential gains larger, than for public-spirited, global ends. To achieve their objectives, distributional coalitions must use their lobbying power to influence government policy or their collusive power to influence the market . . .

[9] For a useful treatment of the neoclassical approach, see Srinivasan 1986.

'Someone has to administer the increasingly complex regulations that result . . . This increases the scale of bureaucracy and government' (Olson 1982: 69, 71).

The third strand of criticism is rooted in Douglas North's historical application of the property rights literature. The right role for the state is to establish and defend rules for control over assets that will promote efficient transactions; unfortunately, rulers will follow their own narrower agendas of revenue maximization at the potential expense of such efficiency. They may be forced to concede a property rights structure able to favour powerful supporting groups; or the costs of collecting taxes may cause them to adopt an inefficient set of property rights. 'These two constraints together account for the wide spread of inefficient property rights. In effect, the property rights structure that will maximize rents to the ruler (or ruling class) is in conflict with that that would produce economic growth' (North 1981: 28).[10]

All three strains of neoclassical political economy share an emphasis upon misallocation through distributional priorities deriving from competition in the political sphere. Entrenched interests, and those contesting for the spoils, defeat even the good intentions of the state. What is efficient in the economic market place, in reducing profits and assuring minimum cost, becomes wasteful in the political arena as the prospect of private gains leads to socially unproductive activity and the wrong set of property rights.

All three strains of neoclassical political economy equally opt for reduced government intervention. For those writing in the rent-seeking tradition, the solution is liberalization and the elimination of rents. In the words of James Buchanan: 'If, however, governmental action moves significantly beyond the limits defined by the minimal or protective state, if government commences, as it has done on a sweeping scale, to interfere in the market adjustment process, the tendency toward the erosion or dissipation of rents is countered and may be shortly blocked' (Buchanan 1980:9, as cited in Srinivasan 1986). In the name of such efficiency, hard measures may be necessary: 'a courageous, ruthless and perhaps undemocratic government is required to ride roughshod over these newly-created special interest groups' (Lal 1983: 33). That done, pluralism can presumably be restored later in the minimalist state.

Olson is more optimistic about the prospects for a democratic consensus doing the right same thing: 'it might simply repeal all special-interest legislation or regulation and at the same time apply rigorous anti-trust laws to every type of cartel or collusion that used its power to obtain prices or wages above competitive levels' (Olson 1982: 236). North, with his historical and

---

[10] North's position is ambivalent. His state, when unleashed, is able perfectly to remedy external economies. Its intervention is perfect. On the other hand, private individuals also organize collectively and are able to reduce transactions costs once property rights are correctly assigned by the state.

positive emphasis and his sympathy for constructive state action, is less overt. Yet the property rights literature from which he starts is clear. There are always possibilities to rearrange private property rights such that individual decisions are the right ones; that defines the correct and minimalist state role.

Neoclassical political economy, not unlike orthodox Marxism, is in fact a theory of the non-state, focusing almost exclusively upon the reactions of private individuals and groups contesting for advantages. The state is a caricature, condemned to failure in its efforts to implement its developmental agenda when such is even conceded. All state-promoted transfer of resources is relegated to unproductive distributionism, even when such reallocation of resources is at the heart of the developmental process. Quantitative restrictions may contribute directly to industrial sector profits and investment rather than to gains by third parties. Second-best instruments are sometimes necessary. The neoclassical school's counterfactual world is harmonious market competition, as though the same special interests that present themselves in the political realm will meekly conform and market solutions will not concentrate power or impede efficiency.

The literature contributes by indicating how state intentions may be checked and constrained. In this respect it is a healthy offset to mere assumption about the capacities of the state to intervene positively. As the Economic Commission for Latin America confessed, 'during much of the 1960's and 1970's, it was assumed that in Latin American countries the State was indeed in a position to play the role assigned to it by the development and economic transformation strategy . . . The main schools of economic thought in Latin America, including ECLAC, have never devoted much of their efforts to analyzing the State' (Maddison 1986: 54, 53).

The neoclassical approach is also a useful counterpoise to the extreme position taken by Chalmers Johnson in his discussion of Japanese development, which emphasizes state effectiveness; economic inefficiency is relegated to a secondary plane. But as the rent-seeking literature emphasizes, inefficiency can also lead to ineffectiveness as yet additional resources are wasted in pursuit of the distortion-provoked spoils (Johnson 1982: 19 ff). More generally, inefficiency weakens the state by reducing its resource base. Even favoured groups will not provide continuing support out of stagnant incomes. Initial objectives will have to be modified or given up, as state effectiveness is limited to a narrower domain. Johnson converts the political economy problem of stimulating economic development into an exclusively political one.

The principal deficiency of the neoclassical approach, however, is its failure to inform about the conditions under which the state can play a positive role. Beyond creating (minimalist) rules to enhance the market, there is no policy advice. Nor, except for resort to authoritarian tutelage, is there guidance about creating and sustaining political support, even for liberalization. There is too much evidence of different types of state action in the course of economic development, successful and unsuccessful, for such a theoretical political economy to suffice. It is a central theme of late-comer development that is not casually dismissed. And, even accepting the conclusion of excess intervention in many countries at the present, there remains the need to establish priorities about what the state should do and not do, and the need to implement them.

There is an opportunity to learn from the divergent East Asian and Latin American experiences.[11] The East Asian cases have been seen as prototypes of developmental states with high degrees of autonomy, and hence with the capacity to choose and implement an economic growth strategy without dilution at the hands of a myriad of contending private interests. Such autonomy was partially the product of an overriding concern with national security, even societal survival. Significant agrarian reform and income equalization removed concerns about inequality from the agenda, permitting concentration upon accumulation. National identity was assured by external threat; foreign penetration of capital was limited by the labour intensity of the manufacturing sector and state support for national firms.

State bureaucracy was focused and insulated. The public sector was not an employer of last resort, nor was it weakened by lack of access to resources. Early external aid inflows were of central importance in Korea and Taiwan. Later, when they ceased, the state benefited from increased revenues as product growth accelerated. Consistent and credible public policy reduced private sector uncertainty and encouraged investment.

All these characteristics helped to promote the switch in strategy in the early 1960s from import substitution to export orientation. The rapid expansion of international trade provided a growing market for the NICs as Japanese exports became more sophisticated. Export promotion was an industrialization strategy that could work for poor, resource-poor economies. The Latin American developmental state took another form, emphasizing import-substituting industrialization. This was for two reasons. First, the Great Depression had aroused an understandable scepticism concerning the opportunities for international trade and a liberal order. The 1930s had also been a period of industrial growth in many countries. Second, export promotion in the resource-rich countries of the region necessarily translated into an emphasis upon the primary sector and reinforcement of the traditional rural élite whose influence industrialization was supposed to diminish. What Latin America was deemed to need was a new, modernizing, urban middle class.

State incentives and a new bureaucratic technocracy would play a

[11]For a comprehensive review of recent literature on the role of the state in East Asia and Latin America, see Haggard 1986.

prominent part in the conscious transformation of society. The continuing power of the Latin American rural élite, not its weakness as in Sachs's version, determined the choice of the exchange rate and the adoption of commercial policy instruments to tax the rural sector and simultaneously redistribute the proceeds to the new industries. Trade policy was not about trade, it was about internal production incentives and finance. The state was interventionist and could set national goals, but it lacked the political power to implement them fully. Indirect techniques were therefore the order of the day. That meant a bias against exports, and also a need to use the inflationary tax to finance an expanding infrastructure investment. By the end of the 1950s the net result in the large countries in the region was an impressive growth in industrial production, accelerating inflation, and balance of payments problems. In the smaller ones, market-size limitations reduced the scope for successful transformation; the efforts to create a regional common market failed.

Greater attention to exports necessarily ensued in Latin America in the 1960s, as discussed in Section 5.1. But the resource-rich and middle-income status of much of the region continued to make the external market a doubtful focus for a development strategy oriented to industrialization. Exports were needed to relieve the balance of payments constraint, not to provide a source of demand for domestic industry. That function was as much true for Brazil, with its more favourable export performance, as for other countries. And it carried over as much to the Latin American military governments as the civilian ones they replaced in the 1960s and 1970s. The Latin American developmental state remained inward looking not only as an expression of its autonomous commitment to industrialization, but also as a result of the rise of an urban society organized around the industrial and public sectors. Nationalism was a strong unifying ideology that was always appealed to. In Latin America, nationalism was equated with protectionism, even though the consumer-durable style of Latin American industrialization required large foreign investment. And protectionism meant support of industrial entrepreneurs and workers and a white-collar service sector. These domestic interests and the continuation of a political and constitutional tradition diluted the technocratic capacities of the state to define an independent development strategy.

As industrialization proceeded in the 1960s and 1970s, there were too many priorities. Pressures were brought to bear from a variety of diverse groups. There was a cancelling of real allocation effects as first one, then another, group received subsidies. The only consequence was a larger fiscal drain. The bureaucracy not only mirrored these divisions but superimposed its own lack of unity. State enterprises multiplied, with their own claims on resources—internal and external. The net consequence was a diminished efficiency of investment, not only of the public sector but also of the private.

At the same time, the distributional issue achieved a new prominence in the region, in part because of World Bank interest, in part because it was a legitimate outlet for the previously repressed populist agenda. Latin American inequality was at the upper reaches of the international scale. Bland assurances of a Kuznets curve that would improve the income distribution as income increased were inadequate. There was a problem of extensive poverty in the midst of plenty: the distribution issue was more fundamental than rent-seeking or special interest coalitions. And it did not have an immediate or simple solution.

The task of the Latin American developmental state has therefore been more complicated than its East Asian counterpart. Frustrated expectations have frequently exaggerated state efforts to stimulate growth, while at the same time evoking more divisive societal responses. At the same time, state capacities have been consistently more limited. Fiscal deficits and the resort to the inflation tax are a measure of that weakness. It is no wonder that external resources seemed the ideal solution, routed as they predominantly were to the public sector. In a larger sense they also averted a tradeoff between consumption growth and the domestic saving required to maintain high growth rates. A risky strategy was preferable to one of immediate adjustment that could not be implemented.

Indeed, a hallmark of Latin American economic policy is its heterodox quality. The state has been charged with achieving multiple goals, but granted only limited instruments. Economic agents are not only sceptical about policy effectiveness, they have constructed defences of their relative incomes. Novelty, and frequency of action, are the attempted means of reconciliation. Note that even when the Southern Cone countries went to liberalization, they did so in a special and extreme way that relied upon international responses to enforce internal discipline. And they did so incompletely, even in the midst of military repression.

The correct solution to deal with the continuing problem of economic recovery in Latin America is not the uniform application of orthodox remedies: that would be to draw the wrong lesson from East Asia by focusing narrowly on specific exchange rate, interest rate, and other policy instruments. Likewise, it would be to ignore the evidence of inadequate adjustment under IMF auspices. The right question is how to reconstruct a Latin American developmental state that can consistently implement the right policies, not just register the right prices. State direction is not enough because it was sometimes too much. But moving to a minimal state is to treat symptoms rather than the problem. Reforms must have a domestic basis in a sustainable societal consensus. That is the challenge facing the new democracies in the region, doubled by virtue of the immediate pressing requirements of the debt crisis.

5.5 A FINAL WORD

The increasingly divergent East Asian and Latin American economic performances in the 1970s and 1980s are a rich experience from which not only academics will draw conclusions, but also policy-makers. The challenge is to get the inferences right.

That means posing the comparison of the long-term growth records and the effects of external shocks correctly. It also means a careful look at the way market forces have worked to stimulate export growth, as well as at the appropriateness of export-led development for all. But above all, it necessarily involves a more systematic understanding of the political economy basis for a development strategy. It is not sufficient any longer to conduct the discussion around the theme of whether the East Asian states intervene, or even about how they do so: we must also understand what economic policies are effective and feasible in different settings, and how they contribute to altering the political space.

6

Worlds within the Third World: Labour Market Institutions in Asia and Latin America

Tariq Banuri and Edward J. Amadeo

It has become a commonplace, in the macroeconomic literature on *industrialized* countries, to regard differences in labour market institutions as critical determinants of macroeconomic performance.[1] Yet, the far greater variety of institutional arrangements in the Third World has almost entirely been neglected as an explanator of the equally divergent macroeconomic performance.[2] Recent writings in the field of development continue to identify government policies as the primary, if not the sole, determinant of cross-country differences in macroeconomic outcomes.[3] The disregard of institutional differences has become a serious problem in today's world, where much of the development profession is engaged in exhorting 'unsuccessful' developing countries to adopt the policies of 'successful' countries, without taking account of the costs which would be entailed in such an adaptation, or of constraints which might render such an exercise entirely infeasible.

This paper will seek to address some questions raised by this omission, by looking closely at labour market institutions in three regions of the Third World: Latin America, South Asia, and South–South-East Asia. We have argued in Chapter 2 that institutional arrangements place constraints upon policy-making and should be taken into account in policy prescriptions. Here we wish to extend the argument by showing that the feasible range of institutional change is also circumscribed and constrained by historical and social factors peculiar to each country or region. To invoke a concept which has recently come into vogue in the macroeconomics literature, labour

---

[1] Calmfors and Driffil (1987:1) observe, for example, that 'is has gradually become recognized that wage-setting may be as important for macroeconomic performance as policies on the part of the government'. Several other recent studies explain the success of a small number of industrial countries—Austria, Finland, Norway, Sweden, and often Japan and Switzerland as well—in terms of their 'corporatist' structures; see e.g. Rowthorn and Glyn 1990; Bruno and Sachs 1985; Goldthorpe 1984. For a theoretical treatment and critique, see Przeworski 1987.

[2] Notable exceptions include Fields 1984, which is discussed below.

[3] A striking example of asymmetric treatment of industrialized and Third World countries can be seen in the writing of Jeffrey Sachs, who relies on differences in wage-setting institutions to explain differential macroeconomic performance in OECD countries (Bruno and Sachs 1985), but ignores them entirely in a similar comparative study of Third World countries (Sachs 1985).

market institutions introduce 'hysteresis' into the analysis of policy effectiveness.[4] In other words, because of the existence of these institutions, the nature of current economic relationships is affected by past economic history. The effect of government policies on macroeconomic variables is determined, in part, by the history of economic variables, economic policies, and economic institutions; and the ability of governments and social groups to introduce successful institutional change is conditioned, in part, by the history of economic and political relationships and economic and socio-political conflict.

The key feature of labour market institutions, as identified by economists writing about industrialized countries, is the centralization of wage-setting arrangements and of labour organization in general. Many of these writers have therefore tried to construct numerical 'indices' of centralization as a means to explaining differential economic performance.[5] We believe, however, that given the extreme diversity of the relevant structures in the Third World, little purpose would be served by attempting to construct such a precise numerical index for this group of countries. We introduce instead a qualitative taxonomy which places countries into one of four different categories or 'models' of labour market institutions, in increasing order of centralization: 'decentralized', 'pluralist', 'polarized', and 'social corporatist'.[6]

The difference between this approach and other recent attempts to compare economic performance in Third World countries (e.g. Balassa 1985a; Sachs 1985), lies in the fact that our taxonomy does not treat either policy or institutions as exogenous; indeed, our attempt is precisely to discover the causes of differences in policy choice and economic performance as well as those in differential patterns of institutional development. Our description also differs from that of Gary Fields (1984), who has argued that government wage *policy* is a key determinant of institutional change, and therefore of macroeconomic success, in small open economies.[7] We argue, on

---

[4] The concept of 'hysteresis' was first employed by the physicist James Ewing to describe electromagnetic properties of ferric metals. In economics, while the idea can be traced back to Josef Schumpeter, it has been employed most extensively in recent Keynesian explanations of the unemployment performance of industrialized countries. For a detailed discussion, see Cross 1988, esp. chs. 1–3.

[5] Such indices have been constructed by several economists including Bruno and Sachs (1985) and Calmfors and Driffil (1987). Among political scientists, Crouch (1985), Blyth (1979), and Schmitter (1981) are particularly notable.

[6] As in contemporary studies of industrialized countries, we distinguish 'social corporatism'— with its social democratic and participatory implications—from 'corporatism' or 'corporativism', which has élitist and statist connotations, particularly in Latin America (cf. Bergquist 1986: 149–82; Erickson and Middlebrook 1982).

[7] Fields (1984) identifies four institutional forces which determine macroeconomic success. Two of these—minimum-wage legislation and government pay policy—are pure policy instruments, and he argues that even the others—strength of labour unions and multinational corporations—are determined by the tacit or explicit support provided by the government. He sees labour union strength as deriving either from government encouragement to the unions, or simply from the latters' affiliation with the party in power. Similarly, he claims that

the other hand, that these outcomes are determined by social, political, cultural, and historical factors which underlie wage-setting institutions, and over which the government has little control.

This construction is used to make four points: First, apart from a few notable exceptions, countries within the same region share institutional characteristics which distinguish them from countries in other regions.[8] Second, these institutional differences are related to growth and adjustment performance in important ways; specifically, there seems to be a hump-shaped relationship between labour market centralization and growth and stabilization performance.[9] Third, institutional differences are themselves explained by underlying historical, social, cultural, and ideological factors (which are often shared by countries within the same geographical region). Lastly, as has been mentioned already, the feasible range of institutional change is limited, and restrained by historical factors.

More importantly, it brings out the fact that successful macroeconomic performance is a function not of the 'tightness' or 'laxity' of the government's wage-policies, but rather of the priority placed by governments on maintaining social peace. Given that the requirements for maintaining social peace will differ from country to country—depending upon the economic, political, cultural, and historical factors mentioned earlier—successful policies will also generally differ from country to country. Proposals based on the East Asian experience, to 'liberalize' labour markets (see Krueger 1986; Balassa 1986a), or to introduce 'tight' wage policies (see Fields 1984), miss the point entirely. While it is fair to say that governments in East Asian countries place a large premium on the maintenance of social peace—and, if one is willing to overlook the moral aspects of the issue, that they have managed to accomplish this task quite efficiently—it is facile as well as erroneous to assume that social peace can be procured in all circumstances through the centralized, élitist, and statist methods popular with these governments. The special historical and political, not to mention the cultural, background which facilitated this outcome is clearly absent in Latin America, and may be in the process of disappearing from East Asia as well.

While governments can try to initiate a move towards structural and institutional changes which create the possibilities for effective policy-making, this move has to take account of the nature of political forces in society. Where there is a long history of conflict and struggle, the imposition

---

multinational corporations pay high wages only to appease governments in order to avoid expropriation or explusion. See Fields 1984: 80.

[8] Of course, given the strong cultural and social affinities of such countries (e.g. a common language or lingua franca), as well as their shared history of conflict and struggle (e.g. against colonial domination), this is entirely to be expected.

[9] Similar hump-shaped relationships have been discovered for industrialized countries. See e.g. Calmfors and Driffil 1987.

of strict wage policies is likely to lead to political instability rather than to economic growth. In such circumstances, effectiveness of policy can be enhanced only by bringing disaffected social groups into the decision-making process, rather than by ignoring, suppressing, or disenfranchising them.

6.1 TAXONOMY OF LABOUR MARKET INSTITUTIONS

In order to analyse and describe labour market institutions in various countries, we need information on the nature and the strength of the labour movement. This is a function of two things (a) the existence of legal arrangements protecting the rights of workers to organize and to undertake political action in defence of their interests; and (b) the history of organization, resistance, and success, which on the one hand shapes perception of political possibilities and political expectations, and on the other contributes to the improvement, through learning-by-doing, of the 'technology' of organization and mass mobilization.

Information on legal arrangements is presented mainly as a background to the more pertinent discussion of historical developments, since the extent of legislative protection at any point in time provides only a rough guide to the strength of the labour movement. This is so mainly because changes in political regimes in the last two decades have led to a certain amount of convergence across countries of the legal rights of industrial workers. On the one hand, the emergence of authoritarian regimes in Latin America in the 1960s and 1970s was accompanied by a crackdown on the activities of organized labour; and on the other hand, increasing resistance against repressive state policies in South Korea has resulted in a gradual relaxation of the severest of controls. Nevertheless, clear differences along this dimension continue to exist between the different sets of countries, since even the most authoritarian regimes did not roll back most of the important institution protections; nor did the relaxation of controls translate immediately into substantive changes. Be that as it may, we look for answers to the following questions:

LEGAL ARRANGEMENTS
Unions and strikes
1. Do workers have a *right to organize* unions?
2. What is the highest level of union organization (plant, industry, region country)? Are *nation-wide* unions legally allowed? Do they exist?
3. What *percentage* of the labour force is organized in labour unions?
4. Is there a *closed shop* system where only one union is legally permitted to organize the workers in a particular plant, industry, or region?
5. Do workers have the *right to strike*?
6. What is the level of *strike activity*?

Wage-setting
   7. What is the level (plant, industry, region, country) at which the actual
       wage-bargaining takes place?
   8. Is there direct participation by workers in the form of *voting* on the
       wage-bargain?
   9. Is there a legal *minimum wage*?
  10. *Cost of living allowances?*
  11. *Other*, e.g. bonuses, social security, pensions, unemployment compen-
       sation, child care, etc.?

History
  12. When did the labour movement first make an appearance in the
       country? When were unions organized? When did widespread strikes
       first take place?
  13. What were the periods of political repression of workers?
  14. When did the countries have pro-labour governments? When were
       comprehensive labour laws first introduced?

Detailed information on the above questions is presented in the Appendix.
Salient features relevant for the analysis of policy issues are discussed below.
Specifically, we use the information to place countries into one of the four
categories of 'ideal types' according to the centralization and strength of
their labour organizations; and show that the classification is correlated not
only with familiar indices of the political power of organized labour—the
level of unionization, the right to strike (*de jure* and in practice), and income
protection arrangements—but also with observed macroeconomic performance.

6.1.1 Centralization of wage setting

By now, although the right to form unions is recognized almost everywhere,
it is often heavily encumbered with various forms of legal and political
restrictions. In particular, governments of almost all Third World countries
use legal or extra-legal methods to discourage the formation of genuine, over-
arching national unions or federations, presumably out of a fear of the
political strength of workers. This is so even though the example of Social
Democratic countries in Scandinavia and elsewhere illustrates that such
institutions can help replace conflict with co-operation by allowing an
effective representation of the interests of industrial workers in national-
level decision-making (see Rowthorn and Glyn 1990). Using the level of
centralization of worker organization as an index, Third World countries can
be grouped into three categories or 'models', which are described below,
along with the 'social corporatist' model prevalent in Social Democratic
countries.

1. *Decentralized model.* Strongly circumscribed and divided labour movement with diffuse influence in some areas of the country; does not play a major part in national politics, nor is able to confront employers in any significant sense. Wage bargaining is always at the enterprise level. Operation of labour laws and labour rights considerably circumscribed. Right to strike is strongly limited in practice even when it exists legally. In many cases, a national union is established by the government to supervise organized workers and to regulate union activities.

2. *Pluralist model.* Organized labour in a somewhat dependent situation; labour groups wield power only through alliance with other identifiable political groups, most importantly established political parties or ethnic groups.

3. *Polarized model.* Broad-based labour movement with a long history of mobilization, organization, conflict, and success; but with internal divisions along regional, craft, skill, or industry lines. Thus, while organized labour is capable of imposing real costs on the economy in the defence of its interests, it is not strong enough to impose a co-operative solution at the national level.[10]

4. *Social corporatist model.* Functional groups wield power and transact affairs in their own right and, more importantly, are organized even at the national level. In addition, the institutional and organizational resources of the state are used to facilitate co-operation between labour and capital. Thus, the political strength of organized labour can be used for negotiating a 'national' compromise, increasing productivity, maintaining stability, and ensuring social peace.[11]

'Decentralized' and 'pluralist' countries appear to be similar because wage-negotiation in both takes place at the plant level, but the similarity is only superficial. Whereas workers in different firms in pluralist countries are connected to each other through their affiliation with political parties, there are no comparable vertical or horizontal linkages in 'decentralized' countries, except through the auspices of the government or a government-controlled labour federation. In Latin America, even though many governments have tried to push wage negotiations down to the plant level, the representative form of conflict continues to be at the level of the industry or of a region.

Table 6.1 summarizes the information in the Appendix regarding the degree of centralization of the worker movement, and presents a comparable

---

[10] As in Latin American countries in the 1970s and 1980s, these institutions can lead to a suboptimal stalemate, rather than to a resolution of conflicts through centralized and consensual arrangements.

[11] Consequently, it is possible for the state to pursue full employment and distributional goals without necessarily undermining productive and market efficiency. In the political science literature, this model is also referred to as 'concertationist'. A recent discussion of corporatist arrangements and their role in facilitating adjustment to external shocks is to be found in Goldthorpe 1984. A more succinct source of references is Rowthorn and Glyn 1990.

Table 6.1 Taxonomy of labour market institutions

Model	Third World	Industrial countries
Decentralized	Thailand, Malaysia, S. Korea, Indonesia	Japan, Switzerland
Pluralist	South Asia	US, Canada, Italy, France
Polarized	Latin America, the Philippines	UK, Netherlands, Belgium
Corporatist	None	Scandinavia, Austria

Source: Third World: appendix to this chapter. Industrial countries: Calmfors and Driffil 1987.

picture of industrialized countries. It turns out that besides the Philippines, the groupings in the Third World correspond to the geographical position of a country: Latin American countries considered here are very much alike, so are South Asian and East–South-East Asian countries. It may be noted, here, however, that Indonesia shared some characteristics of pluralist countries, but its decentralized character has become increasingly dominant over the last two decades.

6.1.2 Strength of union activity

As mentioned earlier, indicators of union strength are likely to be somewhat flawed since legal provisions often change in periods of economic or political uncertainty. As such, the presence or absence of a particular legal right in a given type of country is best seen in probabilistic terms: although it is more likely to be present among polarized rather than in pluralist or decentralized countries, it will not necessarily be present in all of the former, nor necessarily be absent from all of the latter. In Table 6.2, we look at three indicators of the political strength of organized workers: (a) the percentage of workers belonging to trade unions; (b) whether there is legal support for a closed union shop (in other words, whether the law allows only one union per enterprise); and (c) whether workers are legally allowed to strike.

The higher rate of unionization in 'polarized' countries relative to the others is quite obvious, and need not be dwelt upon. A clarification is, however, called for in the case of Sri Lanka, where the large percentage of workers in labour unions might suggest an exaggerated estimate of the strength of organized labour. The largest union, the Ceylon Workers' Congress (CWC), is more of an 'ethnic' political group than a labour union. Representing the half million 'Indian' Tamil workers in Sri Lankan tea plantations,[12] it has

[12] These workers were imported from South India into Sri Lanka (then Ceylon) as plantation labour by British colonial rulers in the nineteenth century. They have a distinct cultural identity, different not only from the majority Sinhalese population, but also from the 'Sri Lankan' Tamils

Table 6.2 Labour union strength indictors, 1983

	% unionized	Closed shop	Right to strike
Polarized			
Argentina	16.6	y	y
Brazil	48.6	n	y
Chile	28.5	n	l
Mexico	23.6	y	y
Venezuela	44.5	n	y
Colombia	24.0	n	y
Peru	3.4	y	y
Uruguay	...	y	n
Philippine	24.0	y	y
Pluralist			
Bangladesh	3.0	n	y
India	4.5	n	y
Pakistan	3.5	n	y
Sri Lanka	30.0	n	y
Decentralized			
Indonesia	4.8	n	l
S. Korea	7.0	y	l
Taiwan	17.3	y	l
Malaysia	8.7	n	l
Thailand	1.1	n	l

Notes: y = yes; n = no; l = limited.
Source: *Far East Economic Review* 1987: 44, International Labor Affairs Bureau and Kurian 1982.

constantly projected an ethnic group rather than a working-class perspective in national politics, and its revered leader, Savumyamoorthy Thondaman, is himself the owner of a tea plantation and a government minister.[13] As a result, the CWC, the strongest labour union in Sri Lanka, representing over one-third of all organized workers, has never made common cause with the rest of the labour movement.

The closed shop system is a more complicated indicator of the power of organized labour, since it appears in countries at both ends of the spectrum of the centralization of labour organizations: in the strong unions of 'polarized'

who migrated to the island centuries ago. The 'Indian' Tamils have not taken an active part in the recent Tamil–Sinhalese ethnic conflict.

[13] Indeed, the name CWC was adopted only after independence. At its founding, with the help of Nehru and Gandhi, who visited the island for this purpose in 1939, it was called the Ceylon Indian Congress (CIC), and was conceived of as a means of propagating Indian nationalism and as a political arm of the Indian National Congress.

countries, and in the relatively weak plant unions of 'decentralized' countries. Whereas in the former case this law is essentially a reflection of the strength of organized workers to protect themselves against efforts to fragment and divide them, in the latter case it is invariably an indicator of the weakness of the labour movement, since it ensures that workers do not form independent organizations to challenge pro-government 'legal' unions. In South Korea and Taiwan, for example, since the government has the discretionary power to certify legal unions, the closed shop system enables the government to register only loyal unions, and to prevent them from being challenged or replaced by independent unions.

With regard to the legal right to strike, even though recent trends in Latin American and East Asian countries appear to be leading towards a certain amount of convergence, the two regions are still remarkably different in this respect. The total prohibition of strikes has been relaxed somewhat in all East Asian countries in recent years. The Taiwanese government allowed this right for the first time in July 1988 when it revised the Arbitration Dispute Law. In South Korea, while technically the right to strike—'within the scope of the law'—was granted under the 1980 constitution, the web of restrictive laws has made almost every labour dispute since then illegal (*Far East Economic Review*, 27 Aug. 1987:15). Strikes were tolerated (and led to successes) only when the government faced widespread and popular opposition, as in 1979–80 or 1985–6.

Similarly, there are elaborate preconditions for 'legal' strikes in Malaysia, Thailand, and Indonesia.[14] The major sanction against illegal strikes is the government's insistence on firing and punishing strike leaders even in instances where the management does not so insist, and/or when the protest is not only successful but also appears justified. In any event, illegal strikes in East Asian countries are rarely prolonged events, nor do government crackdowns on organized workers appear to last too long. In South Korea, there was a brief period of strike activity in the early 1970s following the self-immolation of a young worker in protest of working conditions, but these strikes were suppressed very severely (see Irwan 1987), and large-scale unrest did not take place until the late 1980s.

In Latin America, on the other hand, the right to strike was recognized in various countries as early as the 1920s and 1930s, but has increasingly been restricted in the last two decades by authoritarian governments—such as Argentina (1966–71, 1976–82), Brazil (1964–85), Chile (1964–70, 1973–present), and Uruguay (1974—present)—during episodes of 'economic liberalization'. Yet, the new legal restrictions were obeyed only at the peak of the repressive phase. The Brazilian military government limited the right to

---

[14] Preconditions for legal strikes include: a notification to the Labour Ministry, a 20-day cooling-off period, conciliation, mediation, and arbitration. For a description of current labour unrest, see *Far East Economic Review*, 27 Aug. 1987.

strike at the time of the military coup in 1964, and as a result of the repression that followed there were no major strikes in the ten-year period 1968–78; but workers began carefully constructed job-action programmes, which would register their dissatisfaction and pressure employers, yet remain within the letter of the law. Subsequently, in 1978, labour strikes over wage demands started again, first in São Paulo and spreading to other areas. The government increasingly tolerated them despite the terms of the tough anti-strike decree laws then in force. Similarly, strikes were tolerated in Chile in the 1960s and early 1970s even though up to 80 per cent did not fulfil the legal requirements. Later, in 1973, the Pinochet government disbanded the major trade union federation (CUTC) and severely curtailed labour rights including the right to strike, yet illegal strikes continue to take place. All Venezuelan strikes in 1977 or 1978 (and all but one in 1979) were illegal, yet there were no jailings of labour leaders or participants in this period.

The underlying legal arrangements are reflected in the level of strike activity. Table 6.3, which gives figures on the number of man-days lost due to labour disputes, reveals quite clearly the high level of labour-militancy in polarized and pluralist countries, and the very low levels in decentralized East Asian economies. While a large number of strikes does not, by itself,

Table 6.3 Number of mandays lost due to labour disputes (average per year per 1,000 labour force members)

Country	Period	Days lost
Polarized		
Argentina	1974	60
Chile	1980–1	158
Venezuela	1980–4	70
Philippines	1980–4	61
Pluralist		
Bangladesh	1980–4	28
India	1980–4	153
Indonesia	1980–2	1
Pakistan	1980–4	21.5
Sri Lanka	1980–4	80
Decentralized		
South Korea	1980–2	2
Malaysia	1980–3	2.5
Thailand	1980–3	4
Memo: United States	1955–80	342*

Source: International Labour Statistics
* US figures are average per 1,000 employees.

indicate a strong labour movement (indeed, it could reflect exactly the opposite), these data complement other indicators of the relatively greater power of organized labour in Latin America.

6.1.3 Legal income-protection arrangements

Information on income protection arrangements in various countries is summarized in Table 6.4. Almost all Latin American countries have legislated minimum wages, mandatory cost of living allowances (COLAs), and mandatory bonuses, although some backtracking has taken place in recent years during military dictatorships and/or stabilization episodes. In Asia, only the Philippines has a long history of similar legislated benefits. South Asian countries had piecemeal legislation during the colonial period, but the laws are still very selective, subject to discretionary interpretation, and loosely enforced.[15]

Table 6.4 Wage-setting institutions, 1988

	Minimum wage	Cost of living allowance (COLA)	Bonus
Polarized			
Argentina	y	y	1 month
Brazil	y	y	1 month
Chile	y	y	1 month
Colombia	y	n	1 month
Mexico	y	y	share
Uruguay	y	y	1 month
Venezuela	y	y	1 week–2 months
Philippines	y	y	1 month
Decentralized			
Indonesia	n	n	n
Korea	l	n	n
Malaysia	l	n	n
Thailand	l	n	n
Pluralist			
Bangladesh	w	n	n
India	w	n	4%–20%
Pakistan	n	n	n
Sri Lanka	y	y	n

Notes: y = yes; n = no; l = limited; w = weak.
Source: Kurian 1982.

---

[15] India and Pakistan have a practice of 'dearness allowances', which are introduced by the government from time to time, and which result in an *ex post* indexation, ranging from 100 per cent for the lowest income levels to about 40 per cent for upper income brackets.

South Korea and Taiwan initiated the process of legal reform only in the 1980s (without much consultation even with official labour unions), and have not begun to enforce the new laws forcefully. The South Korean government initiated a policy of minimum wage guidelines between 1974 and 1979, but the practice was abandoned during the adjustment to the 1979 shocks; subsequently, a complicated minimum wage legislation was passed in January 1988, but it has yet to acquire full force.[16] Taiwan instituted a minimum wage as part of the Labour Standards Law passed in 1984 but enforcement is lax. Other Asian countries (Malaysia, Thailand) have legislated minimum wages, but they apply only to selected sectors. The absence of COLAs is easier to understand in Asian countries because of their moderate levels of inflation. However, even in Latin America these innovations pre-dated the period of high inflation.

6.2 CONTEMPORARY DETERMINANTS OF LABOUR MARKET INSTITUTIONS

Why is labour better organized and better protected in Latin American than in Asian countries? The neoclassical answer, as we have noted already, is that these differences emerge from the inclination of Latin American governments to intervene in potentially free-functioning labour markets, to encourage labour organization for political purposes, and to enact legislation protecting the rights of industrial workers. This appears to us to be a rather one-sided portrait of historical realities, focusing as it does on the autonomous role of the government rather than on popular needs and concerns which make organized activity necessary; in particular, it ignores the fact that the acquiescence of governments to workers' demands as well as the emergence of pro-labour governments occurred generally as a consequence of the political strength of labour rather than the other way around.

Therefore, the interesting questions pertain to the factors which contribute to the ability of workers to forge a strong and organized movement at the national level, to develop a workers' perspective on political and economic issues, and to provide a blueprint not only for a one-shot redistribution of income and wealth, but also for sustainable and healthy development for the future. Two sets of factors, different but not mutually exclusive, present themselves. (*a*) The longer *history* of mobilization in defence of economic and political rights, such as in Latin American, can contribute to the development of leadership and organizational abilities, to the emergence of a workers' political and social identity, to the legitimacy, popularity, and credibility of organized activities, and thus to a greater measure of influence in national decision-making. (*b*) Some economic and social *institutions* are relatively more

[16] For a criticism of this legislation, see Park 1988: 110.

congenial to the forging of a national labour movement, partly by lowering the costs of forming organizations and partly by increasing the expected benefits from this activity.

We leave the question of historical determinants until a later section. Here, we argue that three features of the society—the existence of a (political or economic) centre of gravity of the society, socio-economic inequality, and socio-cultural homogeneity—are positively related to the perceived costs and benefits of creating and joining organizations, and that these are prominent in countries where organized labour is relatively more powerful. We also argue that the government attitude towards labour rights is influenced to a marked degree by these features of society.

6.2.1 Centralization

The issue we are interested in is not that workers can form trade unions at some or all enterprises to bargain for wages or other benefits. The issue is whether workers in a particular country can forge a movement of a national character with a consistent vision of the good life; a movement which can influence political choices in such a way as to minimize the need for local conflicts, to increase the effectiveness of local or national agreements, and to introduce on the one hand, political participation and on the other, political responsibility.

The ability to construct a national movement would be enhanced in countries where there is an identifiable political or economic 'centre', as compared with a situation where political or economic power is effectively decentralized. Two examples can be given to elaborate this idea. First, consider the situation in most South American countries in the first half of this century, where relatively small and concentrated export sectors were of critical importance in the functioning of the polity as well as the society.[17]

It is possible to think of these sectors—nitrate (and later, copper) mining in Chile, oil in Mexico and Venezuela, meat-packing in Argentina, coffee in Colombia, or the metal industry in Brazil—as the 'centres' of the national economies. They provided the bulk of the foreign exchange, and thus the ability to purchase the imported consumer and investment goods on which the economy had rapidly become dependent. More important, they constituted the major source of revenue for the rapidly expanding state, which became equally dependent on them. This twin dependence facilitated the forging of a national labour movement, since from the very start any action by organized workers in the export sector (or in the ancillary, and equally critical, transportation sectors) was elevated to a national issue, given its ability to disrupt the entire economic and political system of the country.[18]

[17] The following paragraph borrows heavily from an argument made by Bergquist (1986).
[18] As Bergquist (1986) noted, the differences in the nature and effectiveness of organized labour activity in different Latin American countries can be traced in important respects to the

Not surprisingly, these organizational efforts were met with virulent public and private repression, but this provided even greater incentives for organization and resistance, with the result that ultimately the state was forced to accommodate workers' interests. Another consequence was that workers in general, but in these industries in particular, became conscious of their predicament, their power, and their responsibility.

This type of an 'economic' centre was absent in the large agrarian South Asian countries when they embarked upon the path of industrialization and worker organization. The only exception was Sri Lanka, where a similar (albeit less significant) dependence on tea exports had developed by the early years of this century; here, the plantation workers did organize themselves into a powerful union, but as has been mentioned earlier, they expressed ethnic rather than a workers' perspective, and did not therefore provide a leadership for workers in other sectors. Of the East Asian countries, only two developed significant export dependence: the Philippines, where a labour movement did emerge by the turn of the century; and Malaysia, where, notwithstanding the anti-British insurgency in 1948–57, the emergence of a strong labour movement was hindered by several factors, including the politically decentralized nature of colonial rule in Malaysia, the existence of ethnic differences and the prominent role of ethnic Chinese in the labour movement, and the limited legitimacy of terrorist actions during the insurgency by a leadership which was popularly thought of as being subject to foreign control.

A second type of centralization is related to the level of urbanization of a country, particularly to the extent of the domination of the largest city in national political and economic life. In such countries, since open urban conflict has the potential of paralysing the entire economy, there would be a greater premium on maintaining social peace. In contrast, in geographically diffuse societies, even if a particular city is closed down, the rest of the country could function without any problems.

Generally speaking, the level of urbanization of a country contributes to the ability of organized political groups to defend or promote their interests, particularly when the urban population is heavily concentrated in one 'primate' city—such as Mexico City with 32 per cent of the national population, or Buenos Aires with 45 per cent. In these cases, since it is often difficult for the government to localize and contains conflicts, organized political action becomes more feasible as well as more effective. Joining or forming an organization becomes not only more beneficial, it often becomes a necessity simply for defending oneself oneself from the adverse effects of political actions of other organized groups.

structural conditions in its export industry. Thus, Chilean mines and Venezuelan oilfields facilitated unionization, whereas Colombian coffee plantations and Argentinian cattle ranches delayed it.

Table 6.5 Urbanization in Latin America and Asia

Country	% urban (1985)	% largest city (1980)
Latin America		
Big Four		
Argentina	84	45
Brazil	73	15
Chile	83	44
Mexico	69	32
Andean countries		
Venezuela	85	26
Colombia	67	26
Ecuador	52	29
Peru	68	39
Bolivia	44	44
Uruguay	85	52
Paraguay	41	44
Central America		
Panama	50	66
Nicaragua	56	47
El Salvador	43	22
Honduras	39	33
Costa Rica	45	64
Guatemala	41	36
Asia		
East Asia		
China	22	6
S. Korea	64	41
Taiwan	. .	. .
South East Asia		
Philippines	39	30
Malaysia	38	27
Thailand	18	69
Indonesia	25	23
South Asia		
Burma	24	23
Pakistan	29	21
Sri Lanka	21	16
Bangladesh	18	30
Nepal	7	27
India	25	6

Source: World Bank 1987.

As Table 6.5 reveals, a larger percentage of the total population in Latin American countries lives in urban areas, particularly in the largest city, than that of Asian countries (except for South Korea and the Philippines). Thus, it would make sense for Latin American workers to organize themselves, and for their governments to become sensitive to their grievances.

6.2.2 *Inequality*

Another factor which can influence labour organization and labour legislation is the existence of significant socio-economic inequalities. A social perception of unfair inequality can lead to social frustration and thus to greater incentives for joining a political group. Widespread social frustration will render political action more efficacious, because of the greater possibility of attracting allies from other disaffected members of the society. Given a favourable political environment, such alliances can lead to the establishment of governments which are relatively more responsive to the concerns of popular groups, and inclined towards the enactment of legislation favouring these groups.

More often than not, however, such legislation has taken the form of income protection arrangements rather than pure distributive actions, given the fears of populist governments that pure redistribution can be destabilizing because of its association with greater social mobilization and growing expectations. An interesting exception to this rule is provided by the success of land redistribution policies after the Second World War in South Korea and Taiwan, which did not need a mobilization of the rural populace since the expropriated persons had already left. Thus, the land redistribution lowered the level of social frustration in the short run (by equalizing incomes) without bringing about an increase in social frustration in the long run by promoting mass mobilization and social aspirations.

Data on income distribution in different countries are notoriously unreliable. However, Table 6.6 does indicate that the level of inequality in Asian countries is much lower than in Latin American countries. The exceptions are the Philippines and Malaysia.

The control of oligarchic groups over Latin American governments up to the early twentieth century had much to do with high levels of inequality prevailing there, particularly in facilitating an extremely unequal distribution of agricultural land, the main form of wealth. In Asian countries, land was not as unequally distributed, even in colonial periods. An interesting research issue, which cannot unfortunately be dealt with in this paper, is why and how did most countries preserve their income distributional profiles over the last forty years despite extremely rapid structural change and industrialization.

Table 6.6 Income distribution

Country	Year	% of total-income	
		Lowest 40% of households	Highest 20% of households
Latin America			
Argentina	1970	14.1	50.3
Brazil	1972	7.0	66.6
Chile	1968	13.4	51.4
Mexico	1977	9.9	57.7
Venezuela	1970	10.3	54.0
Peru	1972	7.0	61.0
East Asia			
Philippines	1970	14.2	54.0
S. Korea	1976	16.9	45.3
Taiwan	1971	21.9	39.2
Malaysia	1973	11.2	56.1
Thailand	1975	15.2	49.8
South Asia			
Indonesia	1976	14.4	49.4
Bangladesh	1976	17.1	46.9
India	1975	16.2	49.4

Source: World Bank 1987.

6.2.3 Cultural homogeneity

The relationship between cultural homogeneity and labour organization is a complicated one. At a simple level, a high level of cultural homogeneity among workers reduces the chances of internal divisions and conflicts and thus enhances the prospect of organizational unity along functional lines, partly because the likelihood of non-economic conflicts diverting attention away from conflicts over economic issues will be smaller. Moreover, if the homogeneity is developed along an identification with Western countries, economic conflicts will be intensified because of aspiration towards Western standards of living and Western institutions by the élite and non-élite alike.

On the other hand, cultural heterogeneity can also exacerbate conflict, mainly in circumstances where economic and political resources are distributed unequally between various cultural or ethnic groups. In terms of worker organization, cultural heterogeneity will stimulate collective action if workers and employers belong to different cultural groups. However, this depends crucially on the degree of politicization of underprivileged cultural groups. Where there is a high level of politicization, as in South Asia, there is

Table 6.7 Ethnic, linguistic, and religious heterogeneity

Country	Ranking	Index %
Latin America		
Argentina	71	69
Bolivia	63	32
Brazil	109	93
Chile	96	86
Colombia	112	94
Mexico	72	70
Uruguay	84	80
Venezuela	107	89
South Asia		
Bangladesh	129	98
India	4	11
Pakistan	40	36
Sri Lanka	57	53
East Asia		
Korea	135	100
Indonesia	16	14
Malaysia	25	18
Philippines	21	26
Thailand	37	34

Source: Kurian 1982.

a greater likelihood of finding 'soft' states—states which are incapable of pushing through on a controversial course of action because of the ever-present danger of civil strife.[19] In any event, given the last point, it would be difficult to generalize on the issue of cultural homogeneity and worker mobilization. Yet, it is not unsafe to suggest that in the absence of a close correlation between cultural and functional divisions, cultural homogeneity will be associated with a greater degree of organizational capacity.

In Table 6.7, we give George Kurian's estimate of the index of homogeneity in various countries, based on a ranking of 135 countries, with Tanzania number 1 (most heterogeneous) and North and South Korea number 135 (most homogeneous). From these figures it seems that, except for the very unusual properties of South Korea and Bangladesh, Asian countries are much more ethnically diverse than Latin American countries, and hence possess a greater potential for non-economic conflicts[20] and a lesser one for organizational unity along functional lines.

[19] The concept of 'soft' and 'hard' states was first introduced by Gunnar Myrdal (1968: 895–900). See also the discussion in ch. 2, this volume.
[20] This observation seems to be borne out by the rapid escalation of ethnic violence in these countries, acquiring a pandemic nature in the last decade.

The degree of cultural identification with the West is also much more pronounced in Latin American than in Asian countries, the Philippines being a striking exception once again. This is quite evident in the much more extensive adoption of the Catholic religion in these countries, as also in the language (Spanish or Portuguese in Latin America, and English in the Philippines), and the acceptance of political and social institutions from the United States. Among other things, this identification has also helped foster the notion of cultural homogeneity in these societies. In South Asia, while the ruling élite do identify with the West, the strength of indigenous culture is fairly strong even among this group, and even more so in the larger population which continues to adhere to its traditional world-views despite two centuries of colonial rule.

The extremely varied colonial experience of East and South-East Asian countries does not lend itself to many confident generalizations. Nevertheless, it could be said that while the Latin American intellectual heritage involves a conflict between anarcho-syndicalism at the bottom and state-corporatism and militarism at the top (see Bergquist 1986, O'Donnell 1973), and the South Asian tradition between anarchism at the bottom and liberalism and militarism at the top (see Myrdel 1968), the East Asian legacy is much more profoundly coloured by state corporatism. This is explained not only by the fact that almost all these countries suffered colonization or wartime occupation by Japan,[21] which is also said to have a state-corporatist orientation. Rather, the reason is the survival of indigenous cultural traditions during colonial rule, which was either short and confrontational (Korea, Taiwan), or long and superficial (Burma, Malaysia, Indonesia), unlike the strongly hegemonic British colonial rule in India.[22] Filipino society is the only one which developed an explicit identification with the West through its colonial heritage.

Two possible consequences of a strong cultural identification with the West are relevant to our analysis. First, it is likely to push up the consumption standards of the rich (in emulation of those in the West) as well as the aspirations of the poor, thus increasing not only inequality itself, but more importantly the perception of inequality by the poor who would compare their lot with that of the rich of the United States. In addition to this effect, Westernization can also help introduce and legitimize the individual-istic ethic of the West, interfere with social or cultural arrangements which

---

[21] Or, in the case of Thailand, concluded wartime agreements with Japan.

[22] Besides Thailand, which was never colonized, two countries—Korea (1910–45) and Taiwan (1895–1945)—were occupied by Japan; another two (Burma, Malaysia) suffered approximately a century of British colonial rule (which was not only shorter but also less extensive and far-reaching than British rule in India) as well as wartime Japanese occupation; the Philippines were colonized by Spain in the sixteenth century, by the United States in 1898, and by Japan during the Second World War; and Indonesia experienced two centuries of Dutch colonial rule as well as wartime Japanese occupation.

create social harmony through ascriptive identifications, and thus increase the legitimacy of organizational affiliation.

6.2.4 Attitude of government

It has been maintained by some writers that the differences of institutional arrangements in different countries derives directly from the attitudes of respective governments towards intervention in market arrangements. In our view, a more fruitful perspective on institutional development as well as the governments' attitude is provided by the notion of social peace. Even if all governments placed the same priority upon the maintenance of social peace, the resulting policies would be different if the underlying socio-political conditions were different.

This can be illustrated through a specific example of government attitudes. Pranab Bardhan (1984) has argued in a well-known work that the Indian government is 'inflation sensitive'—i.e. its policies reflect a high priority on maintaining a low rate of inflation. This argument can be interpreted in terms of the priority of social peace by noting that inflation is costly in countries like India because it exacerbates the most pronounced conflict, namely the conflict between urban and rural areas. It can also be contrasted to a notion that Latin American governments are 'growth sensitive'—sensitive to growth of employment as well as to growth of consumption—because the fundamental conflict in these countries is in the urban industrialized areas, and the only way to manage this conflict is through growth in employment and growth in consumption.

These countries can also be said not to be as inflation sensitive as Asian governments, because they have institutions which can facilitate adaptation to changes in distribution introduced by inflation (i.e. indexation, minimum wages, unions), but do not have equivalent institutions to facilitate adaptation to unemployment. Notice that in urban areas there is a dichotomous situation, whereby the worker who loses his/her job has no access to consumption, while changes in the price level bring about only continuous changes in ability to consume. In South Asian 'pluralist' countries, on the other hand, the greater inflation sensitivity reflects the fact that the culture enables adjustment to unemployment, but not to inflation. There are no indexation or other arrangements, but the extended family arrangement may provide a slight cushion for the unemployed.

6.3 HISTORICAL DETERMINANTS

Not only does Latin American labour have more effective organizations and more extensive rights and benefits than East or South Asian labour, it achieved all this much earlier than the other two regions, and through an entirely different sequence of stages. In most Latin American countries, three distinct stages of social polarization can be identified, the first characterized by state-corporatist accommodation, the second by bureaucratic-authoritarian repression, and the third, which is still upon us, by muddling through.

The consciousness and articulation of workers' collective interests in Latin America began, in the late nineteenth century, with the formation of numerous 'mutual aid societies', followed by more sustained organizational efforts in the first quarter of the present century. The virulent public and private repression which greeted these efforts led to growing polarization and instability, but found, ultimately, a cathartic denouement in an accommodationist phase. In this stage, populist regimes introduced comprehensive laws to guarantee economic and political benefits to workers, in return for the legitimization of governments' right to control and regulate union activity. Subsequently, however, the denial of direct political participation to highly politicized workers introduced another period of polarization and confrontation, which ended, in most cases, not in a renewed attempt at dialogue and accommodation, but rather in a phase of social repression with the emergence of 'bureaucratic-authoritarian' regimes of the 1960s and the 'liberalization' experiments of the 1970s. After another quiescent period, the resurgence of political articulation and worker mobilization has created a new stalemate, further complicated by the debt crisis and the terms of trade shocks. It is this stalemate which must be resolved.

While the historical experience of East Asian countries is extremely diverse, some common elements do exist. For various reasons—late industrialization, the absence of a political or economic 'centre' (see Section 6.3.1), ethnic and cultural heterogeneity—the labour movement did not acquire the political strength and national identity that it did in Latin America; nor did the labour movements of this region (or any popular movements for that matter) meet with any measure of political success until the 1980s. Second, in most countries, labour organizations were effectively destroyed during internal or international conflicts—Korea, 1931–45, 1951–3; Malaysia, 1948–57; Indonesia, 1965–6—or wartime occupation. Given the weak state of unionization at the time of independence, post-colonial states were successful in controlling the labour movement through state-corporatist institutions and laws (and, in some cases, emergency decrees), which are only now beginning to be challenged.

The historical experience of the workers' movement in South Asia was very different. Here, in the first stage, there was accommodation and encouragement rather than repression and undermining, thanks to a colonial government which promoted the development of 'rational' political institutions and to nationalist political leaders who sought to expand their political base. Moreover, unlike their Latin American contemporaries, South Asian workers never had the ability to paralyse the entire colonial economy. As a result, worker protest and resistance was sporadic unless mobilized by nationalist political parties. Thus, post-colonial governments inherited a large but fragmented labour movement which did not have a national voice despite a long history of mobilization and organization. As a result, unions have been treated with a kind of benign neglect at the national level, except on the rare occasions when their actions threatened the national economy— e.g. the Indian railway strike of 1974, or the epidemic of industrial strikes in Pakistan in the early 1970s.

In the following pages, we shall try to bring out these differences more concretely by examining a few historical features in more detail. When does the activity of organized labour date from, and what were its determining characteristics? When did it acquire a measure of political strength and of political and legislative success? What were the periods of retrenchment and renewal?

6.3.1 Latin America

The history of collective action in Latin America is at least a century old.[23] It began with the emergence of numerous 'mutual aid societies',[24] subsequently transformed into powerful formal organizations with a coherent national identity.[25] Despite several cycles of repression, confrontation, and accommodation, workers in Latin American countries managed to obtain legal recognition, democratic rights, and income stability much earlier than those in any other country now in the Third World; and, even now, after a long period of retrogression and quiescence, their organizations are more dynamic than those of most other Third World countries, and their rights and benefits still compare favourably with workers of other regions.

These successes are illustrated by the enactment, from 1924 onwards, of wide-ranging sets of laws by populist governments, on the one hand to protect the rights and interests of industrial workers—minimum wages, COLAs, bonuses, right to organize, right to strike—and on the other hand, to regulate and direct worker activism—legal requirements for forming unions or going on strike, government supervision of union activities and control of finances. In Chile, the home of Latin America's oldest labour

---

[23] Some information is collected in the appendix to this chapter. For more details, see the sources cited here.

[24] These societies, such as the Chilean *mancommunales*, derived their support from widespread anarchist sentiments. They were generally built on ethnic lines and provided a variety of social services to their members; later, they also formed the basis of 'resistance' societies which were instrumental in presenting workers' demands for better working conditions and compensation.

[25] As noted in Section 6.3.1, this was largely due to the critical importance of primary exports in the national economy.

movement, the government adopted a detailed Labour Code in 1924–5. Other countries soon followed suit: Mexico in 1931, Venezuela in 1936, Brazil in 1943, Argentina in 1946, and Colombia in 1950. In contrast, similar legislation emerged in South Asian countries only in the 1960s, and even later in East and South-east Asia.

The reforms were designed to distribute equitably the fruits of production, particularly the economic rents in the export trade, and thus to ensure the co-operation of organized labour in industrialization and import substitution. Ironically, however, they came at a time when the central importance of export industries in the domestic economies of most countries (Mexico and Venezuela being the outstanding exceptions) was beginning to disappear due to changes in international market conditions. This created unanticipated problems. Since the reforms were premissed in the need to increase labour's share in national income, and to 'protect' their incomes from the vicissitudes of the international markets, they could hardly be used to introduce the wage flexibility demanded by international market conditions. Rather than look for a fresh compromise, most governments chose to accomplish precisely the latter goal by using their newly acquired regulatory power to curb and restrain organized labour. In this endeavour, they were opposed by political groups which were more committed to the egalitarian aspects of the reforms.

In a path-breaking analysis, Guillermo O'Donnell (1973) argued that this conflict reflected an incompatibility between the logic of capitalist develop-ment—i.e. the need to turn towards an advanced stage of import substitu-tion, namely that of capital goods—and the actual political environment, particularly the high level of political mobilization among the working classes, leading to the emergence of 'bureaucratic-authoritarian' regimes all over Latin America. These regimes embarked upon a more determined exploitation of the regulatory powers granted to governments under the existing labour legislation, with the intent to replace political activity with bureaucratic control of unions and other organizations. Nevertheless, even these regimes did not try to abolish the important institutional protections of workers' incomes. (See Weffort 1978; O'Donnell 1973; Fishlow, this volume).

In the 1970s, some of these regimes embarked upon a more ambitious programme, of 'liberalization' of their economies, which did seek to roll back workers' rights and benefits, and to destroy popular institutions developed over a century or so. By analogy to O'Donnell's framework, it could be argued that these policies were attempts to resolve the incompatibility between the logic of a new wave of export-oriented development and a persistently high degree of worker mobilization. As a result, while the authoritarianism of the 1960s succeeded in introducing a brief phase of political quiescence and economic improvement (Brazil, 1964–78), liberaliza-tion attempts of the 1970s were accompanied by brutal police repression

(Chile 1973–present; Argentina, 1976–83), continued confrontation and polarization, and persistent economic dysfunctioning.

In Brazil, the set of laws which guides the behavior of labour unions and establishes the institutional setting for wage-negotiations is the Consolidaçao das Leis Trabalho (CLT). The CLT was enacted in 1943 during the populist Vargas government (1930–45), and represents the most concerted, 'state-corporatist', effort by any Latin American government.[26] These reforms can be viewed as having three different aspects: bureaucratic, participatory, and protectionist. The first confers on the government the right to direct and regulate the labour movement; the second provides encouragement to unionization and organizational efforts; and the third guarantees economic benefits and income protection. The law provides for strong 'industry' unions united into eight national federations, but discourages shop-floor unions,[27] and until 1985, the formation of a single national federation.[28] Government control is exercised by a 1931 law which allows the Labour Ministry to 'intervene' in any union, i.e. to replace elected officials with appointed ones. Moreover, union funds are collected by the government, and distributed to unions according to a pre-determined formula.

These laws created the basis for a period of unprecedented growth in the Brazilian economy which ended only in 1977. However, it was not smooth-sailing all the way. During the 1950s, considerable conflict centred around the 'participatory' and 'bureaucratic' aspects of the reforms, reaching a climax in the militant workers' rally which preceded, and may have precipitated, the military coup of 1964 that ultimately imposed a bureaucratic solution. In the immediate aftermath, union leaders were arrested, strikes banned, and a lid placed on union activity. Later, while the extreme measures were withdrawn, government control over labour organizations was tightened.

Two consequences of the bureaucratic solution can be noted. First, wage-bargaining rights were taken away from unions by a 1966 decree which established a wage-setting formula (see Erickson and Middlebrook 1982:240). However, although the formula was designed to adjust nominal wages in line with inflation and productivity growth, the government consciously under reported inflation, and brought about a sustained downward movement of real wages in general and the real minimum wage in particular.[29] During

[26] This description is based on Camargo 1986. Some details on the structure of laws and rights are given in the appendix to this chapter.

[27] The discouragement of the shop-floor unions operates, first, through the law which does not protect union activities in a firm, and second, by denying union funds to these activities.

[28] Although the law was silent on the question of a single national union, it was interpreted as prohibiting it. However, in the 1960s, the CGT functioned practically as a national union. In 1985, the CGT was recognized as a national federation (as was the CUT).

[29] The minimum wage, established by the Vargas government in 1940 to retain the support of urban workers, has become an index of income distribution as well as a unit of account in inflationary periods. Its establishment pre-dated the enactment of the CLT, and it was

stabilization periods, the indexation level was reduced, thus lowering real wages even further. The index of the real minimum wage fell from 100 in 1964 to 78.7 in 1971, rose during the economic boom of the 1970s to reach 87.1 by 1980, but fell again during the stabilization episodes of the 1980s to 70.8 in 1984.

Second, because of the more consistent use of government's powers to regulate strike activity, the number of strikes fell dramatically.[30] This is paradoxical, since the right to strike on economic issues was recognized for the first time under a military decree of 1964. Strikes were strictly regulated during the Vargas dictatorship, when the government retained discretionary powers, often exercised on the basis of political expediency, to judge the legality of strikes. The 1946 constitution recognized an unfettered legal right for the first time, but since the Congress never passed the necessary enabling legislation (*regulamento*), nor repealed the earlier law prohibiting strikes, the constitutional right did not come into force until the military decree of 1964—at which time, however, it was superseded by other laws and regulations. While overt strike activity declined during 1964–78, workers began to engage in carefully defined job action programs which would remain within the letter of the law and yet challenge employers. Finally, in May 1978, metalworkers in São Paulo held a major strike which effectively broke the strike ban initiating a new period of strike activity.

In Brazil (and also in Argentina), the labour movement quickly recovered its power and organizational structure during the redemocratization process; workers have begun to play important roles at the national level, not only in questions associated with the determination of wages and the distribution of income but also in larger political matters, including changes in laws which affect the structure of the labour movement.

6.3.2 Pluralist South Asia

The distinguishing pattern of the labour movement in South Asian countries is an absence of unity and national identity despite a long history of labour activism, and strong union presence at the local level. While there was a vigorous trade union movement in South Asia by the end of the First World War, three of its attributes distinguish it from the parallel movement in Latin America. First, it remained, in an important sense, an adjunct to the political movement for independence from British colonial rule; second, much of the labour legislation was a boon from above, as it were, rather than the result of a struggle from below, a consequence of the colonial administration being an

---

introduced in response to the pressure from an increasingly demanding urban labour force, in order to guarantee a minimum standard of living for the labour classes in an economy with a significantly elastic labour supply.

[30] In São Paulo state, the number of strikes fell from a high of 302 in 1963 to 25 in 1965, 12 in 1970, and none in 1971. See Erickson and Middlebrook 1982.

extension of that in the mother country; third, and most importantly, the movement failed to acquire a unified national character, partly because of the absence of a political or economic 'centre' (see Section 6.3.1), and partly because of the relatively small size and the diffuse and agrarian nature of the export economy.

The result is that despite its venerable antecedents, the labour movement in South Asia is relatively 'young': it is fragmented vertically as well as horizontally; it has never presented a challenge to the state; it did not begin to develop its own identity and voice until well after independence, and still represents mainly the political and ethnic divisions of the larger society;and while unions may have a great deal of power at the local level, they are relatively weak and ineffective at the national level. Most labour unions are affiliated to federations which are offshoots of political parties. There is a proliferation of unions and federations, since any seven workers can legally form an association or join a national federation (collective wage-bargaining is conducted at the enterprise level by the union which wins a biennial referendum).

The colonial state, seeing itself as an extension of the British government, imitated British laws and institutions, even though employers were able to ignore many of the laws with impunity because of inadequate supervision. These included piecemeal legislation on working conditions and safety requirements in factories, passed as early as the late nineteenth century; and recognition of unions, strikes, and other rights of workers under the Trade Unions Act of 1926. An equally important reason for this benign attitude was the fact that the labour movement did not pose a serious threat to the government, unlike, say, contemporary Latin American labour movements, or the Indian independence movement. This explains why strikes and labour activism did not summon the extreme government repression, such as that visited upon independence struggles or even large-scale peasant uprisings.[31]

A second consequence of colonial history is the reciprocal contributions of the labour movement and the independence movement to each other. While organized urban workers strengthened the independence movement by providing a mass base for protest activities, the reverse linkage was the significant one: leaders of nationalist political parties took part in the organizational and resistance activities of unions, gave them national publicity, and lent their status and prestige to the resolution of industrial disputes.

In India, labour activism is at least seventy years old. There is evidence of strikes even before the First World War—the most prominent was the

---

[31] On the other hand, it may be noted that since South Asian countries did not suffer a total disruption of civil life due to wartime occupation or civil war—as in East and South-East Asia— trade unions and other organizations of the civil society continued to function and grow throughout the twentieth century.

Bombay textile-mills workers' strike of 1913 (see *Far East Economic Review*, 27 Aug. 1987: 63)—and it picked up after the war years. A strong impetus was provided by the founding of the ILO in 1919, of which British India was a member. In the first half of 1920 alone, there were 200 strikes in India affecting over a million workers (see Wolpert 1977: 304). The All-India Trade Union Congress (AITUC) was set up in 1920 with the blessing of the leading nationalist party, the Indian National Congress (INC), and began organizational work in earnest. By 1929, there were more than 100 trade unions in India, with almost a quarter of a million paying members.

The AITUC was soon dominated by communist groups, which it is to this day, whose leadership came mainly from the eastern provinces of Bengal and Kerala, where the labour movement has been the strongest historically. (Indeed, these provinces have had communist governments since independence.) After independence, the Congress government sponsored a rival federation, the Indian National Trade Union Congress (INTUC) in order to counter the hold of opposition political groups, particularly the communists, over the AITUC. Today, the INTUC is the largest labour central, followed by the AITUC. Given the legacy of opposition politics among trade unions, and the almost complete political dominance of the Congress in national politics, even this federation has drifted away from government control. Relations were strained even further when the Indira Gandhi government put down the 1974 railway strike with police and military assistance.

Pakistan and Bangladesh, united as one country from 1947 to 1971, had very little industry at the time of independence—and very little industrial labour. While Bangladesh had experience of labour unrest, such as the tea plantation strike of 1920, Pakistani labour was largely unorganized. In these countries, the AITUC had been succeeded, in 1947, by regional trade union federations, the East- and West-Pakistan Trade Union Federations (EPTUF and WPTUF). These were largely ineffective in pushing for change until the period of unrest in the 1960s. Independent or militant leaders were frequently jailed in the 1950s and replaced with more congenial types. Strong unions, such as the two railway workers' unions or the Karachi port handlers unions, were closely watched.

Although Pakistan signed the ILO conventions on the rights of workers to organize (1948) and to bargain collectively (1949), there was no internal pressure for legislation, and the government was moved into action only after massive civil unrest brought down the unpopular Ayub regime in 1969. The successor military regime passed a comprehensive set of labour laws in a bid to appease workers who had played a prominent role in the civil uprising. These laws recognized the right to organize, bargain, and strike, and mandated various other benefits for organized workers, to be provided by the employers.

By the time Bangladesh seceded from Pakistan in 1971, the situation had changed considerably. Unions were not only recognized legally, they were no longer considered centres of treasonous activities; and they had just contributed to the success of a major popular movement—for the independence of Bangladesh in one wing, and for democratization and renewal of civil liberties in the other. This did not, however, lead to a unification of the labour movement in either of the two countries. In Bangladesh, the EPTUF split into five factions along political lines, in 1971. More than 70 per cent of the workers organized in 2,614 registered unions are affiliated to political parties. The labour movement in Pakistan divided into several groups: a left wing group, federated under the Pakistan Federation of Trade Unions (PFTU), allied to the People's Party which ruled the country from 1971 to 1977; a right-wing Islamic group, the Islamic National Labour Federation (INLF), allied to the fundamentalist Jamaat Islami; and several centrist groups, most notably the All-Pakistan Federation of Trade Unions (APFTU), and the Pakistan National Federation of Trade Unions (PNFTU). These four groups cover more than two-thirds of total membership in 8,300 unions in the country. Notably, despite frequent impositions of martial law, the rights of the workers to organize or to strike on economic issues has not been greatly interfered with in either country.

In Sri Lanka, as noted already, the oldest labour union, the CWC, was formed in 1939 among people of Indian descent working in tea plantations. The union was supposed to be an ethnic party as well as an arm of the INC. Its character as an ethnic party remains to this day; this explains why it has not been able to serve as a catalyst for the formation of a national labour movement, despite its early organizational success and continuing political strength. The remaining unions are affiliated with political parties, including the ruling UNP. As a result, the labour movement is fragmented vertically as well as horizontally, as it is in Bangladesh, India, or Pakistan.

6.3.3 Decentralized East Asia

The labour market in East and South-East Asian countries is characterized by a strong degree of state control over fragmented local organizations. Although a national unity of sorts exists in these countries, it has been imposed from above and bureaucratically administered, rather than emerging through popular mobilization and participation. The effectiveness of government control can be gauged from the quiescence and loyalty of these unions, the rarity of periods of independence and resistance—e.g. Malaysia, 1948–57; Indonesia 1960–6; South Korea, 1976–9, 1987–8—and the ease and effectiveness with which they have been suppressed.

While there is evidence of pre-Second World War collective labour activity, particularly in connection with anti-colonial movements in Indonesia, Korea, Malaysia, and the Philippines, it was either weak

(Indonesia, Malaysia), or was severely crushed and marginalized (Korea).[32] Furthermore, these countries did not have a sufficiently long peaceful period in which popular organizations could take root.

Among the shared historical reasons for this outcome are late industrialization, the absence of an economic 'centre' of critical importance to the national economy, and the limited hegemonic influence of Western culture. More importantly, the labour movement in particular and local popular movements in general do not have a history of successes. Labour laws have typically been enacted in response to international pressure or for corporatist purposes, but almost never as a response to irresistible workers' demands.

In a recent survey of labour market arrangements, the authoritative East Asian news magazine, *The Far East Economic Review*, reported that 'the South Korean worker has one of the longest work-weeks in the world. He, or she, is among the most likely to be killed or injured on the job—and one of the least likely to be represented by a union' (27 Aug. 1987: 14). Until 1987, South Korea had no minimum wage legislation, unemployment insurance, or universal superannuation.[33] Although child labour is prohibited, the violations are generally winked at. Similarly, laws pertaining to hours of work are often said to be grossly violated; in South Korea it is not unusual for textile workers to work 12–15 hours per day with only one day off per month, despite the legal maximum of 50 hours per week.

However, there are elaborate laws governing the formation of trade unions, the settlement of labour disputes, and the conduct of collective bargaining.[34] Indeed, South Korea is a classic example of the state-corporatist system which Latin American governments tried to perfect in their countries in the 1930s and the 1940s. The Labour Union Law allows only one union at a work place, and all the unions are controlled and directed by the Federation of Korean Trade Unions (FKTU), which in turn is directly controlled by the Office of Labour Affairs (Irwan 1987: 401–2). Any one attempting to organize or mobilize workers outside of the state-controlled sphere is faced with severe punitive action by the firm, the government, or by government-backed 'action squads' (ibid. 401–3; Soo 1978).

Besides direct controls over union activity, labour laws discourage

---

[32] The Korean labour unions were essentially adjuncts to the anti-colonial political movement; they had to go underground in 1931 because of suppression by the colonial administration. Later, the division of the country and the civil war destroyed popular political forces. In Indonesia, the brief civil war and the massacre of 1966 saw the destruction of left-wing trade unions.

[33] The following description is drawn from Dee 1986.

[34] The major laws affecting the labour movement are the Labour Union Law, the Labour Dispute Adjustment Law (which made strikes illegal and prescribed expensive and lengthy procedures for government mediation of labour–management disputes), the Labour Committee Law, and the Labour–Management Council Law. For the anti-labour bias of these laws, see Irwan 1987: 403.

resistance in other ways as well. The procedure for settlement of disputes is extremely tedious and discouraging towards labour militancy. The tripartite Labour Committees, consisting of representatives of labour, management, and the 'public interest', which were established to mediate labour disputes, were also biased against labour, because members of the 'public interest' were appointed by the government. Labour–management councils were set up in enterprises to supplant existing unions, or to inhibit their founding in plants without unions. Union activities themselves are restricted to individual companies, and outside legal advice, even by the FKTU, is prohibited. The limited freedom for dispute and collective bargaining were also suspended during the turbulent period of the 1970s.

The weakness of the labour movement in South Korea is rooted in historical factors. Early instances of organized collective action were related to opposition to Japanese influence,[35] which began with the opening up of diplomatic relations in 1876 and culminated in the establishment of colonial rule in 1910. Two well-known anti-Japanese insurrections, the Tonghak peasant rebellion of 1894 and the Mansei rebellion of 1919, were brutally suppressed with the aid of Japanese troops (see Reeve 1963: 16–19). The labour movement in this period was also closely tied to the independence movement and had to go underground in 1931. However, this popular movement did not succeed in its objectives, and independence had to wait for the Japanese defeat in the Second World War.

After independence, the society was disrupted by the partition of the country and by the Korean War. Since much of the heavy industry was in the northern half of the country, the partition contributed to the weakening of workers' organizations. Moreover, the war disrupted civic organizations of all types, and would have necessitated reconstruction efforts anyhow. However, these efforts were hindered because of possible accusation of connections with North Korea. To fill this vacuum in organization, the government (with the assistance of the AFL-CIO, the major labour federation in the United States) stepped into the breach and began organizing loyal unions, united under a government-controlled federation, the Korean Federation of Labour Unions, later renamed the Federation of Korean Trade Unions (FKTU). Throughout the 1950s, the ruling Liberal party controlled unions through the FKTU. Indeed, labour organizations are conspicuous by their absence in descriptions of the popular uprising which helped overthrow the Liberal government in April 1960.

[35] The period of direct colonial rule over Korea is relatively small and relatively recent. From 1388 to 1910, Korea was ruled by the indigenous Yi dynasty, even though the government accepted the suzerainty of successive Chinese empires until the late nineteenth century, and considerable Japanese influence thereafter, the latter leading to the Japanese colonial occupation in 1910. In 1637, the Korean king promised allegiance to the Manchu court; two and a half centuries of peace ensued, coming to an end only with the initiation of Japanese influence in the 1870s. See Reeve 1963: ch. 2.

The Park regime (1961–80) banned unions for a brief period, but then returned to relying on the FKTU to control and supervise union activity; this practice was enshrined in the labour laws included in the Yushin Constitution in 1973. After 1976, however, industrial labour became increasingly assertive after a young worker immolated himself to protest the repressive conditions; but before an organized protest could develop fully, President Park Chung-Hee the target of the protests, was assassinated by one of his aides. The new regime, led by General Chun Doo-Hwan, introduced even more repressive labour laws in 1980 and used them to suppress union activism until 1987, when a new outbreak of strikes led to political and economic concessions.

In Taiwan, the nationalist government has similarly maintained rigid control over labour independence through its corporatist labour central, the CFL, which moved to the island in 1949. Emergency decrees and martial law have also helped to stifle dissent. Since unions and union leaders have to be approved by the local committee of the ruling KMT, the likelihood of union activism has been low all along. Taiwan is also distinguished by the fact that its modern sector consists mainly of small, family-type enterprises, and of relatively cordial relations between workers and employers. Effective and independent union activities have begun to develop only after the lifting of martial law in 1984.

In Thailand, which has never been colonized, the trade union movement dates back only to the 1970s, when the government for the first time decreed the right to organize. Initially, the unions were fragmented local organizations, but when they succeeded in forming a national federation (the LCT), the government managed to take it over. However, a new central (the TTUC) has since gained prominence, and has become the largest federation in the country.

The Malaysian labour movement dates back to the formation in 1934 of the Malaysian General Labour Union. Unions were tolerated, even encouraged by the colonial authorities. However, they were concentrated in the urban areas (Singapore, Kuala Lumpur) and tin mines, and consisted mainly of ethnic Chinese workers. Ethnic divisions between Malays, Chinese, and Indians have created obstacles in the ability of the union movement to forge a national identity. Communist influence was strong in the unions, and was responsible for maintaining organized resistance against Japanese occupation in 1942–5. After the war, when the grant of independence was delayed by the British, these groups began a guerrilla insurrection for obtaining independence, but the fact that they had a narrow popular base and were believed to be controlled by mainland Chinese leaders made their operations extremely vulnerable. The British declared a state of emergency from 1948 until the grant of independence in 1957, and destroyed the organizational basis of the resistance. Subsequently, even though unions were revived, they never recovered their earlier strength.

In Indonesia, labour organization had begun during the Dutch colonial period, but acquired momentum only in the decade after independence. Once again, communist groups were influential, particularly among the ethnic Chinese minority. President Sukarno (1948–66) was moving towards an accommodation with these groups when the abortive coup and the massacres of 1966 effectively destroyed their organization and leadership. The Suharto government, which has been in power since then, instituted state-corporatist reforms through which it creates and controls labour unions within the umbrella of the ruling Golkar Party. These arrangements continue to this day, without much visible friction.

6.4 DEMOCRACY, GOVERNANCE AND HYSTERESIS

As mentioned in the introductory section, this paper has been motivated by a curious asymmetry in the recent analyses of cross-country differences in macroeconomic performance. There is a striking contrast between the excessive attention paid to the effect of variations in labour market institutions in industrialized countries and the almost total neglect of an even richer variety in the Third World. The bulk of this paper has been devoted to bringing out this variety and to articulating the determinant causes which lie behind it.

In this endeavour, however, we have tried to stay away from simplistic and monocausal perspectives, which see government policy as the sole determinant of institutional development. Instead, we have emphasized the fundamental role of popular groups and democratic movements, and the effect which the history of earlier conflicts, successes, and failures has on current possibilities. We found, not surprisingly, that there are strong similarities between institutions of countries within the same geographical region, and that these similarities followed from similar structural conditions as well as common historical developments.

Since recent macroeconomic performance as well as labour market institutions have a clear regional pattern, we need not dwell upon the empirical association of the two variables. As a look at Table 6.8 will reveal, countries which, in our classification, are charcterized by a 'polarized' labour market, have had serious growth and adjustment problems, while those with 'decentralized' or 'pluralist' institutions have fared much better. Several points can be noted from this table. First is the unique decline in recent GDP growth rates of countries whose labour market institutions have been described as 'polarized' (Latin America and the Philippines). The improvement of growth rates in pluralist South Asian countries and the maintenance of the earlier growth record in decentralized East Asia is also apparent. Thus, a regional explanation of the recent economic crisis appears to be more accurate than ones based on policy choices.

Table 6.8 GDP growth rates: selected countries

Country	1960–70	1970–80	1980–5
Polarized			
Argentina	4.2	2.2	–1.4
Brazil	5.4	8.4	1.3
Chile	4.5	2.4	–1.1
Colombia	5.1	5.9	1.9
Mexico	7.2	5.2	0.8
Peru	4.9	3.0	–1.6
Venezuela	6.0	5.0	–1.6
Philippines	5.1	6.3	–0.5
Decentralized			
Indonesia	3.9	7.6	3.5
South Korea	8.6	9.5	7.9
Malaysia	6.5	7.8	5.5
Taiwan	. . .	. . .	. . .
Thailand	8.4	7.2	5.1
Pluralist			
Bangladesh	3.7	3.9	3.6
India	3.4	3.6	5.2
Pakistan	6.7	4.7	6.0
Sri Lanka	4.6	4.1	5.1

Source: World Bank 1987.

Second, even among Latin American countries, it will be noted that periods of slow growth coincided with political conflicts and with the erosion of elaborate legal arrangements instituted during the 1930s and 1940s. Growth in Chile and Argentina slowed down in the 1970s, with the initiation of periods of severe suppression of workers and popular groups. In Brazil, although an equally authoritarian government was in power from 1964–78, its success in using the legal arrangements established during populist rule resulted in a successful growth performance. Slowdown of growth in Brazil and the remaining countries of this group took place only after 1980, with the onset of the debt crisis and political resurgence of worker groups.

Behind this rather simplistic point, however, lie more subtle issues pertaining to policy choices and possible solutions. In order to look at these issues, we have to take a step backwards and ask what is the role of government policy in economic performance. Two types of answers have been popular in the literature: the neoclassical answer identifies the role of the government to be one of ensuring the freedom of exchange, while the radical answer sees the government as the main instrument of social change. Neither of these perspectives gives priority to a problem which was, for example, of central interest to Keynes in his writings; this is the problem of 'governance', namely the creation and maintenance of political and economic stability.

Thus, neoclassical economists look at the current crisis and analyse it mainly in terms of the need for the 'liberalization' of commodity, product, financial, and labour markets, and therefore for reducing government intervention into these markets; paradoxically, however, they have increasingly argued for using the power of the government to destroy economic and political institutions, in other words as an agent of social and political change, and thereby helped to increase rather than decrease the government's role in society. On the other hand, many radical economists have argued for an increase in government intervention and central planning in order to facilitate the joint pursuit of economic growth and other social welfare targets.

Both sides have looked at the (selective) experience of 'successful' East Asian economies, particularly the South Korean economy, for a vindication of their argument: the neoclassical economists look to the relatively open trade regime and the unfettered labour markets in South Korea, and the radical economists to the dirigistic nature of its economy and polity. Often, the two groups have converged in prescribing what can be called the 'Koreanization' of the Third world, although some writers have used the analysis to bring out the undesirable or non-replicable aspects of South Korean development, and thus to warn against the general trend.

There is, however, another way of looking at the issue, which places priority upon 'governance' and sees the primary function of the government to be the maintenance of economic, social, and political stability in a situation characterized by social differentiation and conflict. The first and obvious point in this perspective is that since the nature and intensity of conflict differs from society to society, a single solution cannot suffice for all possible times and places. The demands of economic and political stability must be dramatically different in a Latin American country with its long history of conflict, confrontation and accommodation, and an East Asian country with a more limited and recent experience of such divisiveness. Moreover, the demands for maintaining stability will change with time—South Korea in the 1980s is very different from South Korea in the 1960s.

In other words, it is simply not *possible* for Latin American countries to 'become like South Korea', without the payment of immeasurable social, political, and *economic* costs, and in all probability not even then. The demands of social co-operation in a polity composed of highly politicized and articulate groups are extremely different from those in a society where mass popular mobilization does not have a long history. Rather than push Latin American societies into sterile discussions of the costs and benefits of this intellectual cul de sac, or to coerce their governments into new and seemingly futile experiments of social engineering, it would be more fruitful to ask where these societies are going, and how can this direction of progress contribute to social goals valued by economists.

There is an additional point here. In an important sense, the mainstream debate over liberalization as an answer to all economic problems has managed to obscure a great deal, and actually to reverse social priorities—from economic growth as a means to maintaining a harmonious society, to growth and efficiency as ends in themselves. Now, the pursuit of economic growth, or other goals of importance to economists, by authoritarian governments will not lead to social peace,[36] but the pursuit of social peace as a primary goal by pragmatic governments will often bring about economic prosperity.

Indeed, even the 'successful' East Asian experience can be interpreted as a lesson in maintaining social peace—partly, it is correct, through the morally repugnant measures of intimidation and repression, but also, and more importantly, through an effective and vigilant government. As we have described in detail, the labour market institutions of East Asian countries are strongly reminiscent of the 'corporativist' arrangements which populist governments in Latin America tried to perfect in the 1930s and 1940s. In other words, East Asian governments have simply been more successful in facilitating co-operation between social groups; and they managed to do so not through the market, but rather through the mediation of effective, state-supervised institutions. The question, therefore, for Latin America, is not how, or whether, to 'liberalize' or 'Koreanize' its economies, but how to create the conditions for the type of successful social co-operation achieved elsewhere, by a better understanding of its own history and social and political institutions.

In this respect, it is simply a myth that economic efficiency, rapid growth, or immunity to external shocks is achievable only through the destruction of popular organizations. Among Western countries, for example, the ones which have been the most successful in riding out the recent economic crises with the least disruption of their economies or polities are precisely those which have the most well-organized and powerful labour groups (and other political groups as well). These countries—Austria, Finland, Norway, Sweden—are designated as 'star performers' by Bob Rowthorn and Andrew Glyn (1990), and as 'social corporatist' by other commentators.[37] They are characterized by powerful and articulate functional groups, national-level wage-bargaining, participation by representative social groups in national economic decision-making, and extensive social welfare arrangements, all

---

[36] The recent unrest in South Korea is an illustration. Other examples abound: Pakistan in the 1960s, and then again during the recent military rule; the Philippines in the 1970s; Iran under the Shah.

[37] See Rowthorn and Glyn 1990. For the discussion of social corporatism see Calmfors and Driffil 1987.

under the umbrella of a social democratic consensus shared not only by the ruling Social Democratic parties, but also by much of the opposition.

The Indian philosopher Ashis Nandy once described 'the inability to imagine alternatives' as the surest defence of oppression. The above discussion was intended to suggest not that social corporatism is *the* solution for Latin America, but to demonstrate, rather, that the possibilities for the future are not exhausted by the combination of economic liberalism and political authoritarianism. Indeed, the reference to the experience of social corporatism was meant to suggest that in this instance we are not even called upon to imagine alternatives. Furthermore, social corporatism, as a solution for the impasse between labour and capital is, like all other social solutions, a time-bound innovation. It will simply help to neutralize the most potent form of the conflict in today's world. The conflict will not disappear, and new solutions will have to be found tomorrow. Nor will the emergence of these institutions help to resolve all forms of conflicts—many will have to be dealt with through the well-known process of trial and error.

However, there is one clear advantage that this path possesses over that suggested by the advocates of liberalization. It does not attempt to write off the history of struggle and reform as an egregious error committed by unwise and irrational societies. By the same token, it does not seek to bring about a fresh change in society by imposing a draconian reign of terror, or by unleashing untold misery upon populations for which nobody in the economics profession, least of all expatriate advisers from powerful international institutions, is willing to take responsibility.

APPENDIX:
WAGE-SETTING INSTITUTIONS

The following pages try to present, in an extremely summarized form, information on labour market institutions in Latin American and Asian countries, in particular the legal situation, and to the extent possible, an impression of the workings of the law in practice. Since legislative change has been particularly rapid in recent years, it is likely that the information is not entirely up to date in all cases. While the sources of the information are quite varied, those which have been consulted more frequently include: Bergquist 1986; Deyo, Haggard, and Koo 1987; Erickson and Middlebrook 1982; Irwan 1987; Reeve 1963; and several issues of the *Far East Economic Review* (particularly 3 Apr. 1986, 27 Aug. 1987, and 8 Sept. 1988). In addition, Montek Ahluwalia, Jose Camargo, Jose-Antonio Ocampo, Sebastian Saez, and Carlos Winograd helped to vet some of the information, but are not responsible for any errors.

LATIN AMERICA

Argentina

History. In Argentina, as in the rest of Latin America, labour organization started in the nineteenth century in the form of mutual aid societies. These covered almost half the labour force of Buenos Aires by 1913, and played a significant role in the huge general strikes that shook the city in 1902 and 1909. Structural obstacles to effective labour organization in the critical export sector—the meat-packing industry—delayed organizational success despite several 'organizational' strikes, which began as early as 1894 but gained momentum after 1915. These efforts were more successful in transportation industries, where major strikes in 1917 led to the formation of powerful unions of railroad (FOF) and maritime (FOM) workers. The most prominent labour central, the Confederacion General de los Trabajadores (CGT) was founded in 1930. Enlightened labour reform proposals were made twice by concerned ministries after periods of labour mobilization and general strikes, in 1902 and 1919, but were shelved after the crisis subsided. Although piecemeal legislation was introduced during the 1920s, it was not until 1946, after a protracted period of labour unrest, that a comprehensive labour law was promulgated by the populist government of Juan Domingo Peron. The fall of the Peron government in 1955 led to another period of government repression of organized labour, to the 'anarchization' of conflict, and thus to an effective stalemate between labour and capital. Only recently, with the restoration of democratic institutions, is the possibility of a new labour–capital compromise beginning to re-emerge.

National union. No. The largest trade union federation, the CGT, covers approximately 25 per cent of the labour force.

Closed shop. Yes.

Right to strike. Yes. Banned in 1976. Restored.

Minimum wage. Yes. Set by government. Covers all employees. Many changes in the law since 1976 *coup d'état.*

COLAs. Yes. Indexation implicit before the Plan Austral. Targets in terms of expected inflation thereafter.

Other legal national wage-setting. Mandatory bonus of one month's pay.

Workers vote on contract. No.

Basic level of wage bargaining. Trade union federation (e.g. CGT).

Brazil

History. In Brazil, mutual aid societies had come into existence in the nineteenth century. However, the evolution of labour institutions and labour laws began in earnest after the revolution of 1930 and the ascendancy of President Getulio Vargas (1930–45, 1950–4). In line with Vargas's vision of state-dominated harmonious relations between labour and capital, laws were introduced in 1931 to regulate and control labour organizations through a hierarchical system of functional *sindicatos*, an affiliated system of labour courts, and the institutionalization of social welfare arrangements; these laws were revised and expanded in 1934, revised again and restricted somewhat in 1939, and finally promulgated in consolidated form in 1943 as the Consolidaçao das Leis Trabalho (CLT). Following more and more stringent control of the unions by the government in the late 1950s, there began a series of strikes of increasing intensity, particularly in 1961 to 1963; but instead of a resolution, the process was truncated by the military coup of 1964. As a result of the following repression, strike activity came to a halt; it picked up again in 1978 after a spontaneous series of job actions by metalworkers in São Paulo. The resulting unrest contributed, eventually, to the withdrawal of the military from the government.

National union. No. Basic union level is occupational at municipal level. There were no nation-wide confederations until 1985. Unions cannot exist (bargain or receive collections) outside state-sponsored structure. Ministry of Labour closely controls union operations; in particular, it bans strike funds, and encourages unions to allocate funds for the social welfare of workers.

Closed shop. No.

Right to strike. Yes. Severely limited in 1964. No major strikes in 1968–78. Anti-strike decree increasingly violated after 1978, beginning in São Paulo and spreading to other areas.

Minimum wage. Yes. Set by government. Used as standard for all other wages in the economy.

Mandatory COLAs. Yes.

Other legal national wage-setting. Mandatory bonus of one month's pay; social security; child care.

Workers vote on contract. No.

Basic level of wage bargaining. Municipal. Plant-level unions have little impact. Wage bargains are greatly conditioned and influenced by minimum wage movements and COLA.

Chile

History. Chile boasts the oldest labour movement in Latin America. As in other countries, it started in the form of mutual aid societies (called *mancommunales* in Chile) in the nineteenth century. Organized collective action in the critical nitrate-mining sector began in 1890. It increased in intensity and frequency in the first decade of the twentieth century, culminating in the massive general strike of 1907 in the nitrate zone, and the large-scale massacre of striking workers by government troops at Iquique. The first labour central, the Gran Federacion de Obreros de Chile (GFOC) was founded by railroad workers in 1909. Following more than a decade of worker protests and resistance, a comprehensive labour reform bill was introduced by the newly elected liberal alliance in 1921, and passed in 1924. Although neither side was totally happy with the reforms, strike activity declined somewhat as they began to work within the new legal framework. Labour organization received a boost in the late 1930s when the Confederacion de Trabajadores Chilenos (CTC) was founded to bring miners, transport workers, and manufacturing sector workers within one organization. Later, in 1953, the Central Unica de Trabajadores de Chile (CUTC) brought in white-collar workers, and eventually agricultural workers. The military dictatorship which came to power in 1973 banned the national centrals, prohibited strikes, rolled back some elements of labour legislation, and instituted a wage freeze which reduced real wages by 40 per cent.

National union. No. Largest union, CUTC, disbanded in 1973, but there are still 150 federations and 30 confederations nation-wide. Single enterprise as well as multi-company unions.

Closed shop. Not after 1973.

Right to strike. Yes, with some restrictions. Banned in 1973. Subject to various limitations today, including a maximum period of 60 days.

Minimum wage. Yes. Different in different regions. Covers all employees. Revised annually. Set by tripartite commissions.

Mandatory COLAs. Yes, until 1982.

Other legal national wage-setting. Mandatory bonus of one month's pay until 1982. Thereafter at the government's discretion.

Workers vote on contract. Varies.

Basic level of wage bargaining. Only single-enterprise contracts allowed by law. Treated as legal contracts, and allowed to deal with narrow issues, pay systems, cash benefits, conditions of employment. Government monitors wage-bargaining, but is not formally involved, except in strategic sectors.

Colombia

History. Colombia's major export industry, coffee, has severe structural obstacles to labour organization. As a result, social conflict on coffee estates has generally taken the form of widespread insurgency and social unrest, as in the late 1920s–early 1930s, without leading to organizational improvements. Labour organization before the First World War centred around mutual aid societies among the artisans of larger cities. Formal unions were first established by workers in the railway and river transport sectors, and by urban artisans. These three groups of workers organized a general strike in 1918 in Barraquilla; even though the strike itself was crushed, the government moved quickly (in 1920) to regulate strike activity through legislation, and to set up, in 1923, a separate Office of Labour. After a short recess, strike activity resumed; in 1928, massive strikes in the oil and banana industries shook the society. The ensuing 'banana massacre' of December 1928 is perhaps the most well known event in the violent history of this country. A comprehensive Labour Law was passed in 1931, and was perfected by various amendments over the next fifteen years of Liberal government. This period was followed, however, by one of repression of organized labour under Conservative rule during the late 1940s and the 1950s, when strikes were forcibly put down, and a new restrictive Labour Code adopted in 1950. At the same time, a reformist labour central, the Union de Trabajadores Colombianos (UTC) was established with government blessing, and went on to become the largest labour federation. The period 1948–63 witnessed a bloody civil war in Colombia—initially an urban conflict between Liberal and Conservative groups and between the two groups and the military, and later a rural conflict between the state forces and armed gangs in the coffee areas in the countryside—collectively known as *La Violencia*. In some respects the more recent period of violent conflict, centred around narcotics production and export, are a continuation of the last phase of *La Violencia*.

National union. There are national confederations, like UTC, CTC, CSTC, and the CGT. However, independent unions and federations cover more than 50 per cent of the organized workers, particularly in the government sector. Unions are classified as 'de base' (plant), 'de industria', 'gremials' (craft), or 'de oficios varios' (mixed trades).

Closed shop. No.

Right to strike. Yes.

Minimum wage. Yes. Set by government.

COLAs. Not officially.

Other legal national wage-setting. Detailed provisions in Labour Code, 1950.

Workers vote on contract. No.

Basic level of wage bargaining. Plant level as a legal requirement. Government may get involved directly to obtain settlement. Labour minister often plays active personal role.

Mexico

History. In Mexico, the labour movement started as mutual aid societies in the nineteenth century. At that time, labour unions and formally organized labour existed only illegally, since unions and strikes were outlawed and severely repressed during the *Porfiriato*—the Porfirio Diaz regime, 1877–1910. After the Mexican revolution, 1910–17, organized labour began to play a more prominent role in political events. Article 123 of the revolutionary constitution (1917) granted fundamental organizational and bargaining rights to workers and established welfare norms and social security arrangements. These rights were enacted into law in 1931 (revised and amended in 1971). Among other things, these laws enabled governments to influence the activities of organized labour, particularly in key industries, through the establishment of the main labour central, the Confederacion de Trabajadores Mexicana (CTM) in 1936, which was made a partner in the ruling coalition by the charismatic President Lazaro Cardenas. The CTM's hegemony was challenged briefly in the late 1940s, when workers organized a rival central, the Confederacion Unica de Trabajadores (CUT), but its position was quickly undermined by repressive state action. The state–labour partnership helped restrain strike activity for a quarter of a century, but as unions became increasingly independent of the government in the 1970s, strike activity picked up again.

National union. The umbrella-like Congreso del Trabajo (CT) covers 85 per cent of all union organizations (mainly plant unions, federated into national, regional, or state level) with very diverse political orientations, including a number of opposition-oriented unions. The largest member of the CT is the CTM, which has twenty-five constituent members (industrial or national industrial unions, or state or regional federations).

Closed shop. Yes.

Right to strike. Yes. But few strikes in practice, and they rarely last very long.

Minimum wage. Yes, different for different (111) areas. Set by tripartite commission. Revised annually. Non-compliance very high (30–80 per cent) outside of Mexico City.

COLAs. Yes.

Other legal national wage-setting. Mandatory bonus, share of profits.

Workers vote on contract. No.

Basic level of wage bargaining. Mainly plant level. Industry-wide in sugar, textiles, and petroleum. Government not directly involved.

Uruguay

National union. No. Nation-wide unions are against the law, although the illegal CNT covers 40 per cent of labour force. Only non-political unions allowed.

Closed shop. No.

Right to strike. Banned in 1973.

Minimum wage. Yes. Fairly comprehensive national wage laws, setting minimum *and maximum* wage limits since 1968. Set by tripartite National Commission on Productivity, Prices, and Incomes.

COLAs. Yes.

Other legal national wage-setting. Mandatory bonus of one month's pay, unemployment compensation, pensions.

Workers vote on contract. No.

Basic level of wage bargaining. In effect national, since plant-level bargaining operates within limits set by national commission.

Venezuela

History. The centre of the Venezuelan labour movement is the oil industry, which came into being in 1918 and soon became the largest oil exporter (after the US) and the second biggest oil producer in the world, a position it maintained until the emergence of the Middle East oil producers in the 1950s. Despite significant obstacles to organization in this industry, rudimentary and 'invisible' mutual aid societies soon sprang up, and were instrumental in the 'spontaneous' strike of 1925. A decade of sporadic unrest in the oil industry and elsewhere was followed by the massive general strike of June 1936. Although the strike was severely crushed, it jolted the government into legislating, only a month later, the most comprehensive and liberal set of labour laws in Latin America. Soon, a federation of unions representing artisans, transport workers, and other individual workers in Caracas was founded and legalized under the name of Confederacion Sindical Obreros de Venezuela (CSOV). However, because of the special position of the oil industry, it was another decade before the same recognition was accorded to the oilworkers in 1946. During the latter period of heightened labour mobilization, the number of legal unions in the country went up from 215 to 757 (including 264 rural unions), and of labour federations from 0 to 13. A year later, in 1947, the Central de Trabajadores Venezolanos (CTV) was set up with government blessing.

National union. There are several labour federations, of which the most important is the CTV, covering a majority of the organized workers.

Closed shop. No.

Right to strike. Yes, but only after conciliation channels have been exhausted. Most strikes are technically illegal, but are seldom the basis of prosecution.

Minimum wage. Yes, since 1974, covering all employees. Set by the government.

COLAs. No.

Other legal national wage-setting. Mandatory bonus of 1 week–2 months' salary.

Workers vote on contract. No.

Basic level of wage bargaining. Plant level. No direct government intervention.

SOUTH ASIA

Bangladesh

History. The history of the labour movement in Bangladesh is related to that of Pakistan (1947–71) and India (pre-1947). The earliest record of workers' action is the revolt of the tea plantation labour in 1920. Initially, unions were affiliated to the All-India Trade Congress, formed in 1920; later, this became the East Pakistan Trade Unions Federation (EPTUF). The trade union movement played a role in the independence movement in the 1940s, and was much more significant in the movement against the Pakistani government in the 1960s. The anti-government stance from this experience still continues, and as much as 70 per cent of the unions in the organized industrial sector are affiliated to opposition political parties. Although martial law has been imposed twice in Bangladesh, the right of workers to form and elect unions and to negotiate with employers has not been severely curtailed by the government.

National union. Several. National federations of unions, based on political or regional affiliations, play an influential role in national politics.

Closed shop. No. There are several unions in one plant.

Right to strike. Yes, except in essential industries. Banned in 1972, 1975.

Minimum wage. Yes, but ineffective. In 1987, it stood at a level of Taka 650 ($22) per month, which is at, if not below, the subsistence level. Government supervision is also lax.

COLAs. No.

Other legal national wage-setting. Variable bonus.

Workers vote on contract. No. But they vote on the preferred union, which becomes the representative until the next election or recall.

Basic level of wage bargaining. Enterprise. Government often plays mediational role, depending on the political affiliation of the union involved.

India

History. The trade union movement began as an adjunct to the anti-British freedom struggle. While there were strikes before the First World War—the most famous one being the Bombay Textile workers' strike in 1913—the activities were stepped up after the war with the formation of the International Labor Organization, with British India as a member, in 1919. In 1920, the first national co-ordination body, the All-India Trade Union Congress (AITUC), was founded by the Indian National Congress, the leading anti-colonial political force in the country. Today, the AITUC is a left-wing organization, and is no longer controlled or influenced by the Congress government; it has 3.1 million members, and is second in size only to the reformist INTUC, which was founded in 1947 at the behest of the new national government. Several other federations, most of them affiliated with national political parties, co-exist with these two. The government's role in wage-setting, however, is restricted to mediation in disputes—including prevention, investigation, and settlement, in case of the failure of bilateral negotiations—except in cases of major public sector industries, such as the railway strike of 1974 which was forcibly crushed by police action. Factory laws and piecemeal labour legislation date back almost 100 years, and they have been revised and amended from time to time. The Trade Union Act 1926 granted the right to form associations to seven or more workers, not necessarily in a single enterprise. Other laws covering working hours, leave, and the working environment were introduced later; but supervision is lax, except in the relatively small unionized sector.

National union. Several. There is no national apex body. Every political party engaged in trades union activity has its own national co-ordination body, although some of the major national affiliations (such as bank employees, railwaymen, telecommunications workers, and civil servants) function autonomously. Competing unions (with different political affiliations) seek election of their candidate slates for fixed terms (except for recalls). During the term of one union, other unions continue to operate, but do not have the right to bargain with employers. Almost all organized workers are affiliated to one of seven major national federations.

Closed shop. No. More than one union per plant is common.

Right to strike. Yes, but protracted strikes are rare because of government discouragement and the unions' lack of financial strength.

Minimum wage. Yes, but low/ineffective.

COLAs. Not officially. But most factory workers are on a system of payment of 'dearness allowance' for each 1 per cent increase in the twelve-month average of the CPI. This gives 100 per cent indexation at the lowest level, going up to about 40 per cent at the top.

Other legal national wage-setting. No. However, changes in wage and salary levels of government employees have an important influence on industrial wage bargains.

Workers vote on contract. No.

Basic level of wage bargaining. Plant. Influenced by the political strength/affiliation of respective union. Wildcat strikes are also common, and union control over membership is weak.

Pakistan

History. Before 1947, Pakistan was a part of colonial India, and shared in the history of the trade union movement of that country. At independence, however, the area comprising Pakistan and Bangladesh was primarily agricultural, and had only 75 out of the 1,087 unions registered in undivided India at the time. Like India, Pakistan inherited much of its labour legislation from the colonial period. Subsequently, even though the government signed the 1948 ILO convention on the right of workers to organize and the 1949 convention on collective bargaining, detailed legislation on workers' rights was not enacted until the 1969 Industrial Relations Act. Under this law, the right to organize and bargain were recognized, protection against arbitrary firings were instituted, and an industrial relations commission was established to adjudicate labour disputes. These rights were restricted during the martial law period 1977–85. In general, union power and legitimacy increased during the 1960s and 1970s, and were instrumental in bringing down an unpopular government in 1969. Today, there are 8,300 registered labour unions affiliated with various national federations.

National union. Several. Every major political party has its own national co-ordination body for trade unions, in addition to which there are autonomous organizations as well. Eight federations are better organized than the others, and claim about two-thirds of total union membership. These include the right-of-centre All-Pakistan Federation of Trade Unions (APFTU) and the Pakistan National Federation of Trade Unions (PNFTU); the fundamentalist religious Islamic National Labour Federation (INLF); and the left-wing Pakistan Federation of Trade Unions (PFTU).

Closed shop. No. There are several unions in one plant.

Right to strike. Yes, except in essential industries.

Minimum wage. Yes, but ineffective.

COLAs. No.

Other legal national wage-setting. Variable bonus.

Workers vote on contract. No. But they vote on the preferred union, which becomes the representative until the next election or recall.

Basic level of age bargaining. Enterprise. Government often plays mediational role, depending on the political affiliation of the union involved. Claims are often settled by the quasi-judicial body, the National Industrial Relations Commission (NIRC).

Sri Lanka

History. The Sri Lankan trade union movement has its roots in the collective action of Indian Tamils imported by British colonial rulers to work in tea plantations. As a result, the most powerful trade union to this day is the Ceylon Workers Congress (CWC), which represents plantation workers. Savumyamoorthy Thondaman, the septuagenarian leader of the CWC, enjoys a unique position in Sri Lanka, as leader of an ethnic group, government minister, as well as trade unionist; although radical groups have challenged his dominance of the union in recent years. Other unions are generally affiliated with political parties. The current ruling party, the UNP, began building a trade-union base many years ago, and now commands the Jathika Sevaka Sangamaya (National Employees' Union), one of the most powerful in the public sector. Sri Lanka has a vast corpus of labour legislation, going back to the colonial period. The 1970s also witnessed the formation of the Employers' Federation of Ceylon, which has started entering into collective agreements with unions. Companies that do not belong to the employers' federation often follow the agreements' guidelines.

National union. No. However, the Ceylon Workers Congress (CWC) represents about half a million members (one-third of organized workers), mainly Indians and Tamils in Sri Lankan tea plantations.

Closed shop. No.

Right to strike. Yes, except in essential industries. However, the government has reacted severely to strikes outsides the plantation sector. As a result, most strike activity is among plantation workers (75 of the 91 strikes in 1974).

Minimum wage. Yes. Set by National Wage Board. Annual adjustment with COLAs.

COLAs. Yes; see above.

Other legal national wage-setting. No.

Workers vote on contract. No. Collective bargaining not allowed.

Basic level of wage-bargaining. Collective bargaining not allowed. Wage or other disputes settled through compulsory quasi-legal process involving arbitration, wage boards, tribunals, and labour courts.

EAST/SOUTH-EAST ASIA

Indonesia

History. Labour movement dates back to the colonial period, when unions were active in the independence struggle through strong ties to political parties. Later, the Communist party (PKI) became influential among labour unions, until it was decimated during the 1965 abortive coup and ensuing massacre. The Suharto government banned unions upon assuming office in 1968. Since then, the government has tried to replace the militant labour movement with a more conciliatory political force through the establishment of a tripartite relationship between labour, capital and government, in which the latter has the upper hand and the introduction of the 'Pancasila Industrial Relations' philosophy. It restored union activity in 1973, but in a strongly circumscribed and controlled fashion, and established the

All-Indonesia Labor Unions' Federation (FBSI), a national federation dominated by the ruling Golkar party. In November 1985, the FBSI was reorganized into 10 'departments'—presumably to make it more responsive to government direction— and renamed the All-Indonesia Union of Workers (SPSI). Workers are guaranteed most basic rights through a large number of individual laws, some from the Dutch colonial period. These include the right to form unions, collective bargaining, strike, overtime pay, safe working conditions, annual leave, and protection from firing. Several provisions are circumscribed in practice, however. Unions were banned during 1968–73.

National union. Yes. Strongly controlled by the government. The All-Indonesia Union of Workers (SPSI) has 2.9 million members, and consists of 21 craft unions which, in turn, are loose confederations of plant-based unions. The SPSI, like its predecessor the FBSI, is dominated by the ruling Golkar party through its control of the executive board, and also by virtue of the fact that union expenses are paid by the government.

Closed shop. Yes.

Right to strike. Yes, but heavily circumscribed in practice, because of the requirement of prior approval by the minister of manpower. No right to strike in extensive list of essential industries. However, there are hundreds of illegal/wildcat strikes on local issues every year, most of which are unpublicized. It is expected that the government will reorganize the SPSI so as to further restrict the power of local unions to take independent action.

Minimum wage. No.

COLAs. No.

Other legal national wage-setting. No. But arbitration awards are used as standards by employers for wage-setting.

Workers vote on contract. No.

Basic level of wage bargaining. Only plant-level bargaining allowed, in a tripartite context. Wages set in one collective labour agreement (CLA) have often acted as standards in other industries as well.

South Korea

History. The first labour unions in (unified) Korea were formed soon after the Japanese occupation in 1910. The labour movement became the focus of anti-Japanese actions by workers during the 1920s, and was consequently forced underground in 1931. After the departure of the Japanese in 1945, a militant, socialist union movement in South Korea, grouped under the National Council of Korean Labour Unions (NCKL), was destroyed during the American occupation and replaced by plant-level unions under the anti-communist and pro-government Korean Federation of Labour Unions (KFLU), later renamed (after reorganization in 1955) as the Federation of Korean Trade Unions (FKTU) and linked directly to the ruling Liberal party. With the imposition of martial law in 1961, all unions were banned, but were soon re-established under a more centralized and government-controlled FKTU. Although labour laws became even more restrictive after the adoption of the Yushin constitution in 1973, labour militancy picked up in the late 1970s, reaching a peak in 1980. The Chun regime (1980–7) introduced a wholesale revision of labour laws in 1980, as national and industry-wide bargaining was formally eliminated, and all intervention by third parties in collective bargaining (including that by the FKTU) forbidden. Growing labour militancy in 1987 and 1988 has already led to concessions.

National union. Seventeen national federations affiliated to the officially sponsored FKTU, which covers 60 per cent of the (1 million) organized non-agricultural workers, and 8 per cent of all the eligible workers.

Closed shop. Yes.

Right to strike. None during 1961–4, and 1971–80; severely restricted thereafter.

Minimum wage. The first comprehensive minimum-wage law was introduced in 1988. However, there is a large variation of wages even within the same industry for the same occupation.

COLAs. No.

Other legal national wage-setting: Government participation in tripartite dispute adjustment procedures through the Office of Labour Affairs.

Workers vote on contract. No.

Basic level of wage bargaining. Where workers are organized, wages are set through bargaining/arbitration. Where workers are not organized, employers set them.

Malaysia

History. The Malaysian labour movement dates back to the formation, in 1934, of the Malayan General Labour Union, mainly by Chinese workers in British-owned plantations and mines. Influenced by political developments in China, labour unions organized widespread strikes and played a significant role in the low level anti-colonial guerrilla insurgency which started in 1948 and lasted up to the grant of independence in 1957. During the insurgency, all unions were banned under a state of emergency. Today, labour relations are regulated by the Trade Unions Act, 1959 (extensively amended in 1981), and the Industrial Relations Act, 1967.

National union. Not allowed. Since organized workers are almost entirely Indians (in industry) or Chinese (in commerce), a national union is seen as destabilizing because of its implications for ethnic conflict. Two national federations, which merged in 1985, cover about three-fourths of all unionized workers. These are: the Malaysian Trade Union Congress (MTUC), with 100 affiliates and 282,000 members; and the Congress of Unions of Employees in the Public, Administrative and Civil Services (CUEPACS), whose 53 affiliates represent 115,000 government workers.

Closed shop. No.

Right to strike. Yes.

Minimum wage. Limited sectoral minimum wages, mainly in mining.

COLAs. No.

Other legal national wage-setting. No.

Workers vote on contract. No.

Basic level of wage bargaining. Plant level.

Philippines

History. Labour relations in the Philippines were governed by the Industrial Peace Act of 1952, which was subsequently replaced by the 1974 Labour Code during the martial law period. The code granted unions the right to bargain collectively with employers, to own property, and to provide welfare programmes for workers.

National union. Seven trade union federations cover all the workers. The four largest, including the Trade Union Congress of the Philippines (TUCP) represent 62 per cent of all workers. The TUCP, which covers 100 federations under its umbrella, acts as a supervisory body to provide guidance and set policies; it also settles disputes between other federations or national unions.

Closed shop. Yes. Enacted in 1974, but its constitutionality was challenged in the Supreme Court in 1978. The court has not given a verdict.

Right to strike. Limited strike activity during 1972–7 despite 1972 ban, increasing subsequently. Later, began to increase with political unrest, and reaching such a high level in 1984 and 1985 that the then President Marcos considered imposing a state of emergency because of worker unrest. Largest number of strikes per capita in any Asian country since 1980.

Minimum wage. Since 1974. Extensive coverage.

COLAs. Since 1975. Adjusted quarterly.

Other legal national wage-setting. Mandatory bonus of one month's pay.

Workers vote on contract. No.

Basic level of wage bargaining. Plant. Before 1972, collective bargaining was mandatory. Subsequently, it was made illegal and arbitration procedures instituted.

Taiwan

History. Taiwan experienced its first series of major strikes in 1987, when martial law was lifted after thirty-eight years. The ruling party, the Kuomintang (KMT), had imposed martial law in 1949 when it first moved to Taiwan from the Chinese mainland, and had used its provisions to forbid strikes, marches, picket lines, or demonstrations, and to maintain a tight grip on unions. Although workers were given the right to form unions, in practice every union and its leader had to be approved by the local KMT committee. Moreover, all unions were combined under the government-controlled national federation, the Chinese Federation of Labour (CFL) which also moved to the island in 1949. As a result, unions have not had much say in controversial issues, and have focused their actions mainly upon organizing workers' leisure activities and providing credit services. The Taiwanese situation is further complicated by the fact that most of the enterprises are small-scale family businesses, where union formation is relatively difficult. On the legal side, a detailed Labour Standards Law was passed in 1984 after ten years of deliberation in which, interestingly, the CFL did not play any prominent role. The law guarantees a minimum wage, a 48-hour work week, pension and insurance benefits, and severance pay. It is, however, still not very effective due to employers' opposition to various provisions. For example, since employers are opposed to the fact that the burden of creating a social security system has been placed upon them, progress in this direction has been rather insignificant.

National union. Yes. All plant unions are combined into a unified county or city union, then a provincial union, and finally, at the national level, the government-controlled CFL. Also, the Taiwan Provincial Federation of Labour, which is nominally affiliated to the CFL, has often acted independently; it has more than twenty unions and a number of craft federations among its members, and has been active through the post-war period.

Closed shop. Yes.

Right to strike. None during 1949–88. Allowed for the first time under the Arbitration Dispute Law passed on 17 June 1988. Workers can now strike after a first round of mediation, but are still required to return to work if a second, arbitration, phase is called by the government; in the only example of a legal strike so far, the second phase was called after only three hours, and the workers, who refused to return to work, were declared to be in violation of the law. It is thus still almost impossible to have a legal strike.

Minimum wage. Yes. Enacted in 1984. Still ineffective.

COLAs. No.

Other legal national wage-setting. No.

Workers vote on contract. No.

Basic level of wage-bargaining. Enterprise. Wages are set unilaterally by management. Unions generally do not participate in any bargaining over wages. The predominant object of labour unrest is a more thorough enforcement of the Labour Standards Law.

Thailand

History. Thailand's trade union movement dates only from the early 1970s. The organization of workers' associations (by any ten employees) was first allowed under a revolutionary council decree in 1972, subsequently replaced by the somewhat more restrictive Labour Relations Act, 1975. While the former protected workers as soon as they initiated the process of registering a union, the latter provided this protection only after the union had been duly registered. As a result, employers' intimidation of those seeking to form unions is fairly common, and the level of unionization is low even though there were 433 different unions by 1985. The most influential segment of the Thai labour movement is that of the 93 unions of the state-enterprise sector, who represent more than half of all the organized workers.

National union. More than half the organized workers, including those in most of the state-enterprise unions and in the stronger private ones, are affiliated with two main national centrals: the Labour Congress of Thailand (LCT), with 40 unions and 50–70,000 members; and the Thai Trade Union Congress (TTUC), with 72 unions and 100–120,000 members. Two other centrals, the National Congress of Thai Labour (NCTL) and the National Free Labour Union Congress (NFLUC), cover 80 small unions with about 25,000 members.

Closed shop. No.

Right to strike. No.

Minimum wage. Yes.

COLAs. No.

Other legal National wage-setting. No.

Workers vote on contract. No.

Basic level of wage bargaining. Plant, according to strictly prescribed arbitration procedures.

REFERENCES

Agarwala, Ramgopal (1983) 'Price Distortions and Growth in Developing Countries', World Bank Staff Working Paper No. 575, Washington, DC: World Bank.

Aghazadeh, Esmail, and David Evans (1985) 'Price Distortions, Efficiency, and Growth', Brighton: Institute of Development Studies, Sussex.

Ahluwalia, M. S. (1986) 'Balance-of-Payments Adjustment in India, 1970–71 to 1983–84', *World Development*, 14: 937–62.

Akerlof, George A., and Janet L. Yellen (1986) *Efficiency Wage Models of the Labor Market*, Cambridge: Cambridge University Press.

Amsden, Alice (1986) 'The Direction of Trade—Past and Present—and the "Learning Effects" of Exports to Different Directions', *Journal of Development Economics*, 23: 249–74.

Anglade, Christian, and Carlos Fortin (1987) 'The Role of the State in Latin America's Strategic Options', *CEPAL Review*, 31: 211–34.

Arida, Persio (1986) 'Macroeconomic Issues for Latin America', *Journal of Development Economics*, 22: 171–208.

Armella, Pedro Aspe, R. Dornbusch, and M. Obstfeld, eds. (1983) *Financial Policies and the World Capital Markets: The Problem of Latin American Countries*, Chicago: Chicago University Press.

Asian Development Bank (various years) *Asian Development Bank Indicators*, Manila, Philippines.

Bacha, Edmar L. (1984) 'Growth with Limited Supplies of Foreign Exchange: A Reappraisal of the Two-Gap Model', in Moshe Syrquin, Lance Taylor, and Larry Westphal, eds., *Economic Structure and Performance: Essays in Honor of Hollis B. Chenery*, New York: Academic Press.

—— (1986a) 'Terms of Reference for the Country Studies', *World Development*, 14: 909–18.

—— (1986b) 'External Shocks and Growth Prospects: The Case of Brazil, 1973–89', *World Development*, 14: 919–36.

Bacha, E. L., and Richard E. Feinberg (1986) 'The World Bank and Structural Adjustment in Latin America', *World Development*, 14: 333–46.

Balassa, Bela (1981) *The Newly Industrializing Countries in the World Economy*, New York: Pergamon Press.

—— (1982) *Development Strategies in Semi-Industrial Economies*, Baltimore: Johns Hopkins University Press.

—— (1984) 'Adjustment Policies in Developing Countries', 1979–83, World Bank Staff Working Paper No. 675, Washington, DC: World Bank.

—— (1985a) 'Exports, Policy Choices, and Economic Growth in the Developing Countries After the 1973 Oil Shock', *Journal of Development Economics*, 18: 23–26.

—— (1985b) *Outward Orientation*, Washington, DC: World Bank.

—— (1986a) 'Prices, Incentives, and Economic Growth', in B. Balassa and H. Giersch, eds., *Economic Incentives*, London: Macmillan.

—— (1986b) 'Policy Responses to Exogenous Shocks in Developing Countries', *American Economic Review*, 76: 75–8.

Balassa, Bela, and F. Desmond McCarthy (1984) 'Adjustment Policies in Developing Countries, 1979–83', Washington, DC: World Bank.

Balassa, Bela, and Herbert Giersch, eds. (1986) *Economic Incentives*, London: Macmillan.

Balassa, Bela, Gerardo Bueno, Pedro-Pablo Kuczynski, and Mario Henrique Simonsen (1986) *Toward Renewed Economic Growth in Latin America*, Washington, DC: Institute for International Economics.

Banco de Mexico (annual) *Sistema de Cuentas Nacionales de Mexico*, Mexico.

Banker Research Unit, The (1981) *Banking Structures and Sources of Finance in South America*, London: Financial Times Business Publishing Ltd.

Banks, Gary, and Jan Tumlir (1986) 'The Political Problem of Adjustment', *The World Economy*, 9: 141–52.

Banuri, Tariq (1986) *Macroeconomic Effects of Worker Remittances*, Ph.D. thesis, Harvard University.

—— (1988) 'Black Markets, Openness, and Central Bank Autonomy', Helsinki: WIDER (mimeo).

Barbone, Luca (1985) *Essays on Trade and Macro Policy in Developing Countries*, Ph.D. thesis, Massachusetts Institute of Technology.

Barbone, Luca, and Francisco Rivera-Batiz (1987) 'Foreign Capital and the Contractionary Impact of Currency Devaluation, with an Application to Jamaica', *Journal of Development Economics*, 26: 1–15.

Bardhan, Pranab (1984) *The Political Economy of Development in India*, Oxford: Basil Blackwell.

Barker, T., and V. Brailovsky (1983) 'La politica economica entre 1976 y 1982 y el plan nacional de desarrollo industrial', paper presented at the Seminar on Mexican Economy at El Colegio de Mexico, 8–10 August. Mexico City: El Colegio de Mexico.

Bergquist, Charles (1986) *Labor in Latin America: Comparative Essays on Chile, Argentina, Venezuela, and Colombia*, Stanford, Calif.: Stanford University Press.

Bhagwati, J. N. (1986) 'Rethinking Trade Strategy', in John P. Lewis and Valeriana Kallab, eds., *Development Strategies Reconsidered*, New Brunswick, NJ: Transaction Books.

—— (1969) 'On the Equivalence of Tariffs and Quotas', in *Trade, Tariffs, and Growth*, Cambridge, Mass.: MIT Press.

Bianchi, Andres, Robert Devlin, and Joseph Ramos (1987) 'The Adjustment Process in Latin America, 1981–1986', Santiago, Chile: Economic Commission for Latin America and the Caribbean (mimeo).

Blejer, M. I. (1979) 'Devaluation, Inflation, and the Balance of Payments: A Short-Run Monetary Approach', *Economic Record*, 55: 33–40.

Blyth, C. A. (1979) 'The Interaction Between Collective Bargaining and Government Policies in Selected Member Countries', in OECD, *Collective Bargaining and Government Policies in Ten OECD Countries*, Paris.

Boutros-Ghali, Youssef (1980) *Essays on Structuralism and Development*, Ph.D. thesis, Massachusetts Institute of Technology.

Bowles, Samuel, and Robert Boyer (1987) 'A Wage–Led Employment Regime', in S. A. Marglin and J. B. Schor, eds., *The Golden Age of Capitalism*.

Brailovsky, V. (1981a) *Exchange Rate Policies, Manufactured Exports and the Rate of Inflation*, Mexico: Institute for Industrial Planning, Ministry of Natural Resources and Industrial Development.

—— (1981b) 'Industrialisation and Oil in Mexico: A Long Term Perspective', in T. Barker, and V. Brailovsky, eds., *Oil or Industry? Energy, Industrialization and Economic Policy in Canada, Mexico, Norway, the Netherlands, and the United Kingdom*, London: Academic Press.

Branson, William H. (1983) 'Economic Structure and Policy for External Balance', *IMF Staff Papers*, 30/1: 39–66.

Bruno, Michael, and Jeffrey Sachs (1985) *Economics of Worldwide Stagflation*, Oxford: Basil Blackwell.

Buchanan, James M. (1980) 'Rent Seeking and Profit Seeking', in J. M. Buchanan, R. D. Tollison, and G. Tullock, eds., *Toward a Theory of Rent Seeking Society*, College Station, Texas: Texas A & M University Press.

Buchanan, James M., and Gordon Tullock (1962) *The Calculus of Consent: Logical Foundations of Constitutional Democracy*, Ann Arbor, Mich.: University of Michigan Press.

Buffie, Edward (1986) 'Commercial Policy, Growth, and the Distribution of Income in a Dynamic Trade Model', Philadelphia, Penn.: Department of Economics, University of Pennsylvania.

Burki, S. J. (1984) 'International Migration: Implications for Developing Countries', *The Middle East Journal*, 38/4: 668–84.

Calmfors, Lars, and John Driffill (1987) 'Centralization of Wage Bargaining and Macroeconomic Performance', Seminar Paper No. 402. Stockholm: Institute for International Economic Studies, University of Stockholm.

Camargo, Jose Marcio (1986) 'Brasil: Ajuste estrutural e Distribuicao da Renda', *Documentos de trabadalho 308*, Santiago, Chile: PREALC/ILO.

Central Intelligence Agency (1975–84) *China: International Trade Annual Statistical Supplement*, Washington, DC.

Chenery, Hollis B. (1975) 'The Structuralist Approach to Development Policy', *American Economic Review*, 65: 310–16.

Chenery, Hollis B., and Michael Bruno (1962) 'Development Alternatives in an Open Economy: The Case of Israel', *Economic Journal*, 72: 79–103.

Cheng, Hang-Sheng (1986) *Financial Policy and Reform in Pacific Basin Countries*, Lexington, Mass.: Lexington Books.

Choksi, Armeane M., and Demetris Papageorgiou, eds. (1986) *Economic Liberalization in Developing Countries*, Oxford: Basil Blackwell.

Cline, William R. (1984) *International Debt: Systemic Risk and Policy Response*, Washington, DC: Institute of International Economics.

Coase, Ronald H. (1960) 'The Problem of Social Cost', *Journal of Law and Economics*, 3: 1–44.

Cole, David, and Yung Chul Park (1984) *Financial Development in Korea, 1945–1978*, Cambridge, Mass.: Harvard University Press.

Connolly, M., and D. Taylor (1976) 'Adjustments to Devaluation With Money and Nontraded Goods', *Journal of International Economics*, 6: 289–98.

Cooper, Richard N. (1971) 'An Assessment of Currency Devaluation in Developing

Countries', in G. Ranis, ed., *Government and Economic Development*, New Haven, Conn.: Yale University Press.

Corbo, V., *et al.* (1985) 'What Went Wrong With the Recent Reforms in the Southern Cone', Washington, DC: World Bank (mimeo).

Corden, W. Max (1971) *The Theory of Protection*, New York: Oxford University Press.

Cross, Rod, ed. (1988) *Unemployment, Hysteresis, and the Natural Rate Hypothesis*, Oxford: Basil Blackwell.

Crouch, C. (1985) 'Conditions for Trade Union Wage Restraint', in L. N. Lindberg and C. S. Maier, eds., *The Politics of Inflation and Economic Stagnation*, Washington, DC: Brookings Institution.

Dee, Philippa S. (1986) *Financial Markets and Economic Development: The Economics and Politics of Korean Financial Reform*, Tübingen, W. Germany: Mohr.

Deyo, Frederic, Stephan Haggard, and Hagen Koo (1987) 'Labor in the Political Economy of East Asian Industrialization', *Bulletin of Concerned Asian Scholars*, 19/2: 42–53.

Diaz-Alejandro, Carlos (1981) 'Southern Cone Stabilization Plans', in William Cline and Sidney Weintraub, eds., *Economic Stabilization in Developing Countries*, Washington, DC: Brookings Institution.

—— (1978) 'Delinking North and South: Unshackled or Unhinged?', in Abe Goldman, ed., *Rich and Poor Nations in the World Economy*, New York: McGraw-Hill.

—— (1963) 'A Note on the Impact of Devaluation and the Redistributive Effect', *Journal of Political Economy*, 71: 577–80.

Dornbusch, Rudiger (1981) 'Panel on External Financial Openness and Effects on the National Economy,' in Seminar on External Financial Relations and their impact on Latin American Economies. Santiago, Chile: CIEPLAN–Ford Foundation.

Eastman, Harry, and Stykolt, S. (1962) 'A Model for the Study of Protected Oligopolies', *Economies Journal*, 70: 336–47.

Economic Commission for Latin America (various years) *Annual Survey*, Santiago, Chile.

Erickson, Kenneth Paul, and Kevin J. Middlebrook (1982) 'The State and Organized Labor in Brazil and Mexico', in Sylvia Ann Hewlett and Richard S. Weinert, eds., *Brazil and Mexico: Patterns in Late Development*, Philadelphia: Institute for the Study of Human Issues.

Far Eastern Economic Review (1986) 'Asia's Unions', 3 Apr. 1986: 43–67.

—— (1987) 'Labour Strikes Out', 27 Aug. 1987: 14–19.

Feder, Gershon (1983) 'On Exports and Economic Growth', *Journal of Development Economics*, 12: 59–73.

Fields, Gary (1984) 'Employment, Income Distribution and Economic Growth in Seven Small Open Economies', *Economic Journal*, 94: 74–83.

Fishlow, Albert (1985*a*) 'Coping with the Creeping Crisis of Debt', in M. Wionczek, ed., *Politics and Economics of External Debt Crisis*, Boulder, Colo.: Westview.

—— (1985*b*) 'Revisiting the Great Debt Crisis of 1982', in K. Kim and D. Ruccio, eds., *Debt and Development in Latin America*, Notre Dame, Indiana: Notre Dame University Press.

—— (1985*c*) 'The State of Latin American Economics', ch. 5 in Inter-American

Development Bank, *Economic and Social Progress in Latin America*, Washington, DC.

—— (1986) 'Latin American Adjustment to the Oil Shocks of 1973 and 1979', in J. Hartlyn and S. Morley, eds., *Latin American Political Economy*, Boulder, Colo.: Westview.

Foxley, Alejandro (1983) *Latin American Experiments in Neo-Conservative Economics*, Berkeley, Calif.: University of California Press.

Frankel, Jeffrey, and Kenneth Froot (1986) 'The Dollar as a Speculative Bubble: A Tale of Fundamentalists and Chartists', Working Paper No. 1854. Cambridge, Mass.: National Bureau of Economic Research.

Frenkel, Roberto (1983) 'Mercado financiero, expectativas cambiales, y movimientos de capital', *Trimestro economico*, 50: 2041–76.

Friedman, Milton (1983) ' "No" to More Money for the IMF', *Newsweek*, 14 Nov.

Furtado, Celso (1986 [1976]) *Economic Development of Latin America*, 2nd edn., Cambridge: Cambridge University Press.

George, A. M., and I. H. Giddy (1983) *International Finance Handbook*, New York: John Wiley & Sons.

Glyn, Andrew, Alan Hughes, Alain Lipietz, and Ajit Singh (1990) 'The Rise and Fall of the Golden Age' in S. A. Marglin and J. B. Schor, eds., *The Golden Age of Capitalism*.

Goldthorpe, John H., ed. (1984) *Order and Conflict in Contemporary Capitalism*, Oxford: Clarendon Press.

Hamid, Naved, and Ijaz Nabi (1986) 'Privatizing the Financial Sector in LDCs: Lessons of an Experiment', DRD Discussion Paper. Washington, DC: World Bank.

Haggard, Stephan (1986) 'The Newly Industrializing Countries in the International System', *World Politics*, 38/2: 343–70.

Harberger, Arnold (1959) 'Using the Resources at Hand More Effectively', *American Economic Review*, 49: 134–46.

Helleiner, G. K. (1986) 'Balance-of-Payments Experience and Growth Prospects of Developing Countries: A Synthesis', *World Development*, 14: 877–908.

Hirschman, Albert O. (1958) *The Strategy of Economic Development*, New Haven: Yale University Press.

—— (1981) 'The Turn To Authoritarianism in Latin America and the Search for Economic Determinants', in *Essays in Trespassing*, Cambridge: Cambridge University Press.

—— (1987) 'The Political Economy of Latin American Development: Seven Exercises in Retrospection', *Latin American Research Review*, 22/3: 7–36.

Hobson, John A. (1902) *Imperialism: A Study*, London: J. Nisbet.

Huntington, Samuel P., and Joan M. Nelson (1976) *No Easy Choice: Political Participation in Developing Countries*, Cambridge Mass.: Harvard University Press.

IMF (1984) *World Economic Outlook*, Washington, DC.

—— (1985–7) *International Financial Statistics Yearbook* (annual), Washington, DC.

—— (1986) *Annual Report on Exchange Arrangements and Exchange Restrictions, 1986*, Washington, DC.

Inter-American Development Bank (1985) *Economic and Social Progress in Latin America: External Debt—Crisis and Adjustment*, Washington, DC.

Irwan, Alexander (1987) 'Real Wages and Class Struggle in South Korea', *Journal of Contemporary Asia*, 17/4: 385–408.

Johnson, Chalmers (1982) *MITI and the Japanese Miracle*, Stanford, Calif.: Stanford University Press.

Jorgensen, Steen L., and Martin Paldam (1987) 'Exchange Rates and Domestic Inflation: A Study of Price/Wage Inflation in Eight Latin American Countries', DRD Discussion Paper. Washington, DC: World Bank.

Jung, Woo S., and Payton J. Marshall (1985) 'Exports, Growth, and Causality in Developing Countries', *Journal of Development Economics*, 13: 1–12.

Kaldor, N. (1978), *Further Essays on Applied Economics. Vol. vi of Collected Essays*, New York: Holmes and Meier.

Katseli, Louka (1986) 'Discrete Devaluations as a Signal to Price Setters: Suggested Evidence from Greece', in S. Edwards and L. Ahamed, eds., *Economic Adjustment and Exchange Rates in Developing Countries*, Chicago: University of Chicago Press.

Khan, Mohsin S. (1986) 'Developing Country Exchange Rate Policy Responses to Exogenous Shocks', *American Economic Review*, 76/2: 84–7.

Khan, Mohsin S., and J. Saul Lizondo (1987) 'Devaluation, Fiscal Deficits, and the Real Exchange Rate', *The World Bank Economic Review*, 1: 357–74.

Khan, Mohsin S., and Roberto Zahler (1985) 'Trade and Financial Liberalization Given External Shocks and Inconsistent Domestic Policies', *IMF Staff Papers*, 32: 22–55.

Killick, Tony (1983) 'The Possibilities of Development Planning', in M. P. Todaro, ed., *The Struggle for Economic Development*, New York: Longman.

Kim, Joong-Woong (1985) 'Economic Development and Financial Liberalization in Korea: Policy Reforms and Future Prospects', Working Paper 8514. Seoul, South Korea: Korean Development Institute (mimeo).

Kim, Joong-Woong, and Park Won-Woo (1985) 'Internationalization of Finance and the Role of Foreign Banks in Korea', Working Paper 8505. Seoul, South Korea: Korean Development Institute (mimeo).

Kindleberger, Charles P. (1978) *Manias, Panics and Crashes: A History of Financial Crises*, New York: Basic Books.

—— (1984) *A Financial History of Western Europe*, London: George Allen and Unwin.

—— (1985) 'Historical Perspectives on Today's Third World Debt Problem', *Economies et societés*, 19: 109–34.

Krueger, Anne O. (1974) 'The Political Economy of the Rent-Seeking Society', *American Economic Review*, 64: 291–303.

—— (1978) *Liberalization Attempts and Consequences*. New York: National Bureau of Economics Research.

—— (1986) 'Problems of Liberalization', in A. Choksi and D. Papageorgiou, eds., *Economic Liberalization in Developing Countries*, Oxford: Basil Blackwell.

Krugman, Paul R. (1984) 'Import Substitution as Export Promotion', in Henryk Kierzkowski, ed., *Monopolistic Competition and International Trade*, Oxford: Oxford University Press.

—— (1987) 'Is Free Trade Passé?', *Journal of Economic Perspectives*, 1/2: 131–43.

Krugman, Paul R., and Lance Taylor (1978) 'Contractionary Effects of Devaluation', *Journal of International Economics*, 8: 445–56.

Kurian, George Thomas (1982) *Encyclopedia of the Third World*, New York: Facts on File, Inc.

Kuznets, Simon S. (1966) *Modern Economic Growth*, New Haven: Yale University Press.

Lal, Deepak (1983) *The Poverty of Development Economics*, Cambridge, Mass.: Harvard University Press.

Lall, S. (1982) *Developing Countries as Exporters of Technology*, London: Macmillan.

—— (1984) 'Exports of Technology by the Newly Industrializing Countries: An Overview', *World Development*, 12: 471–80.

Lancaster, Kelvin (1984) 'Protection and Product Differentiation', in Henryk Kierzkowski, ed., *Monopolistic Competition and International Trade*, Oxford: Oxford University Press.

Larson, Eric D., Marc H. Ross, and Robert H. Williams (1986) 'Beyond the Era of Materials', *Scientific American*, 254/6: 34–41.

Linder, Staffan Burenstam (1961) *An Essay on Trade and Transformation*, Stockholm: Almqvist and Wicksell.

Little, Ian M. D., Tibor Scitovsky, and Maurice Scott (1970) *Industry and Trade in Some Developing Countries: A Comparative Study*, London: Oxford University Press.

Lloyd's Bank (1986) *The Lloyd's Bank Economic Report, 1986*, London.

McCarthy, F. Desmond, Lance Taylor, and Cyrus Talati (1987) 'Trade Patterns in Developing Countries, 1964–82', *Journal of Developing Economics*, 27/1–2: 5–39.

McKinnon, Ronald (1973) *Money and Capital in Economic Development*, Washington, DC: Brookings Institution.

Maddison, Angus (1985) *Two Crises: Latin America and Asia, 1929–1938 and 1973–1983*, Paris: OECD Development Centre.

——, ed. (1986) *Latin America, The Caribbean and the OECD*, Paris: OECD Development Centre.

Marglin, Stephen A. (1984) *Growth, Distribution and Prices*, Cambridge, Mass.: Harvard University Press.

—— (1988) 'Losing Touch: The Cultural Conditions of Worker Accommodation and Resistance', Helsinki: Wider (mimeo).

Marglin, Stephen A., and Amit Bhaduri (1990) 'Profit Squeeze and Keynesian Theory', in S. A. Marglin and J. B. Schor, eds., *The Golden Age of Capitalism*.

Marglin, Stephen A., and Juliet B. Schor, eds. (1990) *The Golden Age of Capitalism*, Oxford: Clarendon Press.

Meyer, Milton W. (1976) *South Asia: A Short History of the Subcontinent*, 2nd edn., Totowa, NJ: Littlefield, Adams & Co.

Minsky, Hyman (1975) *John Maynard Keynes*, New York: Colombia University Press.

—— (1982) *Can 'It' Happen Again? Essays on Instability and Finance*, Armonk, NY: M. E. Sharpe.

Modigliani, Franco (1977) 'The Monetarist Controversy or, Should We Forsake Stabilization Policies?', *American Economic Review*, 67: 1–19.

Mussa, Michael (1983) 'On Optimal Economic Integration', in Pedro Aspe Armella, R. Dornbusch, and M. Obstfeld, eds., *Financial Policies and the World Capital Markets*, Chicago: Chicago University Press.

Myrdal, Gunnar (1968) *Asian Drama: An Inquiry Into The Poverty of Nations*, Harmondsworth, Middx: Penguin.

North, Douglass C. (1981) *Structure and Change in Economic History*, New York: W. W. Norton.

Nurkse, Ragnar (1953) *Problems of Capital Formation in Underdeveloped Countries*, Oxford: Basil Blackwell.

Ocampo, J. A. (1986) 'New Developments in Trade Theory and LDCs', *Journal of Development Economics*, 22: 129–70.

—— (1987) 'The Macroeconomic Effects of Import Controls: A Keynesian Analysis', *Journal of Development Economics*, 27: 285–306.

Odle, Maurice A. (1981) *Multinational Banks and Underdevelopment*, New York: Pergamon Press.

O'Donnell, Guillermo (1973) *Modernization and Bureaucratic Authoritarianism: Studies in South American Politics*, Berkeley, Calif.: Institute of International Studies.

OECD (1982) *Controls on International Capital Movements*, Paris.

—— (annual) *External Debt Survey*, Paris.

Okita, Saburo, Lal Jayawardena, and Arjun Sengupta (1986) *The Potential of the Japanese Surplus for World Economic Development*, Helsinki: WIDER.

Olson, Mancur (1982) *The Rise and Decline of Nations*, New Haven: Yale University Press.

Ominami, Carlos (1987) 'More Than Adjustment: The Challenge for Latin America', *Development and South–South Cooperation*, 2: 155–69.

Ortiz, Guillermo (1983) 'Dollarization in Mexico: Causes and Consequences', in Pedro Aspe Armella, R. Dornbusch, and M. Obstfeld, eds., *Financial Policies and the World Capital Markets*, Chicago: Chicago University Press.

Pack, Howard, and Larry Westphal (1986) 'Industrial Strategy and Technological Change: Theory versus Reality', *Journal of Development Economics*, 22: 87–128.

Paldam, Martin, and Luis A. Riveros (1986) 'Minimum Wages and Average Wages: Analyzing the Causality', DRD Discussion Paper. Washington, DC: World Bank.

Park, Se-Il (1988) 'Labour Issues in Korea's Future', *World Development*, 16/1: 99–119.

Park, Yung Chul (1986) 'Foreign Debt, Balance of Payments, and Growth Prospects: The Case of the Republic of Korea, 1965–1988', *World Development*, 14: 1019–58.

Pastor, Manuel, Jr. (1987) 'The Effects of IMF Programs in the Third World: Debate and Evidence from Latin America', *World Development*, 15: 249–62.

Pekkarinen, Jukka (1988) 'Keynesianism and the Scandinavian Models of Economic Policy', Working Paper No. 35. Helsinki: WIDER.

Ponce de Leon, E. Z. (1986) 'Mexico's Recent Balance-of Payments Experience and Prospects for Growth', *World Development*, 14: 963–92.

Prebisch, Raul (1952) 'Problemas teoricas y praticos del crecimiento economico', Santiago, Chile: Economic Commission for Latin America.

Przeworski, Adam (1987) 'Capitalism, Democracy, Pacts', University of Chicago (mimeo).

Raj, K. N. (1984) 'Economic Growth in India 1952–53 to 1982–83', *Economic and Political Weekly*, 19/41: 1801–4.

Raza, M. Ali (1963) *The Industrial Relations System of Pakistan*. Karachi, Pakistan: Bureau of Labour Publications.

Reeve, W. D. (1963) *The Republic of Korea: A Political and Economic Study*, New York: Oxford University Press.

Reisen, H. (1985) *Key Prices for Adjustment Towards Less External Indebtedness*, Paris: OECD Development Centre.

Rodriguez, C. A. (1978) 'A Stylized Model of the Devaluation–Inflation Spiral', *IMF Staff Papers*, 25: 76–89.

Ros, Jaime (1986) 'Mexico from the Oil Boom to the Debt Crisis: An Analysis of Policy Response to External Shocks 1978 to 1985', Mexico City: CIDE.

—— (1987) 'On the Macroeconomics of Heterodox Shocks', Helsinki: WIDER (mimeo).

Rosenstein-Rodan, Paul N. (1943) 'Problems of Industrialization in Eastern and South-Eastern Europe', *Economic Journal*, 53: 202–11.

Rowthorn, B., and Andrew Glyn (1990) 'The Diversity of Unemployment Experience Since 1973', in S. A. Marglin and J. B. Schor, eds., *The Golden Age of Capitalism*.

Sachs, Jeffrey (1982) 'The Current Account in the Macroeconomic Adjustment Process', *Scandinavian Journal of Economics*, 84: 147–59.

—— (1985) 'External Debt and Macroeconomic Performance in Latin America and East Asia', *Brookings Paper on Economic Activity*, 2: 523–64.

—— (1986) 'Managing the LDC Debt Crisis', *Brookings Papers on Economic Activity*, 2: 397–431.

Schmitter, P. C. (1981) 'Interest Intermediation and Regime Governability in Contemporary Western Europe and North America', in S. D. Berger, ed., *Organizing Interests in Western Europe*, Cambridge: Cambridge University Press.

Schumpeter, Josef A. (1934) *The Theory of Economic Development*, Cambridge, Mass.: Harvard University Press.

Scitovsky, Tibor (1954) 'Two Concepts of External Economies', *Journal of Political Economy*, 62: 143–51.

Sheahan, John (1980) 'Market-Oriented Economic Policies and Political Repression in Latin America', *Economic Development and Cultural Change*, 28: 267–92.

Singh, A. (1984) 'The Interrupted Industrial Revolution of the Third World: Prospects and Policies for Resumption', *Industry and Development*, 12: 43–68.

—— (1985a) 'The Impact of World Economic Crisis on Poverty and Rural Development in Western Asia', Report No. E/ECWA/W.b18/11, November. Baghdad: United Nations, Economic Commission for West Asia.

—— (1985b) 'The World Economy and the Comparative Economic Performance of Large Semi-industrial Countries', Bangkok: International Labour Organisation, Asian Regional Team for Employment Promotion (mimeo).

—— (1986a) 'Crisis and Recovery in the Mexican Economy: the Role of the Capital Goods Sector', in M. Fransman, ed., *Machinery and Economic Development*, London: Macmillan.

—— (1986b) 'The World Economic Crisis, Stabilisation and Structural Adjustment: An Overview', *Labour and Society*, 11/3 277–93.

—— (1987) 'Exogenous Shocks and De-Industrialisation in Africa: Prospects and Strategies for Sustained Industrial Development', in *African Economic Crisis*, New Delhi: RISNODEC (Research and Information Systems for the Non-aligned and Other Developing Countries).

Soo, Kim Chang (1978) 'FKTU's Action Squads Battle Korean Workers', *AMPO*, 10/1–2: 38–9.

Srinivasan, T. N. (1986) 'Neoclassical Political Economy, The State and Economic Development', New Haven: Yale University (mimeo).

Stewart, Frances (1984) 'Recent Theories of International Trade: Some Implications for the South', in Henryk Kierzkowski, ed., *Monopolistic Competition and International Trade*, Oxford: Oxford University Press.

Stout, D. K. (1979) 'De-Industrialization and Industrial Policy', in Frank Blackaby, ed., *De-Industrialization*, London: Heinemann.

Streeten, Paul (1959) 'Unbalanced Growth', *Oxford Economic Papers*, 11: 167–90.

Talal, H. B. (1984) 'Manpower Migration in the Middle East: An Overview', *The Middle East Journal*, 38/4: 610–4.

Tanzi, Vito (1986) 'Fiscal Policy Responses to Exogenous Shocks in Developing Countries', *American Economic Review*, 76: 88–91.

Taylor, Lance (1979) *Macro Models for Developing Countries*, New York: McGraw-Hill.

—— (1982) 'Back to Basics: Theory for Rhetoric in the North–South Round', *World Development*, 10: 327–35.

—— (1983) *Structuralist Macroeconomics*, New York: Basic Books.

—— (1985) 'A Stagnationist Model of Economic Growth', *Cambridge Journal of Economics*, 9: 383–403.

—— (1987a) 'Macro Policy in the Tropics: How Sensible People Stand', *World Development*, 15/12: 1407–36.

—— (1987b) 'Orthodox Macroeconomic Stabilization: Temperate Medicine, Tropical Disease', Cambridge, Mass.: Massachusetts Institute of Technology (mimeo).

Taylor, Lance, and Stephen O'Connell (1985) 'A Minsky Crisis', *Quarterly Journal of Economics*, 100: 871–84.

UNIDO (1984) *Industry in a Changing World*, New York.

Weffort, F. (1978) *O Populismo na politica Brasileira*, Rio de Janeiro: Paz e Terra.

Weir, Margaret, and Theda Skocpol (1985) 'State Structures and the Possibilities for "Keynesian" Responses to the Great Depression in Sweden, Britain, and the United States', in P. Evans, D. Rueschemeyer, and T. Skocpol, eds., *Bringing the State Back In*, Cambridge: Cambridge University Press.

Wells, J. (1981) ' "Monetarism" in the UK and the Southern Cone: An Overview', *IDS Bulletin*, 13/1: 14–26.

Westphal, Larry (1981) 'Empirical Justification for Infant Industry Protection', World Bank Staff Working Paper No. 445, Washington DC: World Bank.

van Wijnbergen, Sweder (1986) 'Exchange Rate Management and Stabilization Policies in Developing Countries', *Journal of Development Economics*, 23: 227–48.

Williamson, J. (1985) 'Comment on Sachs', *Brooking Papers on Economic Activity*, 2: 565–70.

Winograd, C. (1983) 'Economia Abierta y tipo de cambio prefijado: Que aprendemos del caso Argentino?', Master's thesis, Pontificia Universidade Catolica, Rio de Janeiro.

Wolpert, Stanley (1977) *A New History of India*, New York: Oxford University Press.

World Bank (annual) *World Development Report*, Washington, DC.

World Debt Tables (annual) Washington, DC: World Bank.

Wyplosz, Charles (1986) 'Capital Controls and Balance of Payments Crises', *Journal of International Money and Finance*, 5: 167–80.

INDEX

Index compiled by Peva Keane